A *Finnegans Wake* Lextionary

Let James Joyce Jazz Up Your Voca(l)bulary

Bill Cole Cliett

A Finnegans Wake Lextionary

Copyright © Bill Cole Cliett, 2011.

All rights reserved.

ISBN-13: 978-1463589455
ISBN-10: 146358945X

Title ID: 3630330

riverruntolivvy.com

Cover Design by Lindsay Cliett
Book Design by Jason & Lindsay Cliett

*For Jason and Lindsay Cliett
who always have a good word*

Contents

Introduction	9
A	29
B	57
C	71
D	89
E	103
F	117
G	129
H	137
I	151
J	161
K	165
L	167
M	177
N	199
O	209
P	215
Q	237
R	241
S	249
T	271
U	285
V	293
W	299
X	311
Y	313
Z	315

All words in double-quotation marks not otherwise attributed are from *Finnegans Wake*.

—An' his language, said the other woman.
—Aw yis.
Here the other woman sighed in her turn
and drew her shawl about her:
—On'y, said she, God bless the gintleman,
he uses the words that you nor me can't
intarpit.

—James Joyce, *Stephen Hero*

"**Dictionary,** n. A malevolent literary device for cramping the growth of a language and making it hard and inelastic. This dictionary, however, is a most useful work."

—Ambrose Bierce
The Devil's Dictionary

Introduction

Finnegans Wake is the most deliberately obscure work in world literature. Why? The reasons are diverse, but one major explanation is so many of its words are outside our dictionaries. They are creative collisions of existing words, concocted collaborations of multi-lingual words, and combinations of both that are the inception of a comprehensive, catholic language all its own, what is generally referred to as Wakese. When asked if English didn't have enough words for him, Joyce replied that it had enough words but they weren't the right ones. Thus his inventive mind conjured up whatever he needed, whenever he needed, as many as he needed. Though not particularly picturing Joyce, Virginia Woolf penned him perfectly when she wrote of "The word-coining genius, as if thought plunged into a sea of words and came up dripping."

So, if you like words, particularly the offbeat and the bizarre, and enjoy adding new ones to your voca(l)bulary, written and spoken, then James Joyce's *Finnegans Wake* is the place to find them. With his final book, Joyce gave Mr. Webster more business than he ever bargained for. Some words are weird and way out, some funny or too funny for words, some 100 letters long. *Wake* words are in an original world of their own, creating their own particular and puzzling "langscape," but that doesn't mean you can't make them a part of your life and let them slip off your pen or tongue to amuse and amaze, psych out and profundicate your family and friends. And since Webster and his competitive compeers have overlooked, if they ever looked over, Mr. Joyce's literary gems, the following words and their definitions are an addendum to all those dictionaries that are content to carry only those words that are safely tried and tiredly true.

Let's begin with a scene seen *Through the Looking Glass*. When Humpty Dumpty recites his poem for Alice, "Twas brillig, and the slithy toves . . . ," he explains that "Slithy means lithe and slimy. You see it's like a portmanteau—there are two meanings packed up into one word." Alice asks doubtfully if words can be made to do so many things, and Humpty confidently replies that it is simply a matter of who is to be master. Joyce certainly proved himself to be the master of words, a lord of language, in the writing of *Finnegans Wake* where he upped Lewis Carroll's ante by packing many, many more than two meanings into the portmanteau of some of his word constructions. If Joyce had limited the *Wake*'s linguistic ambiguity by creating words with no more than two meanings, *Finnegans Wake* would be a relatively easier read than it is.

But things get far more complicated. Humpty tells Alice that when he uses a word "it means exactly what I choose it to mean—neither more nor less." Yet the exact opposite applies to the *Wake*. Joyce meant his words to have extended meanings, evocative with elusive allusions, often illusive, that sometimes seem to stretch infinitively within the dark, dream-filled night that is the setting of this "going forth by black" "in the lingerous longerous book of the dark."

As Rebecca West remarked, "The distinctive attribute of *Work in Progress*, Joyce's working title for *Finnegans Wake*, is that it is not written in English, or in any other language. Most of the words that James Joyce uses are *patés de langue gras*. Each is a paste of words that have been superimposed on one another and worked into a new word that shall be the lowest multiple of them all. These words have been chosen out of innumerable languages, living and dead, either because of some association of ideas or of sound. They are 'portmanteau' words such as Lewis Carroll invented when he wrote 'Jabberwocky.'" The *Wake* tells us that it makes use of "anythongue athall," leaving readers to inquire, "are we speachin d'anglas or are you sprakin Djoytsch?" That is, are we speaking English, German, or Joyce? The answer is "yes," and much more besides.

An oft-asked question is, "How did Joyce know all these languages?" "He did not learn all of them," writes Petr Škrabánek, "but dipped into dictionaries and freely misspelt, inflated into portmanteaux, chopped in fragments, wrote backwards and otherwise mutilated words to suit his artistic plan of riverrun of multiple meanings, euphony ["soundscript"], pun, riddle or allusion."

Joyce, commenting on his own word creation, wrote: "... perhaps it is madness to grind up words in order to extract their substance, or to graft one onto another, to create crossbreeds and unknown variants, to open up unsuspected possibilities for these words, to marry sounds which were not usually joined before, although they were meant for one another, to allow water to speak like water, birds to chirp in the words of birds, to liberate all sounds ... from their servile, contemptible role and to attach them to the feelers of expressions which grope for definitions of the undefined ... With this hash of sounds I am building the great myth of everyday life."

When a friend decried the meanings readers were "discovering" in his work, Joyce replied, "Who's to say they are wrong?" Well aware of the complexities of the *Wake*, Joyce admitted, "for the moment there is at least one person, myself, who can understand what I am writing. I don't however guarantee that in two or three years I'll still be able to." So, in answer to the question, can we read too much into *Finnegans Wake*, L.A.G. Strong writes, "It is odd to be afraid of reading too much into Joyce, when so often one misses at least half of his allusions." I'd say Strong is quite conservative, for most readers miss much more than half. But the wonderful thing is that what one misses another identifies, since all readers come with their own personal perspectives and specific, specialized knowledge and experiences. The *Wake* is truly a democratic book in that everyone can contribute to the increased understanding of its seemingly overwhelming difficulties where we are almost all equally lost together. It takes more than a village to read *Finnegans Wake*; it takes the world.

For Joyce remarked that the only demand he made of his readers was that they spend the rest of their lives studying his books, serving as what the *Wake* identifies as "that ideal reader suffering from an ideal insomnia." "We are," it tells us, "once amore as babes awondering in a wold made fresh." And since we are all, to varying degrees and in different ways, "laden with the loot of learning," our individual efforts are necessary to solve the mystery of what Daniel Boorstin calls this "realist, naturalist, symbolist, parodist, comic epic—of countless levels, embodied and enshrouded in the word."

If you are new to *Finnegans Wake*, don't worry. Almost everyone is. It's no exaggeration to say that the *Wake* is virtually unread. Many would say it's unreadable and, at first glance, that's a pretty fair assessment. Just as at times you can't see the forest for the trees, well here you have trouble seeing the book for the words. But with some patience and good guidance I trust you will soon come to find the fascination of a literary world of words unlike any other and heartily agree that—"Nobirdy aviar soar anyway to eagle it."

So, exactly what is *Finnegans Wake* about? Well, that's a good question with ambiguous answers. William York Tindall's famous response is that *Finnegans Wake* is about *Finnegans Wake*, upon which Samuel Beckett expanded by saying that *Finnegans Wake* "is not *about* something; *it is that something itself.*" In *James Joyce A to Z*, A. Nicholas Fargnoli and Michael Patrick Gillespie sum up the *Wake* in 26 words when they write that "in it Joyce attempted to represent through myth, music, symbol and metaphor a universal and comic synthesis of all human culture—a book about, literally, everything."

Even Joyce seemed, at least at the beginning, a little mystified by what he was attempting with his new work. When asked what he was working on, Joyce replied, "It's hard to say." But he was certain of at least two things: "It's about the night," he said, and "It's meant to make you laugh." He summed these up by referring to what he called "my nocturnal comedy."

When *Ulysses* was published, Harriet Shaw Weaver, Joyce's patroness, asked what he was going to write next. "I think," he wrote her, "I will write a history of the world." Now that's a pretty inclusive statement that fits well with the explanations above. But Joyce confused things when he remarked that he had written *Ulysses* out of next to nothing but was writing *Finnegans Wake* out of nothing at all. So, in some sense, or perhaps in a nonsensical way, the *Wake* is about everything and nothing, making it at once terribly difficult and extremely easy. "If there is any difficulty in reading what I write," Joyce said, "it is because of the material I use. The thought is always simple." Perhaps the best word for his work is "simplexity," the *Wake*-worthy word Ford Motor Company coined to describe its technology-driven Lincoln 2011 MKX.

The *Wake*'s comment on itself is that "It's as simple as A.B.C." So, starting with the simple, *Finnegans Wake* is about a Dublin family, the Earwickers, or perhaps the Porters, who, whatever their name, live over their pub in the Dublin suburb of Chapelizod that borders Phoenix Park. Humphrey Chimpden Earwicker (HCE), his wife Anna Livia Plurabelle (ALP), their twin sons Shem and Shaun, and daughter Issy represent all people of all times, all at the same time, in that space-time continuum of the Eternal Now. (It's not for nothing that HCE's initials appear most famously as "Here Comes Everybody.") As the *Wake* puts it: "Tis as human a little story as paper could well carry."

So, why should a story about an average enough, suburban Dublin family, even if they do represent all people at all times, require such an extensive invented vocabulary? Well, there's a very good answer to that. It seems the action of this *novel* novel, if indeed it is a novel, takes place not only during the dark of night but also within the shifting states of the unconscious, subconscious and, at times perhaps, the semiconscious mind of a sleeper who drifts in and out of a dream. As Joyce remarked to friends, "It's natural things should not be so clear at night, isn't it now?" and "The night world can't be represented by the language of the day."

Trying to calm the concerns of Miss Weaver, Joyce wrote, "One great part of every human existence is passed in a state which cannot be rendered sensible by the use of wideawake language, cutanddry grammar, and goahead plot." While these explanations reveal the reason behind the rhyme, the "sobconscious" style of "this nonday diary, this allnights newseryreel" of a "nightynovel" remains a blurred "mistery" to those readers bravely attempting this new world of words.

Then why attempt it at all? Well, as the lyrics of the Irish-American ballad that furnished the book its title, "Finnegan's Wake," tell it, there is "Lots of fun at Finnegan's Wake." According to Joyce's wife Nora, he often kept her awake at night with his laughing as he wrote. The *Wake* has a word for that state when we laugh so hard that we cry, "laughtears." Joyce saw the world as a joke we might as well enjoy, and *Finnegans Wake* reflects this.

But there's also the challenge involved, the thrill of exploring the difficult and the unknown. For the same reason climbers tackle Mt. Everest, book lovers read the *Wake* because it's there. Richard M. Kain writes that *Finnegans Wake* has, "its own unique compelling force" that offers "an original and significant world view, a multidimensional perspective. There it stands, an Everest of literature, a constant challenge to the courageous and the foolhardy."

Joyce gave potential readers some perspective with the title. Like the tasseled-toothpicked sample of sausage you get in a grocery store, tempting you to pig out and buy a whole package, the words in the title of *Finnegans Wake* give a tiny taste of what is to come. First, the missing apostrophe broadens the scope while still referencing the song. Within the lyrics, a construction worker named Tim Finnegan falls from a ladder while under the influence of drink, breaks his skull, and is carried home where he is laid out on the bed. His friends assemble for his wake and, amid the eating and drinking, an argument develops into a knock-down-drag-out fight. A mug of whiskey is thrown, misses its target, and splashes over Tim who suddenly awakens asking, "Do ye think I'm dead?"

So "wake" has two meanings, a watch over a dead body until burial and the regaining of consciousness after sleep. "Wake" becomes a play on words, the first hint that the book is meant to be punny.

By allowing the same awakening from death that comes naturally after sleep, the cyclical structure of the story is suggested. Finnegan can be broken into *fin* (French for "end") and "again." That is to say that Finnegan will be fine again or, as the *Wake* puts it, "Hohohoho, Mister Finn, you're going to be Mister Finnegan!" The absence of the apostrophe may also make "*Wake*" into a command, turning a noun into a verb, an order to the ancient Irish warriors, the Fianna, who are believed never to have died but are sleeping in a cave, waiting to awaken and redeem Ireland. There's also the image of a wake as a track made by a boat on a river that brings in the book's references to Egyptian mythology and Osiris' body floating in a casket on the Nile, as well as its relation to Shaun's voyage on the Liffey in a Guinness barrel.

The three syllables of "Finnegans" match Books I, II, and III of the *Wake* while the one syllable of "*Wake*" matches the short coda of Book IV. The first three syllables also match the three historical ages of the Italian philosopher Vico who will appear in many of the definitions ahead while the fourth and final syllable, "*Wake*," represents his Ricorso, Italian for "recurring."

Finnegans Wake has been compared to a vast puzzle, an "Allmaziful" maze, and a riddle. According to Petr Škrabánek, "The title contains the key to its riddle. Fin neg answake = find the negative answa, that is the key. The answer is 'no.'" Thus, what the final "Yes" of *Ulysses* affirms, the *Wake* negates. For readers who like this sort of thing, the title is a tip-off to much, much more to come.

If this title tale didn't do you in, you have all the makings of a true Wakean, a member of that small band of readers who have fallen head over heels in love with *Finnegans Wake*. If you are already a Wakean, I trust you will find some fun and possibly a few new insights into the book we find so fascinating. But for those among the 99.99% of readers unfamiliar with the *Wake*, I hope this lextionary will open a window onto a wonderful world of words and stimulate you to read as well as read about Joyce's comic masterpiece.

I became a Wakean from once having read the pronouncement that no one can be considered truly educated without reading at least one page of *Finnegans Wake*. So, if reading only one page of a book could make me truly educated after so many years of grade school and university classes, I was game. I approached the *Wake* without any literary heebie-jeebies, unaware of its formidable reputation as a more-than-difficult text, one that so many critics had labeled "unreadable." True, I had read Joyce's *Ulysses*, considered the greatest novel of the 20th Century, some years before, and it had been a rigorous read. But *Finnegans Wake* went way beyond that. So far in fact that I had no idea what I was reading, or even if what I was doing could be considered reading. I decided that it was the work of either a madman or a genius and, knowing what I did about James Joyce, I came down on the side of genius. I was the one who must come up to his challenge.

So much has been written about *Finnegans Wake* that it's difficult for a newcomer to know where to start, but I'll give you what worked for me in hopes that it will do the same for you. Read the *Wake*'s first page, as I did. If you survive that, then turn to one of the earliest works, *A Skeleton Key to "Finnegans Wake"* by Joseph Campbell & Henry Morton Robinson, published in 1944, to tackle the *Wake* in a way literary laypeople can comprehend. I recommend reading only the first 37 pages, "Introduction to a Strange Subject" and "Synopsis and Demonstration." At that point, at least when compared to the rest of the world's readers, you will be in rarified air, an "expert" on the *Wake*.

If that sets the hook, get a copy of William York Tindall's *A Reader's Guide to "Finnegans Wake"* and Roland McHugh's *Annotations to "Finnegans Wake."* The first gives a most readable introduction to the *Wake* and a chapter-by-chapter discussion of the action, assuming there is any action, while the second, with one page for each page of the *Wake*, gives glosses for many of the words and phrases according to their line-by-line location. Of course there are other ways to begin, yet this is what worked for me. But if this book is your introduction to the *Wake*, you are a step ahead of my starting point. Another suggestion, if Joyce's life and work is absolutely unknown to you, you could not begin better than with David Norris and Carl Flint's *Introducing Joyce*, a combination of text and drawings that offers comprehensive coverage in a condensed but entertaining and informative style. After that there is a rich store of works on *Finnegans Wake* that will lead you deeper and deeper into its delights, round and round and round its inexhaustible storehouse, sparkling with the gems of its literary treasures. My own work, *Riverrun to Livvy: Lots of Fun Reading the First Page of James Joyce's "Finnegans Wake,"* an introduction to the *Wake* for literary laypeople, is highly recommended, by none other than me.

And now, in a few words, here's a history of those books about words known as dictionaries. Dictionaries go way, way back with the first believed to be cuneiform tablets from the Acadian empire around 2300 BCE. The Babylonians and Chinese had ancient dictionaries as well. In the 4th century BCE, Philitas of Cos prepared *Disorderly Words* to explain the meanings of Homeric, literary, and technical words. The first Sanskrit dictionary appeared in the 4th century CE while the oldest existing Japanese dictionary was written around 835 CE. Arabic dictionaries appeared beginning in the 8th century CE. The English were latecomers in the word-defining department with *A Table Alphabeticall* written in 1604. It took the remarkable Samuel Johnson to produce the first "modern" English dictionary, *A Dictionary of the English Language*, in 1755. He defined 40,000 words, including "lexicographer" as a "harmless drudge." Dr. Johnson's work dominated the field until the *Oxford English Dictionary* began appearing part-by-part from 1884 to 1928. It is now updated every three months and is the most comprehensive English language dictionary available.

Dr. Johnson dominated the English definition department for so long his name is almost synonymous with dictionary. He wrote that "Dictionaries are like watches, the worst is better than none and the best cannot be expected to go quite true." (In an interior monologue in *Ulysses*, Molly Bloom thinks, "I never know the time even that watch he gave me never seems to go properly.") As to not going quite true, this is more correct concerning Johnson's dictionary than more modern ones that try to be as objective as possible. If Johnson tried to be objective, he didn't always succeed, and I confess that with some of my definitions I didn't even try. His definition of oats is a classic, quoted above all others: "a grain, which in England is generally given to horses, but in Scotland supports the people." He tells little about the nature of oats and much about his attitude towards the Scots. Still, we are grateful for his contribution, even more so since he said, "To write dictionaries is dull work." If only he'd had James Joyce's headmade words at hand, he might have found the task quite exciting, as I did.

When it comes to personal partialness, Ambrose Bierce's *The Devil's Dictionary* outdoes Dr. Johnson. Bierce's definitions are classics of biting causticity, with his entry for "Egotist" my favorite and which I include in my entry for the *Wake*'s "capItalIsed." But recently, as I wondered whether my attempt to write a lextionary for the *Wake* was madness, I read through Bierce again. His comments concerning the word "Mad" seemed directed at me as well as at himself and tied in neatly with much of the criticism directed at Joyce's production of *Finnegans Wake*. Beginning in general terms, Bierce defines "Mad" as: "Affected with a high degree of intellectual independence; not conforming to standards of thought, speech and action derived by the conformants from study of themselves; at odds with the majority; in short, unusual." That's somewhat flattering. He even takes a swipe at those who call others mad, noting that they offer no evidence indicative of their own sanity. Bierce then gets down to the case at hand, his and mine: "this present (and illustrious) lexicographer is no firmer in the faith of his own sanity than is any inmate of any madhouse in the land; yet for aught he knows to the contrary, instead of the lofty occupation that seems to him to be engaging his powers he may really be beating his hands against the window bars of an asylum and declaring himself Noah Webster, to the innocent delight of many thoughtless spectators." For a minute I wondered if this might describe me. Not likely, I decided. There's nothing wrong with me, wrong with me, wrong with me.

Before moving on, I need to admit that I haven't followed to the letter the definition of dictionary. Wakese, words created from mixing many languages, is not exactly a universally recognized language, and dictionaries are meant to give the meanings, spellings, etymology, etc. of a language. A lexicon, that is a dictionary that focuses on a specific subject field, in this case *Finnegans Wake*, may be a better term. But since the *Wake* combines and creates new words from a wide variety of languages, lextionary comes closest to describing my literary creation. So, despite any confusion it may cause, I've adopted the term *Lextionary* from the title on.

Since *Finnegans Wake* is so very complex, you may have some concerns and questions for me: *Are you a scholar?* No, far from it. *Then at least you have a degree in English Literature?* Actually not. Would Elementary Education do? *OMG! How can you presume to define Joyce's complexly constructed vocabulary?* Because Joyce was clear that he was including us as co-creators of the meanings in his complicated text. This book is no work of scholarship, though it draws widely from scholarly insights. It's one literary layman's individual insights meant for other literary laypeople. And, above all, it's meant to be a fun read, one entertaining way out of many to approach the *Wake* and to enjoy the coruscations from a few of the facets of its multitudinous meanings.

While some have suggested that *Finnegans Wake* is an elaborate hoax, "The joke is not really on us," as R.B. Kershner explains, but "thanks to Joyce's training his readers to be writers, the joke is ineluctably ours as well." Remember Joyce's comment above about the meanings readers were "discovering" in his books—"Who's to say they are wrong?" Well, if Joyce isn't going to judge or begrudge the personal meanings and connections I find in his creations, why should they concern you? After all, you are free to find your own. I find my finest qualification for presenting this work in my agreement with a comment Dylan Thomas made to William York Tindall one day in Cavanaugh's bar, that "he prized the *Wake* above all other books. He liked words."

Allan Metcalf explains that "the vocabulary of a language is not just a haphazard heap of words (a great heap, in the case of English), but an organized whole." While he sees a language as a network or web with words tied to one another, with *Finnegans Wake* Joyce includes a great many of the world's languages, forming a far vaster web of words. Thus the connections and associations multiply exponentially. "Say *cheese*, for example," writes Metcalf, "and a listener will think of mozzarella or mice or photographs; say *cheesecake*, and the listener will think of dessert and perhaps even pinups. Psychologists use word associations to test our preoccupations and also our intelligence, because our knowledge and our thinking depend on the connections we make among words." Sheldon Brivic adds that, "By teaching us that every word has an infinite number of meanings and can be attached to every other word in the universe, the *Wake* expands on all possible techniques."

So, in a way, *Finnegans Wake* is an IQ test, and one in which I certainly don't want to see my score. Yet the *Wake* is an exam where all of us not only can, but are encouraged to look at each other's work and to copy, clarify, and expand on what has been found before us. This is where Roland McHugh's great contribution, *Annotations to "Finnegans Wake,"* comes in with its collected wisdom from generations of scholars and lay readers alike. Whatever we see and however well we see in the *Wake*'s labyrinthine construction comes from standing on the shoulders, so to speak, of the shared studies and knowledge of previous readers.

Despite all this, *Finnegans Wake* was rarely well received. Because Joyce published some sections of *Work in Progress* in small literary magazines during the 17 years of its composition and larger portions as bound books, the critics had ample opportunity to express their displeasure. Even John Joyce felt his favorite son had lost his mind, and Joyce's closest brother, Stanislaus, described the little he read as "the witless wandering of literature before its final extinction." The strange new vocabulary was often the target of complaint. Writing in the *London Evening Standard* on September 19, 1929, Arnold Bennett confessed, "I cannot comprehend a page of it. For it is written in James Joyce's new language, invented by himself. Here are a few words from one page: limpopo, sar, icis, seints, zezere, hambles, blackburry, dwyergray, meanam, meyne, draves, pharphar, uyar." "It ought," he concluded, "to be published with a Joyce dictionary."

On June 3, 1939, *The Irish Times*' negative review of Joyce's completed work suggested that *Finnegans Wake* "permits him to try out the results of his experiments with words without coming too close to the form of a dictionary of outlandish usage" and that "The writer may come to it to dig for words amidst the ruins of the novel." But among the few early defenders, Joseph Campbell and Henry Morton Robinson asserted that Joyce "had to smelt the modern dictionary back to protean plasma and re-enact the 'genesis and mutation of language' in order to deliver his message." As Richard Beckman asserts, it is "in the unstoppable transforming of old words and phrases into new ones" that is, ultimately, "the subject of the *Wake* and its means of expression."

Books are composed of words and, given their vital function, it's only natural that books are also written about words. Most of these are about existing words, old and new, but there is a subsection that deals with invented words in the same vein as Joyce's creations. Since Joyce always maintained that *Finnegans Wake* was meant to be funny, I'll mention only several sources of fictional words with a humorous bent, where playing with words is the author's intent.

Jeffrey and Carole Bloom, who share a name but are not, so far as I can determine, related to Leopold Bloom of *Ulysses* fame, wrote *Bloom's Bouquet of Imaginary Words* in which they invented new words by the simple exercise of adding one letter, taking away one letter, or changing one letter. This process creates words like "Inkspiration: *A writer's need*;" "Penvious: *Jealous of another writer's work*;" and "Inkubation: *The period of time between a literary notion and a finished work.*" One of the Bloom's inventions, "Poortrait: *A really bad painting*," was anticipated by Joyce's "a poor trait of the artless," a pun on the title of his first novel, *A Portrait of the Artist as a Young Man*. The technique adopted by the Blooms is found throughout the *Wake* with words such as "adomic" and "barents," two of many examples I define in the pages ahead.

The *Washington Post* ran a created-word contest applying the same rules as the Blooms and received submissions such as "Ignoranus (n): A person who's both stupid and an asshole." My favorite is "Karmageddon (n): it's like, when everybody is sending off all these really bad vibes, right? And then the Earth explodes and it's like, a really serious bummer." The *Post* also offers a neologism contest in which alternate meanings are supplied for common words. One example is "Flatulence (n): emergency vehicle that picks you up after you are run over by a steamroller." Joyce, naturally, includes his own neologisms such as "bawdy" included below. Joyce began this process earlier in his writing when, in *Ulysses*, Stephen Dedalus defines "Kingstown pier" as "a disappointed bridge."

Created words and inventive definitions were not new with Joyce and will continue long after him. English, well ahead of the pack in the sheer number of its words, continues to put out the welcome mat to new words, creating and collecting them at a dizzying rate. While some languages, French for instance, have a greater concern for the purity of their vocabulary, English simply says, "Ya'll come." Some new terms appear as slang and die as quickly as they come, while others show enough staying power to become permanent fixtures. Staycation, a vacation where one can't afford to travel but must stay at home, was accepted into the dictionary in 2009, right in the middle of the recession that caused its coining.

So many new words were entering the English language in the 1500's that Robert Cawdrey felt compelled in 1604, 150 years before Dr. Johnson, to publish his *Table Alphabeticall* to ease the confusion. Newer books like Cawdrey's are still coming out, but we still confess confusion, what the *Wake* calls "confusion." The "collideorescape" of popular culture collides old words like a particle accelerator to break them apart and see what new terms escape the collision. The tunnel constructed under the English Channel is the Chunnel; a comedy/drama becomes a dramedy; Christine Brooke-Rose refers to our society's sexual permissiveness as a "spermisssive society"; the infotainment film *Religulous* examines what it sees as the ridiculousness of the religious; a revolution inspired by Ernesto

"Che" Guevara is a Chevolution; the food industry is promoting eatertainment; Walter Winchell's *New York Mirror* column called a gangster a "Chicagorilla," and an update on the gorilla theme is the documentary film on North Korea's "Dear Leader," Kim Jong ll, titled *Kimjongilia*; and, as you listen to the political pronouncements from Washington, D.C., are you ever overcome with Deja Moo, the feeling you've heard this bull before?

In the wake of *Finnegans Wake*, no book to my knowledge has been more funnydemently creative in its inventions of words than Julián Ríos's novel *Larva: Midsummer Night's Babel*. It's "textinguished" "textravaganza" of "whirrds spinning around" "the whole wild whirl" may appear to be "glibberish" and "freudulent," a "nightmire" "feastival" of a "cat-and-meowse game," but it's actually a "cosmiccomic" "parodyssey" of "sexcursions" in "holy martyromony" and "unrecoited love," a "pignic" for word lovers everywhere. The directions Ríos gives in *Larva* were anticipated long before by Joyce: "Stretch out the longuage, prop up the leanguage, resuscitate the lunguage, tie up the linkguage, unlock the lockguage, regauge the langauge, till all languages mix and meet their match."

While I do have a great passion for words, I never considered creating one until an unexpected opportunity suddenly arose. I was studying with early-childhood-education teacher and author, the New Zealander Sylvia Ashton-Warner, whose journal *Teacher* and novel *Spinster* received international acclaim. She was then working with a school in Aspen while writing *Spearpoint: "Teacher" in America*. For this new book she coined the word "Wannadowanna" because many of the Aspen children, wanting everything their way, were always saying, "I wanna do this" or "I don't wanna do that." Then, to me, she said, "Listen, Bill, we need a new word right here. What shall we have for a person mutated?" I thought for a moment and offered—"Muperson"—a new person through the mutation of personality. I later found this new word in the published book, though I thought it unlikely I'd ever see it in print again. But, some years later, it appeared in Sylvia's autobiography *I Passed This Way*. No doubt that's the end of it, but it did serve its purpose at those times. As Sylvia puts it in *Spearpoint*, "Somebody has to make the language." James Joyce exhibited no shyness in doing exactly that.

When the idea of defining *Wake* words first came to me, I immediately wondered why it hadn't been done before. Harriet Shaw Weaver suggested early on that Joyce prepare a book of annotations to follow the *Wake*'s publication. Not outliving his final book by very long, Joyce didn't have an opportunity to do so, though Roland McHugh acted on Miss Weaver's request quite brilliantly. Joyce did send his patroness a key to some of the first-page words and phrases in 1926. For the word "rory" in "rory end to the regginbrow" in the third sentence, he explained that *rory* is Irish for "red" and that *roridus* is Latin for "dewy." He added, "At the rainbow's end are dew and the colour red: bloody end to the lie in Anglo-Irish=no lie." (Sometimes his explanations need explaining.) But I soon found that with this dictionary concept, as with everything in *Finnegans Wake*, what is happening now has happened before and will happen again.

Eugene Jolas, whose literary magazine *transition* serialized Joyce's *Work in Progress*, also published in 1933 and 1935 two installments of *The Revolution of the Word Dictionary*. As part of this revolution, Jolas printed some posters, "WANTED: A NEW COMMUNICATIVE LANGUAGE," that declared—"*The old words have reached the age of retirement. Let us pension them off! We need a twentieth century dictionary.*" Earlier in the magazine, Stuart Gilbert argued that a literary revolutionary must be free to compose "new word forms whenever these are necessary to render the nuance at which he aims." Naturally enough, Joyce's creations headed up the list of words Jolas defined for his new dictionary. To take two examples, Jolas defined the *Wake*'s "mielodorous" as "honeyed emphasis of odorous" (See "mielodorous" in my definition of "exqueezit.") and "sojestiveness" as "picaresque suggestiveness," which is a different take on my meaning given below. Commenting on Jolas' work, Michael Finney doubts that Jolas had Joyce's authority for these definitions, but Finney believes Joyce "would almost certainly have resisted pinning single definitions" on these words as "his purpose was to enrich the text, to add, not limit, meaning." Perhaps, between Jolas and me and the lexicographers who will follow us, a more comprehensive *Finnegans Wake* lextionary will eventually evolve though, given Wakese's openness to interpretation, I don't see one ever finding finality.

Clive Hart gives an idea of the challenge that creating such a dictionary offers. His indispensable Wakean resource, *A Concordance to "Finnegans Wake,"* presents an alphabetical list of the *Wake*'s words with their page and line numbers to facilitate their location in the text. The *Concordance* lists 63,924 different words, 51,922 occurring only once. (*Ulysses*, a far larger book, has 29,899 different words, 16,432 occurring only once.) Naturally, many of these singular words are of common English usage, but a scan of a few random pages reveals how many are singular in the sense of being strange, odd, and unusual. Shakespeare is credited with the creation of some 1,700 words (zany, advertising, dawn, bandit, fashionable, etc., plus some *Wake*-like words such as prenzie and scamels that still have scholars scratching their heads), but Joyce's inventions are in the ten's of thousands and have scholars pulling out their hair. My *Lextionary* scarcely scratches the surface with its over 800 definitions.

About these *singular* singular words, Hart writes: "For some time there have been suggestions about the possible appearance one day of a much more ambitious work—a complete 'Dictionary of *Finnegans Wake*.' If prepared with discretion it would clearly save every student of Joyce a great deal of effort and frustration, though the enormous bulk and intricacy of such a volume is terrifying in its absurdity." (To that I can only add, AMEN!) Hart disabuses beginning readers of the *Wake* of the thought that such a dictionary could end all their troubles. He asserts that the obscure vocabulary is only part of the difficulty, and perhaps not the major part. "As one learns from assiduous toil with dictionaries and reference books," Hart adds, "a knowledge of what went into the individual words rarely clarifies anything beyond local cruces. The really difficult work of intelligent critical interpretation still remains to be done." Thankfully, though far from finished, that work has been and continues to be done by scholars and lay readers alike.

Allow me to pause here to explain that I have attempted definitions of only those words that speakers and readers of English might find appropriate at special times to jazz up their voca(l)-bularies. A word such as "chagreenold," which Edmund Lloyd Epstein identifies as a reference to Balzac's *La Peau de Chagrin*, when paired with "doriangrayer" (Oscar Wilde's *The Picture of Dorian Gray*), "also comments on his [Joyce's] threatening blindness with green and gray and black, evoking the three increasingly severe sorts of blindness as described in German—*grüner Star*, *grauter Star*, and *schwarzer Star*," while interesting in its context within the *Wake*, is unlikely to find an everyday application. In the same vein is "Sexaloitez," found in the sentence "There's the Belle for Sexaloitez!" Carola Giedion-Welcker reads this as "There's the beauty for sexual people [*leute*]," explaining that the "bell" is that of the Sechseläuten, the Six o'clock Festival celebrating the arrival of spring in Zurich. "The festival is marked," she writes, "by bell ringing, a procession of the historic town guilds, and a huge bonfire on which a papier-mâché figure representing winter is burned." "There's the Belle for Sexaloitez!" would make a fine *bon mot* to toss into a conversation with fellow Wakeans in Zurich for the festival just as the bells begin to ring but, otherwise, not. I trust you will forgive the omission of words such as these.

If you are a confirmed Wakean, I hope you find some of your favorite words in this unusual *Lextionary*. Certainly you will have different meanings for some of these words, meanings special and specific to you. I hope, as well, that I may give you some new insights that will deepen your knowledge and understanding of the *Wake* and its words. Undoubtedly I've left out words lacking significance for me but which will have personally significant meanings for you. I'd love to learn about these. One by one we can add new layers to James Joyce's baklava of a book.

I am one of those people, perhaps you are, too, who enjoy reading dictionaries. It's fun to pick one up, open it at random, and read a few pages in the hope of finding something new, unusual, strange, or different. Some words I think I already know may have a definition or usage that is unfamiliar. Derivations are often fascinating and were especially interesting to Joyce. Dictionaries like Dr. Johnson's *A Dictionary of the English Language* and the *Oxford English Dictionary* include actual usages of the words from historical, scientific, literary, and other sources. With each *Wake* word I define here, I quote the context in which it is found (most often within parentheses but occasionally worked into the discussion of the word) and, when I can, provide some background on the story, characters, settings, and such. These additional entries will deepen your knowledge of what *Finnegans Wake* is all about so that, if you do decide to tackle the whole work some day, you'll not be totally in the dark. In his book *The Gentle Art of Lexicography*, Eric Partridge tells of an elderly lady "who, on borrowing a dictionary from her municipal library, returned it with the comment, 'A *very* unusual book indeed—but the stories are extremely short, aren't they?'" You will not find this to be true about many of the words in this *Lextionary*.

William Faulkner said of Hemingway's books, "He has never been known to use a word that may require the reader to look for a dictionary." On the other hand, *Finnegans Wake* has scarcely a sentence without one or more words that defy a dictionary to define them. Until now, that is.

A

abbroaching *FW* 324.36 *v.* Coming near or approaching with the intent of beginning a discussion or broaching. ("Birdflights confirm abbroaching nubtials.") McHugh suggests "divination by flight of birds" for "Birdflights" and "nuptials" for "nubtials," with "nub" as slang for "copulation." If anything needed divination, approaching the broaching of nuptials most certainly does, especially since the the topic of copulation is an important concern.

abcedminded *FW* 18.17 *n.* Alphabet-minded or interested in the origin of the letters of the alphabet and their uses in forming words. This suggests an Old English word for alphabet—abecede. The "abcedminded" are apt to become lexicographers or interested in the art of lexicography. With a slight stretch, absent-minded comes to mind, something literary and scholarly types are typically portrayed as being. With an even greater stretch, absinthe-minded brings to mind the mind altered by the consumption of absinthe, a bitter, green, anise-flavored alcoholic drink containing oil of wormwood that once was thought to cause hallucinations and mental derangement. (See **absintheminded.**) *Finnegans Wake* may be referring to my work here with

"(Stoop) if you are abcedminded, to this claybook, what curious of signs (please stoop), in this allaphbed!" Claudette Sartiliot reads "abcedminded" as "both 'absentminded' but also aware of the letters of the alphabet. She maintains that "the reader's mind should be absent, that he or she should understand the text otherwise than with the mind, but also should be aware of the letters as sounds, or, if you will, should be in the same position as the child learning the alphabet." She sees Joyce as "the teacher from whom we learn how to read." One thing is certain. Joyce's new way of writing requires a new way of reading.

abhears *FW* 23.26 *v.* Follows closely or adheres to appearing to tolerate or abear by listening to what one detests or abhors. In order to pass a course, a student often "abhears" to a teacher whom s/he abhors. ("Impalpabunt, he abhears. The soundwaves are his buffeters; they trompe him with their trompes") McHugh provides assistance with the German *abhören* for "listen to" and the French *tromper* for "deceive."

abnihilisation *FW* 353.22 *n.* From nothing, the annihilation or complete destruction of something back to nothing. Joyce maintained that while he created *Ulysses* out of next to nothing, he was creating *Finnegans Wake* out of nothing. The Latin *ab nihil* for "from nothing" and the philosophical meaning of nihilism as the denial of all existence come into play here. The meaning in the *Wake* is to the wiping out of words altogether with "*The abnihilisation of the etym*," as etymon is the original sense or meaning of a word. There is also present the annihilation or splitting of an atom or, in this case, a word to release the great power stored within. Certainly some critics have seen *Finnegans Wake* as an attempt to destroy literature, with Joyce's younger brother Stanislaus describing the *Wake* as the "witless wandering of literature before its final extinction."

abortisement *FW* 181.33 *n.* A paid announcement or advertisement for an abortion or the inducing of a premature birth of a fetus or of some project or idea that fails to develop properly. The first, if done at all, is done discretely, while the second is often seen in politics, especially during campaign seasons. ("He appreciates it. Copies. ABORTISEMENT.")

abought *FW* 415.17 *prep.* Something to do with or about a thing or service that is purchased or bought. Successful haggling over the price of a new car is often a subject friends talk "abought." ("'a thought, abought the Great Sommboddy within the Omniboss") If this passage refers to God within the universe, might it hint that He may be bought?

abovemansioned *FW* 265.4-5 *n.* 1. A large house or mansion that has been spoken about earlier or abovementioned. *v.* 2. The housing of people in a large house or mansion that is overhead or above where they are at present. When Jesus tells his disciples that in his Father's house there are many mansions, they understand that they will be "abovemansioned" in Heaven. ("the loftleaved elm Lefanunian abovemansioned, each, every, all is for the retrospectioner")

absintheminded *FW* 464.17 *adj.* Forgetful, abstracted, or absent-minded from the consumption of absinthe, a bitter, green, anise-flavored alcoholic drink containing oil of wormwood that was once thought to cause hallucinations and mental derangement. The old saying, "absence makes the heart grow fonder," through a play on words, becomes "absinthe makes the heart grow warmer." ("Ah, he's very thoughtful and sympatrico that way is Brother Intelligenius, when he's not absintheminded, with his Paris addresse!") Absinthe is most often associated with artists and poets in Paris such as Wilde, Rimbaud, and Verlaine. Mistakenly considered dangerous, this drink was banned for many years but is now available in upscale liquor stores.

accomplasses *FW* 295.27 *n.* Young women or lasses who knowingly assist each other to accomplish or compass a plot, scheme, or compass, thus becoming accomplices. The two girls who testified about some improper action by HCE one night in Phoenix Park were "accomplasses" if their scheme was to damage his reputation but, on the other hand, they may have been telling the truth. Despite a multitude of scholarly investigations, the picture is still a "mistery." ("And makes us a daintical pair of accomplasses!") McHugh reads "a daintical" as "identical" and provides the slang for "pair of compasses," instruments used for drawing circles, as "human legs." Now I admit this is a stretch, as is *Finnegans Wake*, but the coat of arms of Dublin contains two lasses coyly lifting the hems of their skirts to expose their legs (*"Pair of Sloppy Sluts plainly Showing all the Unmentionability"*) and three castles that have been suggested, respectively, for the two girls and three soldiers ("shot two queans and shook three caskles") in HCE's Phoenix Park "impropriety." With "shot" as slang for "fucked" and "quean" as slang for "whore," these "accomplasses" are compromised as witnesses. Add to this their description as "*Conspirators how they all Tried to Fall him*," the "*him*" being "*Privates Earwicker*," with the suggestion he exposed his privates or genitals, and it looks more and more likely that HCE was framed.

accomplicied *FW* 587.32-33 *adj.* Expert or accomplished in aiding someone in committing a crime or an accomplice. ("Mister Beardall, an accomplicied burgomaster, a great one among the very greatest") Bernie Madoff had some "accomplicied" employees on his payroll.

accorsaired *FW* 600.11 *adj.* Damned or accursed as a Turkish pirate or corsair. Lord Byron was Joyce's favorite poet when he was a schoolboy, even taking a beating for defending Byron's poetry, so Joyce was no doubt familiar with his literary hero's popular poem, "The Corsair," and its concluding couplet: "He left a Corsair's name to other times, / Link'd with one virtue and a thousand crimes." ("the kongdomain of the Alieni, an accorsaired race, infester of Libnud Ocean") "Libnud" is one of several instances in which the letters of Joyce's hometown, Dublin, are scrambled.

achdung *FW* 100.5 *n.* The German *Achtung* for "attention" and English *dung* for "manure or excrement," bids one to heed or pay attention to a substance one would prefer not to step in. In a situation where time, and thus brevity, is of the essence, this compact command serves an important purpose. With more pooper-scooper laws in effect, "Achdung" is heard less often on city sidewalks, but this word still comes in handy in the farmyard and pasture. ("Achdung! Pozor! Attenshune!")

acknuckledownedgment *FW* 344.8 *n.* The admission or acknowledgement that one has worked hard and earnestly or knuckled down in achieving an objective. There is also the suggestion that knuckles came into play in the process, hinting at a fistfight or at least some sort of battle. On the evening of November 4, 2008, John McCain was gracious in giving Barack Obama a sincere "acknuckledownedgment" for his successful presidential campaign. (*"giving his scimmianised twinge in acknuckledownedgment of this cumulikick, strafe from the firetrench"*)

acountstrick *FW* 180.5 *n.* 1. A deception or trick used in the keeping of financial records or accounts. The use of a second set of books is one of the older accounting tricks. There's the joke about the businessman who is interviewing for a new accountant. He asks the first applicant, "What is two and two?" The man replies, "Four." The second applicant is asked the same question and gives the same answer. When the third applicant is asked the sum of two and two he replies, "What do you want it to be?" "The job is yours," says the businessman. 2. A deception or trick having to do with how sounds are heard or acoustics. In *Finnegans Wake* Joyce plays many such tricks, as with the first page's "is retaled early in bed and later on life." Read silently, "retaled" is seen as a tale that is retold but, when only heard, it sounds like 'retailed.' Within the sentence, retailed makes sense since the fall of Wall Street is discussed and, even more so, as the spelling Joyce used in his first draft was "retailed." The fact that the secondary meaning of retail is to tell over again makes this "acountstrick" a neat trick indeed. ("egad, sir, accordant to all acountstrick, he squealed the topsquall")

adomic *FW* 615.6 *adj.* Adam and atom combined. An atom is a small particle from which elements are formed and Adam, with the cooperation of Eve, is an elemental particle from which humanity was formed. Humans are thus composed of atoms and Adam. ("the sameold gamebold adomic structure of our Finnius the old One, as highly charged with electrons") Atomic structure in this phrase is a reminder that Joyce predicted atomic bombs ("pang that would split an atam") well before their use on two Japanese cities during World War II ("whatthough for all appentices it had a mushroom on it . . . nogeysokey first" the "hriosmas, whereas take notice be the relics of the bones"). Pat yourself on the back if you noticed HCE hidden in "highly charged with electrons."

adullescence *FW* 54.35-36 *n.* Not very bright or dull during the period of growth from childhood to adulthood or adolescence. Adolescents must deal with physical changes that often seem to overwhelm their mental development or, in other words, sex takes center stage. ("cordially inwiting the adullescence who he was wising up to do in like manner what all did so as he was able to add")

advauncement *FW* 608.3 *n.* Forward movement, promotion, or advancement by one who boasts, brags, or vaunts about abilities and accomplishments. "I can do anything with language," Joyce once boasted to a friend, but that did little for the "advauncement" of *Finnegans Wake* with the reading public. ("the Brehons Assorceration for the advauncement of scayence") McHugh reads this as the British Association for the Advancement of Science. For me, this sounds like an Association of Sorcerers for the Advancement of Séance, giving it a tinge of Harry Potter's Hogwarts School of Witchcraft and Wizardry. (The word "hogwarts" appears in the *Wake* on page 296, line 19, perhaps a Potter premonition.)

aebel *FW* 303.33 *n*. Cain's brother and killer, Abel, and the Danish *æble* for "apple." Abel was something of a rotten apple. ("He, angel that I thought him, and he not aebel to speel ellyotripes, Mr Tellibly Divilcult!") The reference here is to the English children's game, Angels and Devils, in which Shem tries to guess a color chosen by his sister, Issy, and her rainbow girls. He finds it terribly difficult and is not able to guess the right answer—heliotrope.

afeered *FW* 497.16 *adj*. Frightened or afraid (archaic—afeared) of paying money for some type of service or a fee. In the recession of the first decade of the 21st Century, businesses attempted to recover their losses by charging a bewildering array of fees that added up to exorbitant charges for consumers. As an example, some airline passengers found that special fees for baggage, meals, snacks, pillows, blankets, etc. totaled more than the cost of their tickets. It's enough to make anyone "afeered" to fly. ("afeered he was a gunner but affaird to stay away")

Aferican *FW* 387.2 *n*. African and American combined to give an abbreviated version of African-American. In "Noord Amrikaans and Suid African cattleraiders (so they say) all over like a tiara dullfuoco", McHugh references the Dutch *noord* for "north," the Dutch *Amerikaans* for "American," the Latin *Afer* for "Africa," and "tiara dullfuoco" as Tierra del Fuego in the southernmost part of South America, which is a relatively dull place compared with more metropolitan areas.

affaird *FW* 497.17 *adj*. 1. Frightened or afraid of an affair, whether merely an event, a public or private concern, or an amorous relationship. If the latter affair is illicit, the threat of its disclosure might well make one "affaird." 2. Frightened or afraid to be fair. Given the ubiquitous statement that "Life is not fair," fairness can be seen as a contradiction of natural law and thus something to be "affaired" of violating. ("afeerd he was a gunner but affaird to stay away") In this instance, it is only natural that a gunner, that is someone such as a soldier shooting a gun, might be afraid he was a goner or, in other words, shot dead.

africot *FW* 489.27 *n.* A pale, orange-colored fruit or apricot that grows in Africa. ("I loved that man who has africot lupps with the moonshine in his profile") In this case the man's lips would be either apricot colored or taste like apricots or both combined.

afterworse *FW* 416.10 *adv.* Later or afterwards when that which is more unfavorable, unpleasant, or worse has already occurred. The cliché "from bad to worse" provides the basis for an old pun that is "afterworse"—"from bed to hearse." ("Now whim the sillybilly of a Gracehoper had jingled through a jungle of love and debts and jangled through a jumble of life in doubts afterworse") The reference here is to the *Wake*'s version of Aesop's fable about the ant and the grasshopper, the "Ondt and the Gracehoper." (See **dhrone**.)

agleement *FW* 348.13 *n.* A merry, joyous, or gleeful mutual understanding or agreement. Since glee also means three or more voices singing different parts of a song, a good glee club is always in "agleement." ("Junglemen in agleement, I give thee our greatly swooren")

agreenable *FW* 609.1 *adj.* Ready to have the same feeling or agreeable to the color green. The Irish are not only agreeable people but, with 40 shades of green, are also quite "agreenable." In the context of today's meaning of green in terms of being friendly to the environment, anything "agreenable" would be approved by environmentalists and climate-conscious individuals such as the "agreenable" Al Gore. The original motto of Dublin, Georgia,

"Doubling All the Time," that Joyce translated into Wakese as "doublin their mumper all the time," has now been changed to "Green and Growing." ("It was also agreeable in our sinegear clutchless, touring the no placelike no timelike absolent")

aidress *FW* 568.31   *n.* 1. A speech or an address that addresses the need for assistance or aid. 2. The place or address where aid should be sent, such as P.O. Box 37243, Washington, D.C. 20013 for the American Red Cross. *v.* 3. Speak to or address a person or group about needed assistance or aid. ("he shall aidress to His Serenemost by a speechreading from his miniated vellum")

allfaulters *FW* 355.35 *n.* All the mistakes or faults of God or Our Father. Joyce believed the real original sin ("original sinse") was God's creation of the universe, and James Atherton in *The Books at the Wake* writes that "attribution of Original Sin to God is one of the basic axioms of *Finnegans Wake*." ("We all, for whole men is lepers, have been nobbut wonterers in that chill childerness which is our true name after the allfaulters") McHugh provides the Danish *Alfader* for the god "Odin."

allhorrors eve *FW* 19.25   *n.* The evening before All Saints Day on November 1st or Allhollows, better known as Halloween. This is the night all manner of horrible spirits were thought to abound, hence the scary costumes worn then to ward off these evil creatures and worn today to frighten homeowners into forking over candy and treats under threat of being tricked with horrors such as soaping car windows and toilet-papering trees. ("And a hundreadfilled unleavenweight of liberorumqueue to con an we can till allhorrows eve.")

allieged *FW* 617.31   *v.* To claim or allege to have the right to homage and allegiance from a vassal or liege. ("Well, here's lettering you erronymously anent other clerical fands allieged herewith.") McHugh gives "anent" as meaning "concerning" and "fands" as the Danish *fand* for "devil," so this is letting us know anonymously that, concerning clerical devils, they are alleging the right to allegiance from lieges erroneously. There are other ways this might be read but, given Joyce's rejection of what he considered the erroneous claims of Roman Catholic clerics and their control through threats of the Devil (See the two fire and brimstone sermons in *A Portrait of the Artist as a Young Man*.), "allieged" seems to be an exact expression of his beliefs.

allmaziful *FW* 104.1 *adj.* Astonishing or amazing for being full of labyrinths or mazes. The famous Greek, Daedalus, whose name is suggested in Stephen Dedalus, the protagonist of Joyce's *A Portrait of the Artist as a Young Man*, built a labyrinth on the island of Crete that is legendary for its bewildering complexity. *Finnegans Wake*, as a labyrinth built with words, is truly an "Allmaziful" maze for which readers are still searching for that ball of thread that will successfully lead them through it. ("In the name of Annah the Allmaziful, the Everliving, the Bringer of Plurabilities") This immediately brings to mind Anna Livia Plurabelle (ALP) and, in addition, McHugh references Suras of the Koran beginning: "In the name of Allah, the Merciful, the Compassionate." (See **dazecrazemazed**.)

alma martyrs *FW* 348.11 *n.* The schools, colleges, or alma maters where students have studied and, one hopes, graduated, though with great pain, anguish, and suffering for the sake of learning, making them educational martyrs. ("for all them old boyars that's now boomaringing in waulholler, me alma marthyrs") The mention here of Valhalla, the banqueting hall where Scandinavian heroes slain in battle enjoy their afterlife, suggests there may be a similar reward in store for suffering students.

alphybettyformed *FW* 183.13 *adj.* Shaped or formed by the letters of a language or an alphabet. Words are formed from the letters of an alphabet, allowing written communication of what was previously only verbal. Thoughts and feelings are

allmaziful - altoogooder | 39

also "alphybettyformed" from reading. Joyce's daughter Lucia "alphybettyformed" art from the letters of the alphabet, creating lettrines or illuminated letters, both for the first letters of each of his poems in *Pomes Pennyeach* and her own later alphabet book. Her efforts echo the much earlier efforts of seventh century Irish monks in the richly illuminated letters Joyce so much admired in *The Book of Kells*, considered the most beautiful Irish book in existence. This medieval masterpiece inspired the *Wake*'s design and was so important to Joyce that he carried a reproduction of this ancient testament with him wherever he lived. As Joyce said of *The Book of Kells* ("our book of kills") to a friend, "You can compare much of my work to the intricate designs of its illuminations, and I have pored over its workmanship for hours at a time." ("amygdaloid almonds, rindless raisins, alphybettyformed verbage, vivlical viasses")

alshemist *FW* 185.35 *n*. Shaun's twin brother Shem as one who uses science and magic to transform lead into gold or an alchemist who makes ink from his excrement "through the bowels of his misery . . . and the first till last alshemist wrote over every square inch of the only foolscap available, his own body." For those interested in alchemical allusions in the *Wake*, Barbara DiBernard's *Alchemy and Finnegans Wake* is a perfect resource, especially the last chapter "Shem the 'Alshemist.'"

altared *FW* 331.3 *v*. Changed or altered at a raised and sacred structure or altar of a church, synagogue, or temple. In the context of *Finnegans Wake* ("He's herd of hoarding and her faiths is altared."), it's evident that faith is the thing "altered," but one might also be "altared" by sacraments such as baptism, communion, or marriage. Joyce's faith was certainly "altared" for the worse when a schoolboy, and both *Portrait* and *Ulysses* deal with Stephen's guilt over refusing to accede to his dying mother's request that he perform his Easter duties.

altoogooder *FW* 358.16 *n*. On the whole or altogether too much

(See **mmmmuch.**) of a person who is too anxious to do what is beneficial, right, and good or a do-gooder. As its use in the *Wake* indicates, there is a depreciatory aspect to do-gooders. ("I, my good grief, I am, I am big altoogooder")

amadst *FW* 86.18 *prep.* In the middle of or amidst the insane or mad. There are times when reading *Finnegans Wake* that one feels indeed "amadst." "Sheer madness," muttered Irish playwright George Bernard Shaw on *Finnegans Wake*, and John Joyce, upon looking at the copy of the *Wake* his eldest son sent him, declared, "He is out of his head." The great majority of critics agreed with Shaw and Mr. Joyce. ("they landed their two and a trifling selves, amadst camel and ass, greybeard and suckling, priest and pauper, matrmatron and merrymeg, into the meddle of the mudstorm")

ambijacent *FW* 36.15 *adj.* Adjoining or adjacent to both sides or hands. For an ambidextrous writer, a pen placed in the center of a desk would be "ambijacent" to both the right and left hands. Thomas Jefferson designed his bed at Monticello to fit between two rooms so that when he awoke each morning he would be "ambijacent" to them and could get out of bed into the room he wanted to be in. ("now standing full erect, above the ambijacent floodplain, scene of its happening")

ambullished *FW* 356.30 *v.* Attacked by surprise or ambushed but, when retold, elaborated with imaginary details or embellished to make the ambush seem more dangerous than it was in reality. Soldiers ambushed by ten of the enemy may find in the official report that they were "ambullished" by one-hundred or more. It's probably not just a coincidence that the slang term "bull," as in "that's a bunch of bull," (The second syllable "shit" is often omitted for the sake of propriety.) is embedded in "ambullished." ("It his ambullished with expurgative plates, replete in information and accampaigning the action passiom")

amonkst *FW* 609.30 *prep.* In the company of or amongst members of a religious order centered in a monastery or monks. Laymen making a religious retreat might be be said to be "amonkst." ("An I could peecieve amonkst the gatherings who ever they wolk in process?") The "wolk in process" in this sentence refers to "Work in Progress," the working title of *Finnegans Wake* for seventeen years of its composition.

amoosed *FW* 158.3 *v.* Caused to laugh, smile, or be amused by the activities or antics of a moose. For most of us just looking at a moose can cause amoosement, thus the source of some of the humor of the cartoon character Bullwinkle or the 60's slang saying, "Cool as a moose." A recent YouTube video showed two baby moose playing in a lawn sprinkler in the backyard of a Canadian home while their mother was "amoosed" in watching them. ("For the Mookse, a dogmad Accanite, were not amoosed and the Gripes, a dubliboused Catalick, wis pinefully oblivis-cent.") The reference here is to "The Mookse and The Gripes," the *Wake*'s version of Aesop's fable "The Fox and the Grapes." (See *FW* 152.15—159.18.) Queen Victoria's famous use of the royal "we" in her comment, "We are not amused." is also at work here. A cartoon version of the queen uttering this line pops up often in episodes of *Monty Python's Flying Circus*. In the presidential election of 2008, the moose-hunting Sarah Palin of Alaska provided much amoosement on the campaign trail. Based on the election results, it seems a large majority of voters were not "amoosed" by her political antics.

amotion *FW* 365.27 *n.* A strong feeling or emotion that is particularly moving or in motion. In *Finnegans Wake*, the love scene between Tristram and Iseult aboard the ship carrying them to Cornwall is moving in more ways than one, and their sexual motions are no doubt enhanced by the rocking and rolling motion of the boat. Here's one short sample of such an "amotion:" ". . . as quick, is greased pigskin, Amoricas Champius, with one aragan thrust, druve the massive of virilvigtoury flshpst the both lines forwards (Eburnea's down, boys!) rightjingbangshot into the goal of her gullet." ("No mum has the rod to pud a stub to the lurch of amotion.") This is one of many of the *Wake*'s restatements of a line from a speech by the Irish nationalist leader Charles Stewart Parnell: "No man has a right to fix the boundary of the march of a nation."

amourmeant *FW* 231.8 *n.* Love (French *amour*) meant as a form of entertainment or amusement. Since Eve and Adam, "amourmeant" is without doubt the greatest form of amusement available throughout the history of humanity. Casanova was a prime practitioner of the art of "amourmeant." If the term "love," as is often the case, is used euphemistically for "sex," it outperforms all other amusements. No other evidence is necessary than the speed with which sex came to dominance on the internet. ("*And cloitered for amourmeant in thy boosome shede!*") If "*cloitered*" is translated as cloistered, "*boosome*" as bosom, and "*shede*" as shade, then amusement may be found in the secluded shade of large boobs. Armament may also be suggested since armor is a slang term for a condom, and fighting in armor refers to the wearing of a condom during sex, giving a risqué reference to a knight/ night in armor.

Ampsterdampster *FW* 319.16-17 *n.* A resident of the moist or definitely damp city Amsterdam, the largest city in the Netherlands. ("Save Ampsterdampster that had rheumaniscences in his netherlumbs.") The dampness of Amsterdam could lead to remembrances or reminiscences of rheumatism in one's lower or nether limbs or legs.

amusin *FW* 539.16 *n.* An immoral act or sin that is entertaining or amusing. Bill Clinton's dalliance with Monica Lewinsky comes immediately to mind as an "amusin," but celebrities keep us supplied well beyond our needs. ("The amusin part is, I will say, hotelmen, that since I, over the deep drowner Athacleeath to seek again Irrlanding, shamed in mind")

analectralyse *FW* 67.8 *v.* To examine carefully or analyze the components of a chemical compound that has been decomposed by an electrical current or electrolyzed. This is one *Wake* word you will find difficult to drop into an everyday conversation. ("We might leave that nitrience of oxagiants to take its free of the air and just analectralyse that very chimerical combination, the gasbag where the warderworks.") Since Joyce was so far ahead of his time, he could be referring to electric, anal vibrators that were to come a few decades later.

analist *FW* 395.4 *n.* 1. One who examines critically or analyzes the rectum or the anal area of the body, also know as a proctologist. 2. An annalist who keeps a record of historical events or annals that have to do with the anus. The report that Napoleon's poor performance at Waterloo was partly caused by uncomfortable hemorrhoids is a case in point. ("and all the other analist, the steamships ant the ladies'foursome")

angricultural *FW* 86.20-21 *adj.* Farming or agriculture by people born or living in Ireland who are of English ancestry or the Anglo-Irish. In *Everything Irish*, Jim Patterson writes that "The Anglo-Irish have traditionally played a disproportionate cultural role in Irish Society." Though he is referring to the arts, the same can safely be said of things agricultural since the Anglo-Irish, as opposed to the native Irish, appropriated all the best farmlands for themselves. ("The gathering, convened by the Irish Angricultural and Prepostoral Ouraganisations, to help the Irish muck to look his brother dane in the face") McHugh references this as The Irish Agricultural Organization Society founded by Sir Horace Plunkett, whom Lawrence W. McBride, in *Everything Irish*, identifies as, you guessed it, being an Anglo-Irish aristocrat. McHugh also identifies "muck" in this passage with the Irish *muc* for "pig." Both "muck" as moist, farmyard manure and "muc" as a filthy, farmyard animal, are how many Anglo-Irish viewed the native Irish. (See **Ouraganisations** & **Prepostoral**.)

annaversary *FW* 493.5 *n.* A yearly celebration or anniversary for Anna Livia Plurabelle or ALP, wife of Humphrey Chimpden Earwicker or HCE, and mother of twin sons Shem and Shaun and daughter Issy. Anna is, if not the central character in *Finnegans Wake*, certainly the central female character who is also the personification of the River Liffey. The book begins with her in "riverrun" and concludes with her memorable, moving soliloquy as she flows home to her father, the Irish Sea. Book I, Chapter 8 is devoted entirely to Anna and, without doubt, contains the *Wake*'s most beautiful passages. ("O he never battered one eagle's before paying me his duty on my annaversary")

annoyimgmost *FW* 495.2 *adj.* To be at once troubling or annoying and nameless or anonymous, such as reading "caller unknown" on the caller-identification screen of your telephone. ("wreuter of annoyimgmost letters and skirriless ballets in Parsee Franch")

annuysed *FW* 342.28 *v.* Entertained or amused in a way that also makes one troubled or annoyed. We are more often than not "*annuysed*" watching America's Congress at work. ("*Our lorkmakor he is proformly annuysed.*") McHugh identifies "*lorkmakor*" as "Lord-Mayor" and "*proformly*" as "profoundly," which may indicate that Joyce was profoundly entertained and troubled by Dublin politics. Viewers would have been either amused, annoyed, or "annuysed" when some Trinity College men threw an overripe orange into the face of Dublin's Lord Mayor during the St. Patrick's Day procession of 1900.

anomorous *FW* 112.29-30 *adj.* At once irregular or anomalous (Greek *anomos* for "lawless"), nameless or anonymous, and loving or amorous. ("It is not a hear or say of some anomorous letter") The "anomorous letter" is the famous "litter" that the hen, Biddy Doran, scratches out of the dump or kitchen midden ("kikinmidden" with the Danish *køkken* for "kitchen" and *kik ind* for "peek in") and which ALP believes will prove the innocence of her husband, HCE ("ischt tell the cock's trootabout him"),

annaversary - anthrapologize | 45

against the accusations of his alleged improprieties in Phoenix Park. This letter appears in differing fragments throughout *Finnegans Wake* until finally appearing in full on pages 615-619. Like the *Wake* itself, the "litter" is nothing if not anomalous and is amorous in the sense that it expresses ALP's devotion to HCE. As to its being anonymous, though it's signed by "Alma Luvia, Pollabella," elsewhere there's the suggestion that it was actually written by her twin son Shem or perhaps transcribed by him from his mother's dictation. Scholars have seen this letter as *Finnegans Wake* itself, so it's unlikely its mysteries will ever be completely understood and likely it will continue to be "an illegible downfumbed by an uneligible."

anonymay's *FW* 374.7 *adj.* May or may not be nameless or anonymous, a situation that may trouble, vex, or annoy. The famous forged letter that was meant to implicate Charles Stewart Parnell in the Phoenix Park murders was found to be fraudulently written by a man named Pigott who hoped to remain anonymous but became "Anonymay's" through the courtroom discovery of his misspelling hesitancy as "hesitency." When his anonymity disappeared, he put a bullet through his head, a sobering lesson for schoolchildren who don't study their spelling lessons. ("In preplays to Anonymay's left hinted palinode obviously inspiterebbed by a sibspecious connexion.") (See **hasitate** & **hazeydency**.)

anthrapologize *FW* 151.7 *v.* Express regret or apologize for the science of man or anthropology. So many mistakes, unintentional and sometimes not, have been made in the study of human origins and development, especially racial, along with customs and beliefs, that some apologies are needed. The Aryan racial beliefs of Adolf Hitler, so effectively supported by Heinrich Himmler's sanctioned anthropological studies, are but one glaring example for which there was a need to "anthrapoligze." This sentence from the *Wake* is a case in point: "I need not anthrapologize for any obintentional (I must here correct all that school of neoitalian or paleoparisien schola of tinkers and spanglers who say I'm wrong *parcequeue* out of revolscian from romanitis I want to be) downtrodding on my foes." If Himmler had been able to write in Wakese, one could almost imagine him dictating this sentence to Joyce as he wrote *Finnegans Wake*. It seems to be saying that he need not apologize beforehand (Latin *ob* for "before") for intentionally misusing anthropological studies to trod down (read Holocaust or "the haul it cost") his foes and that he is correcting all the schools of thinkers who express revulsion for his romantic notions. Joyce certainly saw early on exactly what the Nazis (See **folksfiendship**.) had in mind when he wrote his patroness Harriet Shaw Weaver that Europe is "where the gas is really going to be turned on." Remember, *Finnegans Wake* was published in 1939.

aposterioprismically *FW* 612.19 *adv*. A posteriori, or known through experience, and prismatically, or the refraction of light through a prism, thus brightly colored or brilliant knowledge gained through the refracted reflection of direct experience. ("by thiswis aposterioprismically apatstrophied and paralogically periparolysed, celestial from principalest of Iro's Irismans ruinboon pot") A "ruinboon pot" (See **ruinboon**.) here suggests a pot of gold at the end of a rainbow, a glittering gift gained first hand through knowledge of this legend.

apoxyomenously *FW* 353.6 *adv*. Coming close to or approximately threateningly or ominously. Add to this McHugh's provision of the Greek *apaxioumenos* as the participle of "disclaim as unworthy" and the German *apoxy* for "pointed" and this word threatens to point to someone or something as unworthy in a manner that is close to being ominous. ("*but apoxyomenously deturbaned but thems bleachin banes will be after making a bashman's haloday*") This seems to come after a busman's holiday. (See "*haloday*.")

appeers *FW* 570.22 *v*. 1. To come in sight or appear through looking closely so as to see clearly or through peering. 2. Seems to be or appears to be a peer, either an equal or a member of the British nobility or both. ("O yes, Lord Pournterfamilias has been marrying man since so long time in Hurtleforth, where he appeers as our oily the active") "Hurtleforth" refers to Dublin, originally known as "The Town of the Ford of the Hurdles."

applegate *FW* 69.21 *n.* Eve and Adam's fall in the Garden of Eden after eating the forbidden (See **forebitten.**) fruit of the Tree of the Knowledge of Good and Evil, popularly thought of as an apple. This is one of those instances in which Joyce came up with a term that was later to become widely used in popular culture. Instances include Watergate, Contragate, and Monicagate, though in Monicagate the term "gate" assumes an alluded meaning that would require an "R" rating. ("everything was got up for the purpose he put an applegate on the place by no means as some pretext a bedstead") It's been said that the real problem in Eden was not with the apple on the tree but with the pair on the ground.

appraisiation *FW* 41.28 *n.* Favorable criticism or appreciation that is expressed through words of commendation or praise. ("with their priggish mouths all open for the larger appraisiation of this longawaited Messiagh of roaratorios")

apuckalips *FW* 455.1 *n.* The revelation of a cataclysmic upheaval or Apocalypse when you can pucker up your lips and kiss your ass goodbye. ("nor homemade hurricanes in our Cohortyard, no cupahurling nor apuckalips nor no puncheon jodelling nor no nothing") Punch and Judy appear here.

apun *FW* 224.36 *prep.* On or upon the humorous use of a word that has several different meanings or a pun. Answering the question, "Is life worth living?" Mark Twain repied, "It all depends of the liver." Joyce's patroness, Harriet Shaw Weaver, disparagingly called *Finnegans Wake* a "Wholesale Safety Pun

Factory," and Joyce didn't disagree, saying, "Such a book, all in puns!" When asked, "Aren't many of your puns trivial?" Joyce replied, "Yes, and many are quadrivial." John Gross writes that "pure puns, in the sense of double meanings that turn on exact homonyms, are in fact not all that common—i.e., there are probably not more than a dozen or so a page." What he finds far more frequent are "the phantom puns conjured up by the pressure of an idiom, a familiar cadence, a leitmotif, the compound verbal fractures that send splinters of meaning flying off in five or six different directions at once." The *Wake*'s "punns and reedles" are combined in "When is a Pun not a Pun?" The answer is "Isaac," meaning "he laughed," an appropriately humorous name if you remember that Sarah laughed when God told her she would bear a child at the age of 90. The earliest pun I've found so far in Joyce's books is in *Stephen Hero*, his abandoned precursor to *A Portrait of the Artist as a Young Man*. Stephen's friend McCann is described as a "steadfast reader of the *Review of Reviews*." The pun, a slight one, comes from the name of the *Review of Reviews* publisher, William T. Stead. (See **thuartpeatrick**.) ("Apun which his poohoor pricoxity theirs is a little tittertit of hilarity") If any book is built "apun," *Finnegans Wake* is that book.

arboriginally *FW* 314.16 *adv.* Combining the many meanings of arbor as a tree, an orchard, a shaded retreat, and a genealogical tree with aboriginal as the original or earliest know inhabitants, then Eve, Adam, ("our forced payrents") and Eden ("Edenborough") were "arboriginally" our first or original ancestors and home. ("And forthemore let legend go lore of it that mortar scene so cwympty dwympty what a dustydust it razed arboriginally") Humpty Dumpty makes another of his numerous Wakean appearances here, with his fall found in the Welch *cwymp* for "fall."

ardour *FW* 106.5 & 606.10 *n.* Passion or ardor that is also somewhat stern, severe, or dour. The "*Ardour*" of that noble Moor

Othello who loved his wife Desdemona "not wisely but too well" is a perfect example of dour mixed with ardor. ("*He Perssed Me Here with the Ardour of a Tonnoburkes*" & "he meditated continuously with seraphic ardour the primal sacrament of baptism or the regeneration of all man by affusion of water") With the second quote we are reminded of the "ardour" attached to the amount of water some Christians consider necessary for the sacrament of baptism.

arsched *FW* 547.30 *v.* Bent into a curve or arch resembling the human posterior, "ass" in America but "arse" in Great Britain. In more up-to-date American slang, the term "bubble butt" could be considered equivalent to "arsched." ("I cast my tenspan joys on her, arsched overtupped") McHugh references the phrase "arse over tip."

ashaped *FW* 373.13 *adj.* Uncomfortable from an improper action or ashamed enough to correct one's behavior by shaping up. A sense of shame is a fine stimulus to improvement when one is told to "Shape up or ship out." HCE might have been properly "ashaped" by his alleged impropriety in Phoenix Park, if only he could be certain of what exactly he had done. ("— He shook be ashaped of hempshelves, hiding that shepe in his goat.") If, as McHugh suggests, "hemp" stands for "hump" and "shepe in his goat" translates into "shape in his coat," as well as "sheep/goat," then we find a reference to not only HCE's or *Humph*rey's hump on his back but the story of the hunchbacked Norwegian captain who orders a bespoke suit from a Dublin tailor. When the suit doesn't fit, the captain complains that the tailor can't sew, while the tailor claims the captain is impossible to fit. This was one of John Joyce's stock of stories that his son wove into the fabric of *Finnegans Wake*. Perhaps another parallel is to Jacob who should be "ashaped" of himself for stealing his brother Esau's (Esau means hairyman.) birthright by wearing a sheepskin on his hands and neck ("carryin his overgoat under his shulder [German *Shuld* for "guilt"], sheepside out") to fool his blind, old father Isaac ("bland old isaac") into giving him, Jacob, his brother's blessing.

ashipwracked *FW* 275.18-19 *v.* The destruction, ruin, or wrack of a boat or ship wrecked by a storm or collision with rocks, another ship, etc. ("his seaarm strongsround her, her velivole eyne ashipwracked") Robinson Crusoe found himself "ashipwracked."

ashunned *FW* 489.18 *adj.* Disturbed by an improper action or ashamed while being avoided because of dislike or shunned. When the cause of one's shame is known, as in Hawthorne's novel, *The Scarlet Letter*, one is also likely to be shunned. ("He feels he ought to be as asamed of me as me to be ashunned of him.") McHugh identifies Shem in "asamed" and Shaun in "ashunned."

aslimed *FW* 506.7 *adj.* Disturbed by an improper action or ashamed while giving off a sticky substance or slime. ("the Muster of the hoose so as he called down on the Grand Precurser who coiled him crawler of the dupest dye and thundered at him to flatch down off that erection and be aslimed of himself for the bellance of hissech leif") This references God's direction to the serpent in Eden to crawl on his belly in the dust for the rest of his life for encouraging Eve and Adam's disobedience to His command not to eat the fruit from the Tree of the Knowledge of Good and Evil. While the skin of a snake is actually dry, it is commonly thought of as slimy. There is no record as to whether the serpent was "aslimed" of himself, but his hiss can clearly be heard in "hissech." HCE is reversed in "hissech," a reminder of his possibly improper action in Dublin's Phoenix Park, often a stand-in for Eden. McHugh gives the German *flachen* for "flatten" or "level down."

aspolootly *FW* 372.34 *adv.* Without a doubt or absolutely certain to plunder or loot. In earlier times soldiers received whatever they could loot from their enemies and their cities as payment for their military services. Naturally a general got the lion's share, which explains why Julius Caesar often turned his troops loose on cities in Gaul even when citizens surrendered up front without a fight. ("The for eolders were aspolootly at their wetsend in the mailing waters, trying to. Hide! Seek! Hide! Seek!")

assalt *FW* 331.30 *n*. An attack or assault made with sodium chloride or salt. Too much salt in a person's diet is an "assalt" on the system that can cause high blood pressure. In war, a defeated nation sometimes suffered an "assalt" when the victors sowed salt in the ground to prevent food from being grown for years, as when the Romans, determined to put down the Carthaginian threat once and for all, decided on an "assalt" of the fields around the city. ("was it the twylyd or the mounth of the yare or the feint of her smell made the seomen assalt of her") The assault suggested here is the sexual "assalt" of a woman by a man's salty semen. (See **seomen**.)

assideration *FW* 451.36 *n*. Attention, deliberation, or consideration of the stars since *sidereus* is the Latin for "starry." Oscar Wilde demonstrated some "asideration" with his observation that "We are all in the gutter, but some of us are looking at the stars." ("I'd be awful anxious, you understand, about shoepisser and in assideration of the terrible lufsucks wobbling around with the hedrolics in the coold amstophere") Microsoft Word suggested "asseveration" for "assideration," so this gives an additional meaning of a positive or earnest affirmation given to a consideration of the stars, as Wilde so obviously does.

assorceration *FW* 608.2 *n*. A society or association for persons practicing witchcraft or sorcerers and, perhaps, for their apprentices. Harry Potter's Hogwarts School of Witchcraft and Wizardry can be thought of as an "assorceration." Within "the Brehons Assorceration for the advauncement of seayence because, my dear, mentioning of it under the breath, as in pure (what bunkum!) essenesse," McHugh references "Brehon Law:

ancient Ir. legal system" and "British Association for the Advancement of Science" as well as the "hostility of 19th Century scientific bodies to spiritualists" as evidenced by its essence being pure bunkum.

astoneaged *FW* 18.15 *v.* Amazed or astonished by the Stone Age or some aspect of it. Astounding suggestions are surfacing about life during this earliest known time of human culture when stone tools and weapons were used. More recently, the citizens of North Vietnam were no doubt "astoneaged" when President Lyndon Johnson declared his intent to bomb them back into the Stone Age. Within *Finnegans Wake* we find the twins Shem and Shaun, as the cavemen Mutt and Jute, discussing the Battle of Clontarf/ Waterloo: "Mutt.—Ore you astoneaged, jute you?" "Jute.—Oye am thonthorstrok, thing mud." Hearing Thor's thunder, the thunderstruck pair beat a path to the safety of their cave during this first of Vico's three ages, the theocratic. (See **thonthorstrok**.)

Astraylians *FW* 321.9 *n.* Australians who have taken the wrong way or have strayed. In the early days of western settlement of this continent, England shipped many of its convicts to Australia, thus those who had strayed from the path of law and order could properly be called "astraylians." ("breaking and entering, from the outback's dead heart, Glasthule Bourne or Boehernapark Nolagh, by wattsismade or bianconi, astraylians in island") McHugh translates these last three words as "Australians in Ireland," although, through English harshness with Ireland, there were many more Irish in Australia than the reverse.

astunshed *FW* 448.6 *v.* So greatly surprised or astonished as to knock senseless, bewilder, or stun. First-time readers of *Finnegans Wake* are usually "astunshed" by its bewildering word play. ("I shall be very cruelly mistaken indeed if you will not be joshed astunshed to see how you will be meanwhile")

attemption *FW* 364.12 *n.* 1. An effort or attempt at heeding or paying attention. This is generally unsuccessful if a task is dull and is often observed in classrooms where students are not paying attention to the lesson but attempt to appear as if they actually are. ("Dear and lest I forget mergers and bow to you low, marchers! Attemption!") 2. Notice or attention given to a strong attraction or a temptation. It is usually easy to give "attemption" to that which tempts. As Irishman Oscar Wilde remarked, "I can resist everything except temptation."

audorable *FW* 562.33 *adj.* A delightful or adorable sound that can be heard or that is audible. The recording of James Joyce reading from *Finnegans Wake* is absolutely "audorable." ("He is too audorable really, eunique!") Joyce's reading can be found on several internet websites and is available on a CD. What a shame, with his lovely "audorable" tenor voice, Joyce didn't have a recording made of his singing "Finnegan's Wake."

automoboil *FW* 448.29 *n.* A car or automobile in which the radiator has overheated to the point that its water is boiling, as evidenced by steam pouring from around the cap. ("under privy-sealed orders to get me an increase of automoboil and footwear")

aveiled *FW* 375.29 *v.* Made use of or availed to hide the face with thin material or a veil. Women throughout history "aveiled" themselves to disguise their features or simply to hide wrinkles. ("Fummuccumul with a graneen aveiled.") Here we have the legendary Irish hero Finn MacCool whose wife-to-be, Grania, "aveiled" to hide her identity, ran off with MacCool's nephew Dermot, a story somewhat reminiscent of King Mark II of Cornwall who lost his bride-to-be Iseult's love and virginity to his young nephew Tristram who appears on the *Wake*'s first page as "Sir Tristram, violer d'amores," or the violator of love.

avunculusts *FW* 367.14 *adj.* Like an uncle or avuncular combined with a strong sexual desire or lust. It has long been the custom for an older man in the company of a young woman or young man for sexual purposes to pose euphemistically as their "uncle" in an attempt at respectability. ("—I'll gie ye credit for simmence more if ye'll be lymphing. Our four avunculusts.") In this instance the "four avunculusts" are the four evangelists Matthew, Mark, Luke, and John, know in *Finnegans Wake* as "Mamalujo." These four old men sometimes show up in the *Wake* with lust in their hearts as when they spy on ("luistening and listening to the oceans of kissening, with their eyes glistening, all the four") Tristram and Iseult making love on the ship taking them to Cornwall where Iseult is to marry Tristram's uncle, King Mark II, who is not without "avunculusts" feelings for his much younger fiancée.

awailable   *FW* 228.24   *adj.* That which can be secured or is available for a long lament or wail. In some cultures it is the custom to hire professional, "awailable" mourners as one part of funeral services. ("by an alley and detour with farecard awailable getrennty years")

aweghost   *FW* 353.3   *adj.* Inspiring reverence or awe in the sense of august, thus the honorary title given to the Roman Emperor Octavian, Caesar Augustus. His wife, Livia, who may be suggested with the last word on the *Wake*'s first page, "livvy" (Mark Twain's nickname for his wife Olivia was Livy, and the Roman historian Livy was important to the work of Vico.), was given the title Augusta. In a six-degrees-of-separation sense, Augusta is tied to Joyce because his middle name, Augustine, was incorrectly written as Augusta on his birth registration. Finn Fordham describes "Aweghost" as "awe-inspiring like the holy ghost of the Trinity, fiery like high summer (August)." ("And the name of the Most Marsiful, the Aweghost, the Gragious One!") McHugh suggests gracious and egregious for "Gragious."

awethorrorty   *FW* 516.19   *n.* Both dread and reverence or awe for the power of control or authority. Awe for authority is common, often leaving one speechless in the presence of power, as Dorothy, the Scarecrow, the Tin Man, and the Cowardly Lion were in the presence of the Wizard of Oz, that is until they paid attention to the man behind the curtain. ("this is my awethorrorty") McHugh calls attention to the Scandinavian god Thor, whose thundering hammer inspired "awethorrorty" in gods and men alike, in this *Wake* word.

awondering *FW* 336.16 *adj.* Roaming, traveling, or wandering while admiring, marveling, or wondering. If Joyce had written at the time of William Wordsworth, that lake-district poet might have written, "I was awondering lonely as a cloud." ("We are once amore as babes awondering in a wold made fresh where with the hen in the storyaboot we start from scratch.") This sentence describes the readers of *Finnegans Wake* who feel like babes in the wood as they start from scratch trying to make sense of the story about all of human history. It also refers to the letter or "litter" a chicken scratches out of the dump. (See **anomorous, litter,** & **middenst.**)

awristed *FW* 532.27 *v.* Handcuffed at the wrists when apprehended or arrested. It is common police procedure for those taken into custody to be "awristed" and their wrights wread to them. ("I should her have awristed under my duskguise of whipppers")

axecutes *FW* 346.6 *v.* To put to death or execute with a sharp blade fastened to a handle or an ax. Henry VIII is probably known as much or more for the axecutions of two of his wives as for any other acts of his long reign. ("*while the Arumbian Knives Riders axecutes devilances round the jehumispheure*")

ayewitnessed *FW* 254.10 *v.* To have actually seen some act or happening as an eyewitness and thus are able to testify in the affirmative or aye to its occurrence. ("Polycarp and Irenews eye-to-eye ayewitnessed and to Paddy Palmer") As to HCE's alleged crime(s) in Phoenix Park, the two girls and three soldiers who testify aye to being eyewitnesses seem to be as unreliable as so many eyewitnesses in court often prove to be.

ayternitay *FW* 406.28   *n*. An affirmative vote, ay or aye, in favor of tea, pronounced "tay" in Ireland, for all time or eternity. ("Ever of thee, Anne Lynch, he's deeply draiming! Houseanna! Tea is the Highest! For auld lang Ayternitay!") McHugh identifies "Anne Lynch" as a Dublin tea and this first sentence as the song "Ever of Thee I'm fondly dreaming." This is followed by "Hosanna in the highest" and then the standard song for New Year's Eve, "Auld Lang Syne." McHugh also mentions "For All Eternity," a song in John McCormack's repertoire. So, here is a strong statement in favor of tea the way the Irish like it, "strong enough to trot a mouse on," while fondly dreaming of draining a pot of this highest drink forever and ever. In *Ulysses* Haines remarks, "But, I say, Mulligan, you do make strong tea, don't you." Buck Mulligan replies in an old woman's voice, "When I makes tea I makes tea, as old mother Grogan said. And when I makes water I makes water." And Irish fairy tales concluded with, "So they put on the kettle and made tea (tay), and if they don't live happy that you and I may." Tea can even be read into the last word of *Finnegans Wake*, "the," which as *thé* is French for tea. The Liffey was said to be the color of tea from the dumpings of the dye-houses on its banks, and Joyce asked Faber and Faber, the publishers of his Anna Livia Plurabelle book, to print the cover in brown to match the color of the Liffey. So "Ayternitay" is such a strong statement it has an exclamation mark behind it. Summing up how highly tea is considered in British culture, an English churchman once remarked, "I thank God I was not born before tea."

B

baallad *FW* 593.15 *n*. A poem, song, or ballad that tells a story about young sheep or a lamb. The nursery rhyme about Mary's little lamb that broke the rules by following her to school is perhaps the most famous "baallad" of them all, although the "baallad" about the black sheep that had three bags full of wool is equally well known. An English expression for a nice, sweet young person is a "baa-lamb." ("And let Billey Feghin be baallad out of his hummuluation.")

bababadalgharaghtakamminarronnkonnbronntonnerronntuonnthunntrovarrhounawnskawntoohoohoordenenthurnuk! *FW* 3.15-17 *n*. Onomatopoeia for the sound of thunder. This is the first of 10 thunder words in *Finnegans Wake*, it and eight others having 100 letters and the 10th having 101 letters, making 1,001 letters that suggest the *Arabian Nights* or, in Wakese, "this scherzarade of one's thousand and one nightinesses." As a numerical palindrome, 1001 suggests the circular system of Vico and the *Wake*'s never-ending, never-beginning stylistic structure. In Vico's system, the Divine Age is the first of three ages in which humanity hears the voice of God in thunder and, driven by fear ("the fright of light") to hide in caves, pray "Loud, hear us!" "Who in the name of thunder'd ever belevin you were that bolt?" In keeping with this theme, the first thunder word is made up of many words similar to thunder in various languages: "kamminarro" (Japanese *kaminari*); "tuonn" (Italian *tuono*); "bronnto" (Greek *Bronte*); "thurnuk" (Gaelic *tornach*); "awnska" (Swedish *aska*); "tonner" (French *tonnerre* and Latin *tonare*); "tova" (Portuguese *trovao*); and "ton" (Old Rumanian *tun*). There are also words that come close to thunder such as "arag" (French *orage* for "storm") and "tonner" (German *tonen* for "resound"). The letters "bababa" and "toohoohoo" mimic a stutter that is heard throughout the *Wake* as a sign of guilt. Since it is God's voice heard in thunder, this stuttering indicates God's guilt for what Joyce considered the Original Sin, the creation of the world. (See **thuthunder** & **unpeppeppediment**.) There's a ton of other meanings and references to be found in this first thunder word, not to mention the next nine which I haven't included in this dictionary so, if you want to delve more deeply into them, I highly recommend Eric McLuhan's exploration of all 10 of these words in his excellent book, *The Role of Thunder in "Finnegans Wake."* (I'd be willing to bet the pun was intended.)

babbelers *FW* 15.12 *n.* Speakers whose spoken sounds cannot be understood by others as a result of God's destruction of the Tower of Babel or babblers. The diversity of tongues that resulted sounds like babbling to the untutored ear. While God divided one language into hundreds, Joyce reunites almost all of them in *Finnegans Wake*. Critics have inevitably compared the *Wake* to babbling, but those patient readers who have taken the time to studiously peruse it have found a book with, if anything, too much meaning rather than none at all. God has not yet destroyed *Finnegans Wake* as He did the Tower of Babel, probably because He hasn't tried to read it for Himself. The builders of Babel appear as "The babbelers with their thangas vain have been (confusium hold them!) they were and went."

backtowards *FW* 84.30 *adv.* In the direction of or toward the back or backwards with the special sense of moving toward a specific person, place, or thing. In other words, not simply a backwards movement. The film *Back to the Future* or the song lyrics "I was looking back to see if you were looking back to see if I was looking back to see if you were looking back at me" are illustrations in which "backtowards" could be used appropriately. ("wurming along gradually for our savings backtowards motherwaters so many miles from bank and Dublin")

backwords *FW* 73.19, 100.28, 487.32, & 624.18 *n.* Words written backwards as either the letters of a word written backwards or a group of words written in an order opposite to their accustomed or generally recognized way. *Finnegans Wake* has many examples of both, with the words or initials for Humphrey Chimpden Earwicker (HCE) and Anna Livia Plurabelle (ALP) being the most common. ("proceeded with a Hubbleforth slouch in his slips backwords (*Et Cur Heli!*) in the directions of the duff and demb institutions," "hearing his own bauchspeech in backwords, or, more strickly, but tristurned initials," "When Lapac walks backwords he's darkest horse in Capalisoot," & "Bold bet backwords.") The *Wake* itself is "backwords" in the sense that the words at the very back of the book ("A way a lone a last a loved a long the") start the sentence that begins the book ("riverrun, past Eve and Adam's, from swerve of shore to bend of bay, brings us by a commodius vicus of recirculation back to Howth Castle and Environs.") Another example is "Nilbud" or Dublin "backwords."

bankrump *FW* 590.3 *n.* 1. Buttocks or rump one can cash in on or bank on. Jennifer Lopez's rump has helped both her career and bank account. 2. A movie star unable to pay debts or bankrupt from no longer being able to get good roles because his or her "bankrump" went south, also known as a sagging ass. One crucial role of personal trainers is to keep those butts firm. ("what remains of a heptark, leareyed and letterish, weeping worrybound on his bankrump") To use a word from the *Wake*'s first page, an actor's career has been "buttended."

barebarean *FW* 71.30 *n.* A naked or bare uncivilized person or barbarian. The ancient Celts of England were said by the Romans to go into battle wearing nothing more than a coat of blue paint, but for which they would have qualified for the title of "*Barebarean.*" ("*He's None of Me Causin, Barebarean, Peculiar Person*")

baremaids *FW* 526.23 *n.* Naked or bare women who serve alcoholic drinks or barmaids. Topless bars are popular, and it seems the less the ladies pouring drinks wear, the larger their tips. ("Sure I thought it was larking in the trefoll of the furry glans with two stripping baremaids, Stilla Underwood and Moth MacGarry") The "two stripping baremaids" referred to are the two girls on Dublin's coat of arms who are lifting the hems of their dresses to show their bare legs.

barents *FW* 331.12 *n.* Naked or bare fathers and mothers or parents. Eve and Adam would have been the first "barents" if they had refrained from eating an apple, but they were wearing skins by the time Cain and Abel came along. Nudist parents and certain Amazonian tribes best describe today's "barents." ("And you Tim Tommy Melooney, I'll tittle your barents if you stick that pigpin upinto meh!") The nudity implied with "barents" is appropriate with the sexual suggestions in this sentence.

barnacled *FW* 423.22 *v.* Fastened securely, as a salt-water crustacean or a barnacle is to the bottom of a boat. The maiden name of Joyce's wife, Nora, was Barnacle. When John Joyce heard that his son had eloped with a woman named Barnacle, he is said to have remarked, "She'll stick to him," proving that the love of puns ran in the family. McHugh mentions that "barnacled" is also slang for "wearing spectacles," which makes sense in its Wakean context. ("when he made his boo to the public and barnacled up to the eyes when he repented after seven.") This might refer to Joyce whose eyeglasses were quite strong.

barsalooner *FW* 625.11-12 *n.* An establishment serving alcoholic drinks such as a bar or saloon in Barcelona, Spain. ("But you'll have to ask that same four that named them is always snugging in your barsalooner") McHugh writes that Joyce "wore a Borsalino hat" and that a "snug" is a "secluded area in pub." The term "snugging" appears in *A Portrait of the Artist as a Young Man* to describe an activity that caused two students at Stephen's school to be severely punished. Though the subject of unresolved scholarly debate, "snugging" is generally thought to describe some sort of mutually agreeable though unspecified sexual activity between two boys.

bawdy *FW* 547.28 *n.* This is a case of an existing word that Joyce transformed into a new meaning. With bawdy meaning lewd or obscene, in the Wakean context it becomes a lewd or obscene body. ("with all my bawdy did I her whorship") This might be a more appropriate vow for many celebrity marriage ceremonies than the traditional words—"With my body I thee worship." (See **whorship**.)

beaconegg *FW* 382.11 *n.* Anything that is a warning or beacon to an egg. A "beaconegg" posted on Humpty Dumpty's wall might have saved him, as well as all the King's horses and men, a great deal of inconvenience. Humpty's remains, if left there, would serve as a graphic "beaconegg" to future eggs who might contemplate sitting on the wall. ("till that hen of Kaven's shows her beaconegg") Bacon and eggs are also suggested.

bearserk *FW* 582.29 *adv.* 1. To become violently angry or berserk with the wild fury of a maddened bear. *n.* 2. A bear that has gone berserk. Film director Werner Herzog's documentary film, *Grizzly Man* (2005), presents the story of grizzly bear advocate Timothy Treadwell and his girlfriend who are literally eaten alive by a hunger-driven "bearserk." 3. An insanely upset

Wall Street speculator who, believing the stock market will fall, known as a bear, sells all his shares, only to see the market rise to the cheers of the optimists, known as bulls. ("Hokoway, in his hiphigh bearserk!") Asked what the stock market was going to do, financier J. P. Morgan replied, "It will fluctuate." *Finnegans Wake* speaks to this with "Bull igien bear and then bearagain bulligan." This is reminiscent of the famous train-wreck telegraph, "Off again, on again, gone again, Finnegan." The ripples from *Wake* words spread in ever widening circles.

beauhind *FW* 564.8 *n.* A handsome or beautiful (French *beau* for "beautiful") buttocks or behind. Marilyn Monroe walking up the stairs to her apartment in the film *The Seven Year Itch* provides a beautiful view of a female "beauhind." ("Is it not that we are commanding from fullback, woman permitting, a profusely fine birdseye view from beauhind this park?") In this instance it is most probably HCE's bare butt exposed to the three soldiers in Phoenix Park that is on view. (See "***mehind***.") Though HCE's alleged crime that evening in the park was never proven in his trials, all Dublin judged him guilty of something or other.

beautonhole *FW* 350.11 *n.* 1. A beautiful flower worn in the buttonhole of the lapel of a man of fashion, a dandy, or beau such as Beau Brummell. *v.* 2. To be forced to listen or buttonholed by a man of fashion, a dandy, or beau. Beau Brummell was a gentleman with manners as exquisite as his clothes and was never known to "beautonhole" anyone. ("*with a gesture expansive of Mr. Lhugewhite Cadderpollard with sunflawered heautonhole pulled up point blanck by mailbag mundaynism at Oldbally Curf*") McHugh tells us that Oscar Wilde wore a heliotrope flower (one that follows the sun) in his buttonhole at his first trial at the Old Bailey Court and that Lady Campbell described Wilde as a great white caterpillar.

bedst *FW* 356.26, 531.5, & 560.20 *n.* The finest or best furniture designed for sleeping or bed. The Danish *bedst* means "best," but the immediate association for me comes from William Shakespeare's will in which he left his "second best bed" with all its furnishings to his wife. There has been much controversy regarding this apparent slight in that he didn't leave her his "bedst," but it may be simply that their "bedst" was reserved for company and that their marriage bed, while the second best in quality, had first place in matrimonial memories. Joyce was certainly aware of the contents of Shakespeare's will because we find in *Ulysses*—"Leftherhis / Second / Leftherhis / Bestabed / Secabest / Leftabed." I can't leave this without including that wonderful pun from *Ulysses*: "If others have their will Ann hath a way." ("like my good bedst friend," "Master's gunne he warrs the bedst," & "Around the bloombiered, booty with the bedst.") To illustrate the individualized, evocative nature of *Wake* words, when a friend who was reading this book as the manuscript progressed asked what word I was working on and I said "bedst" or best bed, she said the first thing that came to her mind was 'bedstead.' Well, with that I thought I was through with this entry, but then I received an email from the eminent Joycean Brandy Kershner who had been kind enough to give me the page and line number in *Ulysses* for the first quote above. Brandy forwarded a freshly penned limerick just emailed to him by the distinguished Wakean John Gordon:

> He left her the secondbest bed
> Before lying down with the dead;
> 'Twas Will's way to trumpet
> His Anne was a strumpet
> And to rue that the two of them wed.

It seemed a spooky coincidence coming so suddenly after my writing about what is certainly an obscure subject, but then I remembered G. K. Chesterton wrote that "Coincidences are spiritual puns," and somehow it made a strange sort of sense, somewhat like *Finnegans Wake*.

beehiviour *FW* 430.19   *n.* The conduct, deportment, or behavior of insects that make honey or bees in their house, swarming place, or hive. The queen's "beehiviour" keeps the others buzzing. ("goodwill girls on their best beehiviour who all they were girls all rushing sowarmly for the post as buzzy as sie could bie") (See **buzzy** & **sowarmly**.)

beerlitz *FW* 182.7   *n.* A school to study making different varieties of beer, much as the Berlitz Schools offer courses in learning different languages. ("to ensign the colours by the beerlitz in his mathness and his educandees to outhue themselves") Joyce went to Switzerland with Nora in the belief that he had been promised a job as an instructor in English at the Berlitz School in Zurich. When that proved to be false, he moved on, briefly, to the Berlitz School in Pola and then to the one in Trieste until World War I forced him back to Zurich. McHugh gives the following translations that assist with this phrase: French *enseigner* for "to teach" and Italian *educande* for "girl boarders in convent schools." The phrase "to outhue themselves" is obviously Joyce's anticipation of Roland McHugh's *Annotations to "Finnegans Wake"* in which McHugh did outdo himself in providing much needed assistance to struggling readers of the *Wake*.

begottom *FW* 582.1   *v.* Produced, caused to be, or begotten from the lowest part or bottom. Things "begottom" from a barrel are often somewhat crushed or broken from the pressure of all the other objects on top of them. The Caviarteria in New York has advertised "Bottom of the Barrel" caviar at a reduced price. Though the sturgeon eggs are broken, the taste is still superior. ("Yet he begottom.")

belchybubhub *FW* 239.33   *n.* Lucifer or Beelzebub violently shooting out or belching, most likely fire in Hell, with a great uproar or hubbub. ("oaths and screams and bawley groans with a belchybubhub and a hellabelow bedimmed and bediabbled the arimaining lucisphere") McHugh translates "hellabelow" as "hullabaloo" and gives the Spanish *diablo* for "devil" in "bediabbled." Joyce wrote one children's book, *The Cat and the Devil*, for his much loved grandson, Stephen James Joyce. It paints a *purr*fect picture of "belchybubhub."

benefiction *FW* 185.3 *n.* Something imagined, made up, or a fiction that appears to be good or beneficial (Latin *bene* for "well" or "good"). Benediction, the request for God's blessing, and benefaction, a good deed, are suggested here but with the underlying idea that their goodness is not of real benefit. For instance, if there is no God, or at least no personal God who grants individual blessings in the first instance and, in the second instance, charity such as the soup kitchens set up by English Protestants during the Irish potato famine that provided aid to starving Catholics on condition of their religious conversion. The old adage, "If it sounds too good to be true, it probably is," applies to many a "benefiction." ("under his own benefiction of their pastor Father Fammeus Falconer")

besighed *FW* 261.24 *adv.* Nearby or beside one who let out a long, deep breath or sighed. Horatio was "besigned" Hamlet at the graveside when he sighed, "Alas, poor Yorick. I knew him Horatio." ("Ainsoph,[3] this upright one, with that noughty besighed him zeroine.") The symbol "[3]" following "Ainsoph" does not mean that this word is cubed but refers readers to footnote number 3, "Groupname for grapejuice." McHugh identifies "grapejuice" as "Wine in Mass."

betwixtween *FW* 184.7 *prep.* A contraction of the phrase "betwixt and between." Since "betwixt" is archaic for "between" and "betwixt and between" means "in the Middle" or "neither one thing nor another," "betwixtween" can convey the idea of something halfway between the archaic and the modern, such as a typewriter in the middle or between handwriting and word processors, or teenagers who are neither modern children nor archaic adults.

biografiend *FW* 55.6 *n*. An evil-spirited or fiendish writer of a person's life or a biographer. Joyce hand-picked his first biographer, Herbert Gorman. As the only authorized author of Joyce's life, Gorman was also unauthorized to report certain details, such as the marital legal status of Joyce and Nora or the mental problems of their daughter Lucia. Joyce didn't live long enough to read the slew of biographies that followed Gorman's, but each contains material Joyce almost certainly would have disapproved seeing in print, such as the sexual language he used in some letters to Nora. In *Finnegans Wake*, he anticipated these fiends of the biographical arts yet to come with "his biografiend, in fact, kills him verysoon, if yet not, after."

bisexycle *FW* 115.16 *n*. 1. A two-wheeled, pedal-powered vehicle or bicycle for those attracted to both sexes or bisexuals. An example might be a standard boy's bike painted pink with plastic fringe at the end of each handlebar. 2. A bicycle built for two sexes with one half having the horizontal bar between the handlebars and the seat as found on a boy's bike and the other half without that bar as found on a girl's bike, at least those designed for girls in days long ago when they wore skirts and dresses. ("dinky pinks deliberatively summersaulting off her bisexycle")

blanck *FW* 350.11 *adj*. Without any light or black and an empty space or blank. A better name for Black Holes found by physicists in outer space might be "blanck" holes. Joyce was very interested in modern physics and followed Einstein's work with great interest. With "dipdipping downes in blackholes," Joyce came up with the concept of blackholes before Hawking and other scientists. Einstein's relativity equations actually predicted Black Holes, but he refused to believe in them. ("*pulled up point blanck by mailbag mundaynism*")

bleaueyedeal *FW* 384.24 *adj*. The color of a clear, daylight sky or blue and a perfect type or ideal combined as a blue-eyed ideal. Within the *Wake*, this "Gaelic champion, the onliest one of her choice, her bleaueyedeal of a girl's friend" is Iseult's lover, Sir Tristram, who is introduced on the first page as a "violer d'amores," that is a violator of love and a musician of love. His beautiful blue eyes are ideal for making him her ideal man whom she loves a great deal. In his essay in *How Joyce Wrote Finnegans Wake*, Jed Deppman finds "'blow' (bleau), the color blue (blau, bleu), and such higher-level comment-puns as 'eyedeal' (ideal; 'deal' of the eye; 'I'-deal; 'I(solde)-deal'; 'why-deal';'Y(seut)-deal'; 'below-eye-deal'; 'below-ideal'; 'blue-eyed deal'; etc.)" Deppman adds: "Some readers will even see a 'blue-eyed eel' and others anything 'ideally' blue.'" There's more, but why try to outdo the *Oxford English Dictionary*.

blottom *FW* 281.F2 *v.* To dry or blot one's buttocks or bottom. ("poliss it off, there's a nateswipe, on to your blottom pulper") McHugh gives the Latin *nates* for "backside" and reads "blottom pulper" as "blotting paper." The most prominent person to "blottom" in *Finnegans Wake* is the Russian general shot by the Irish sharpshooter Buckley during the Crimean War when he saw the general pick up a piece of sod to wipe his bottom after defecating. (See **gianerant**.) No doubt the general would have preferred a piece of blotting paper.

bluggy *FW* 31.11 *adj.* 1. Covered with blood or bloody and swarming with bugs or buggy. A mosquito can be considered a "bluggy" insect as a swarm of them can make one's body bloody. *n.* 2. As British slang, a bloody little bugger can mean a cursed engager in anal sex. 3. Homicidal maniacs are considered crazy or buggy and leave their victims bloody. 4. An accident involving a light carriage or buggy might turn it into a "bluggy." "Naw, yer maggers, aw war jist cotchin on thon bluggy earwuggers" was HCE's response when the king asked what he was doing one day on the turnpike with pot on a pole. He was catching bloody earwigs. Thus the King gave HCE, sometimes known as Mr. Porter, the surname Earwicker.

boosome *FW* 231.8 *adj.* An intimate or bosom friend during bouts of drinking alcoholic beverages or booze. A "*boosome*" pal is nice to have when on the "bottlefilled." (See **bottlefilled**.) ("*And cloitered for amourmeant in thy boosome shede!*") (See **amourmeant**.)

bottlefilled *FW* 310.26 *n.* Site of a military conflict or a battlefield filled with glass containers for holding liquids or bottles, particularly those containing alcoholic spirits. It was not unusual for soldiers (sailors, too) to indulge in a liberal quantity of wine, brandy, run, etc., what the *Wake* calls "liquid courage," before going into battle. HCE's pub may also be thought of as a battlefield filled with bottles where he fights for his honor against his customers' accusations that he engaged in some improper activities in Phoenix Park. ("till time jings pleas, that host of a bottlefilled, the bulkily hulkwight") Here we hear, thanks to McHugh, HCE announce the closing of his pub with "Time, gents, please." With "bulkily hulkwight," Joyce anticipates the famous wrestler who knows best, Hulk Hogan.

breakfarts *FW* 453.12 *n.* The expelling of gas or farts that escape or break as the result of something eaten at the first meal of the day that breaks the fast of night or breakfast. ("exciting your mucuses, turning breakfarts into lost soupirs") McHugh reads this as turning "breakfasts into Last Suppers." If it was soup served at this last supper, no doubt it was bean soup. (See **fartenoiser**.)

broadcussed *FW* 526.27 *n.* A radio or television transmission or broadcast that is cursed or cussed. A program may be cursed in the sense that it suffers some ill fortune, such as being cancelled or having the star die, or cussed at by the listening or viewing audience who swear it is truly terrible, or filled with a broad range of cuss words, as do most films beyond a "G" rating. ("There was that one that was always mad gone on him, her first king of cloves and the most broadcussed man in Corrack-on-Sharon, County Rosecarmon.") McHugh identifies the "king of cloves" as King Clovis of the Salian Franks and the king of clubs and "mad gone" as "Maud Gonne loved by Yeats."

buttom *FW* 48.18 *n*. The base, buttocks, or bottom of the human body known in the vernacular as the "butt." As a midpoint between bottom and butt, "buttom" is a few degrees more socially acceptable than butt and certainly, at least in polite conversation, far better than ass. ("from tubb to buttom all falsetissues") I read this as "from top to bottom it is all false issues." McHugh identifies the phrase "a tissue of falsehood." But (no pun intended), with Joyce's placing of "butt" in "buttom," I can't help wondering if "falsetissues" might mean unfaithful to the accepted concept of toilet tissues. This, in turn, suggests the story of Buckley and the Russian general. (See **gianerant**.)

buzzy *FW* 430.20 *adj*. Emitting a humming sound or buzz while active or busy. ("rushing sowarmly for the post as buzzy as sie could bie") With the German *sie* for "her" and the Norwegian *bie* for "bee," the old phrases "As busy as she could be," and "As busy as a bee" appear. A humming Winnie-the-Pooh could be described as "buzzy." (See **beehiviour** & **sowarmly**.)

C

canifully *FW* 374.33 *adv*. Carefully, painfully, perhaps fainfully acting in the manner of Cain, who infamously killed his brother, Abel, angrily and jealously after God accepted Abel's offering of animals and rejected Cain's offering of fruits and vegetables. Cain got the murder ball rolling, and men and women have continued killing "Cainfully" ever since. ("Just press this cold brand against your brow for a mow. Cainfully! The sinus the curse.") McHugh references this first sentence with *Genesis* 4:15: "the Lord set a mark upon Cain," and translates the last sentence as "sign of the cross." God made it "Cainfully" clear from the beginning that carnivores are his kind of folks and vegetarians are cursed. Just remember, it was God who ignored PETA's advice and replaced Adam and Eve's fig-leaf couture with the skins of dead animals. As the bumper sticker reads, "I didn't claw my way to the top of the food chain to eat vegetables."

capItalIsed *FW* 120.4 *v*. 1. To have written a letter of the alphabet in its large form, especially the letter "i" written as "I." 2. To place special emphasis on oneself over and above all others or to make one's ego supreme, saying in effect that "I" am the best or of capital importance. In his classic, *The Devil's Dictionary*,

72 | A *Finnegans Wake* Lextionary

Ambrose Bierce defines an egotist as "A person of low taste, more interested in himself than in me." It seems humans have always "capItalIsed" themselves as Individuals.

celescalating *FW* 5.1 *v.* 1. Expanding by stages or escalating the celestial space of the heavens. With the advent of the Hubble Telescope, the universe has continued "celescalating" from the days limited by human sight. Will we one day be able to see far enough to actually witness the origin of the cosmos? Stay tuned. 2. Using "very good" or "beautiful" as one definition of "celestial," *Finnegans Wake* has increasingly been "celescalating" as scholars delve deeper and deeper into its mystic mysteries. ("erigenating from next to nothing and celescalating the himals and all, hierachitectitiptitoploftical") With the German *Himmel* for "sky, heaven," the Big Bang ("Big went the bang") may be referred to or what the *Wake* describes as the "expending umniverse."

celibrate *FW* 600.35 *v.* To honor or celebrate being unmarried or celibate. There's a joke about a monk copying an ancient religious text in a medieval monastery. Worried that a mistake may have been made in an earlier copy that was then repeated over the years, he searches out the original book. Much to his dismay, he finds an egregious error. As he tearfully tells his brother monks, "It says 'celebrate!'" It may have been a misprint like this that caused Joyce to decline an offer to study for the priesthood. ("so who would celibrate the holy mystery upon or that the pirigrim from Mainylands beatnd") (See **sorowbrate**.)

cerebrated *FW* 421.19 *adj.* Distinguished, renowned, or celebrated for thought, reason, or the cerebral rather than emotion, feeling, or action. James Joyce is certainly a "cerebrated" writer whose celebrated works require a cerebral workout from his readers. ("the penmarks used out in sinscript with such hesitancy by your cerebrated brother—excuse me not mentioningahem?")

chaosmos *FW* 118.21 *n.* While the cosmos is considered the

celescalating - charictures[3] | 73

orderly, harmonious system of the universe, "chaosmos" is the exact opposite, the completely confused, disordered, and chaotic universe or the cosmos in chaos. ("every person, place, and thing in the chaosmos of the Alle anyway connected with the gobblydumped") Commenting on this ordered/disordered creation, Finn Fordham writes, "Chaosmos, however, is an aptly disunified concept, voicing the word 'chiasmus,' or 'arch,' that symbol of structural harmony, and in itself a bridge, like many of the *Wake* words themselves, between chaos and cosmos."

charictures[3] *FW* 302.31-32 *n*. An exaggerated drawing or caricature of the personality or character of a person with an emphasis on the person's peculiarities. Joyce drew many such "charictures" with words in *Finnegans Wake*, beginning on the first page with "a bland old isaac" for the blind old Isaac who later becomes "blind old eye-sick." His sons Jacob and Esau become "Jerkoff" and "Eatsoup," "charictures" of Jacob the jerk who cheated his brother and deceived his father and Esau who couldn't hold his hunger but had to eat the soup his younger twin had cooked even at the ridiculously inflated price of his inheritance. ("And ook, ook, ook, fanky! All the charictures[3] in the drame!") Here Joyce invites readers to look, look, look frankly at all the characters and their caricatures in his written drama/dream. (See **drema**.) It can and has been postulated that there are only two characters in the *Wake*, HCE and ALP, and that all the others are merely "charictures" of these two elemental characters. This passage comes in the lessons chapter where the Earwicker's children are doing their homework. Issy provides a footnote here with "[3] Gag his tubes yourself." McHugh translates this as "keep it to yourself," and it does paint a vivid picture of choking a person's speaking tubes to shut them up. It brought to my mind the Valley Girl slang, "Gag me with a spoon," another example of the *Wake*'s referential process. But, given Issy's budding interest in sex, it could refer to a form of birth control where the tubes are tied or gagged or, if the penis is thought of as a tube, birth control in the form of oral sex.

charmaunt *FW* 384.30 *n.* The sister of one's father or mother, wife of one's uncle, or aunt, who is pleasing, fascinating, attractive, or charming. The "charmaunt" in *Finnegans Wake* is Iseult, princess of Ireland, who, on becoming the wife of King Mark II of Cornwall, immediately becomes the aunt of "Sir Tristram" whom readers meet on the *Wake*'s first page. Tristram was entrusted by his uncle the king with escorting Iseult from Ireland to Cornwall where they were to be married. But during the voyage Iseult and Tristram innocently drink a love potion Iseult's mother brewed for her beautiful daughter and King Mark to drink on their wedding day. Needless to say, the steamy shipboard love scenes described so erotically in the *Wake* continue after the wedding day, and Tristram not only cuckolds his uncle but beds his "charmaunt." It may help to know that "aunt" is slang for "whore." Anyway, the medieval tale of Tristram and Iseult flows through *Finnegans Wake* as the Liffey flows through Dublin. ("that was palpably wrong and bulbubly improper, and cuddling her and kissing her, tootyfay charmaunt, in her ensemble of maidenna blue") Moving into the modern day, in *The James Joyce Murder*, a novel by Amanda Cross, the sleuthing scholar Kate Fansler remarks on the young boy in her charge: "And Leo really is my nephew, but the way. No doubt it has already been suggested that he is a small misstep I am passing off in this manner. Is there, by the way, a word for auntly, counterpart to avuncular?" "I doubt it," Mr. Mulligan said. "Perhaps we can invent one. I've always felt certain the major reason Joyce wrote *Finnegans Wake* was to have the fun of making up words. How about auntiary?" (See **avunculusts**.)

charmermaid *FW* 148.24 *n.* A female servant who takes care of bedrooms or a chambermaid who, also, delights, fascinates, or charms. As all Joyceans know, Nora Joyce, nee Barnacle, was a chambermaid at Finn's Hotel in Dublin when Joyce met her on the street and was instantly charmed by her. Nora must have been equally charmed, as she agreed shortly thereafter to leave with Joyce for the continent with only the promise of a job there for him and without the promise of the benefits of clergy for her. ("Did you really never in all our cantalang lives speak clothes to a girl's before? No! Not even to the charmermaid?") After the one and only meeting between Joyce and Marcel Proust at a dinner party in Paris, Joyce remarked that all Proust wanted to talk about was duchesses while he, Joyce, was more interested in their chambermaids. Another charming chambermaid is found in Laurence Sterne's *A Sentimental Journey Through France and Italy*, a book, like *Finnegans Wake*, concluding with a suspended sentence that may have suggested this device to Joyce: "So that when I stretched out my hand, I caught hold of the Fille de Chambre's"

chassetitties *FW* 93.19 *n.* 1. When spoken, "chassetitties" sounds somewhat like chastity which, when taken in its Wakean context ("the chassetitties belles conclaiming") comes across as chastity belts, something appropriate for beautiful women or belles. *v.* 2. McHugh suggests that the French slang *chasser* for "to flirt" may be a good fit here. But another meaning that might apply, if we allow ourselves to degenerate into American slang, is "chasing titties," a situation in which a chastity belt could prove useful to a chaste woman whose flirting has caused her to be chased.

chastemate *FW* 548.7 *n.* A pure, virtuous, or chaste spouse or mate. Since chaste can also mean celibate, a "chastemate" may be a partner in an unconsummated marriage. That this mate may be a woman is suggested by McHugh's reference of *casemate* as French slang for "cunt," one of the *Wake*'s favorite suggested words. ("I chained her chastemate to grippe fiuming snugglers, her chambrett I bestank so to spunish furiosos") What with McHugh providing the French *chamberette* for "little room," the chaining of a "chastemate" bringing in bondage, and the sexual implications of snugging in "snugglers" (See **barsalooner**.), something deviant is definitely in play.

childream's *FW* 219.5 *n.* 1. A very large quantity or reams of young boys and girls or children. 2. Child and dreams combined to make a child's dreams. ("By arraignment, childream's hours, expercatered.") McHugh mentions a B.B.C. radio program called "Children's Hour."

chymerical *FW* 67.8 *adj.* An imaginary, fanciful, or chimerical archaic chymical or chemical. Filled with alchemical allusions, *Finnegans Wake* itself may be the "chymerical" substance that turns the lead of prose into the gold of poetry. ("We might leave that nitrience of oxagiants to take its free of the air and just analectralyse that very chymerical combination, the gasbag where the warderworks.") (See **analectralyse**.)

circumcivicise *FW* 446.35 *v.* To cut around and remove or circumcise those parts of a city and its civic government that are not absolutely necessary for its proper functioning. The city of Detroit is now doing just that as it clears away neighborhoods that have been abandoned from the city's shrinking population. The image of a religious ritual involving the cutting away of a baby boy's foreskin obviously comes to mind here and is certainly apropos. Since a second meaning for circumcise is to purify, to "circumcivicise" a city also makes it easier to keep clean and healthy, one of the practical effects of male circumcision. In addition, the prefix "circum" coming from the Latin *circus* for "circle" or "around," suggests the circular structure of *Finnegans Wake* as well as the history-as-circle theory of Giambattista Vico and the Dublin road named for him which the *Wake* mentions with: "The Vico Road goes round and round to meet where terms begin." (452.21-22) ("We'll circumcivicise all Dublin country.")

circumconversioning *FW* 512.16 *v.* Going around or in a circle concerning a change or a conversion. Political moderates might change their party registrations from Republican to Democrat to Independent and back to Republican as party platforms shift, or candidates might circulate among parties to improve their chances of reelection. Religious "circumconversioning" among denominations may occur, or even circular thinking regarding belief and disbelief in God. In *Finnegans Wake* people, events, and stories all change (yet remain the same or, as the *Wake* puts it: "The seim anew.") as the book itself continues its Viconian circle "a long the ... riverrun." ("It is the circumconversioning of antelithual paganelles by a huggerknut cramwell energumen") The Huguenots and Cromwell appear here in one of the many appearances of HCE's initials.

circuminsistence *FW* 354.14 *n.* 1. A firm stand or insistence on the fact, event, or circumstance of the cutting off of the foreskin or circumcision. God's "circuminsistence" was a symbol of the covenant he made with Abraham. Compared with being sacrificed on an altar, as Abraham was first asked to do to his son, Isaac, circumcision looks pretty good. 2. A firm stand or insistence on going around in a circle, with the prefix "circum" for around or in a circle. Joyce's "circuminsistence" on the *Wake*'s cyclical structure, based upon Vico's "circuminsistence" on the three cycles of human history, may be inferred with this Wakean word. ("*but keenheartened by the circuminsistence of the Parkes O'Rarelys*") "The Ballad of Persse O'Reilly," the incriminating song making the rounds of Dublin to spread the word about HCE's alleged sexual impropriety in Phoenix Park is introduced here.

circumveiloped *FW* 244.15 *v.* Surrounded or encircled by screening devices or veils so that an enveloped person or object may not be seen or observed. If Joyce had a derivation in mind here, it might be the Latin *circumvallatus* for "walled-around." Salomé, in her frustrated desire for John the Baptist, "circumveiloped" her stepfather, King Harod, by performing the dance of the seven veils. After dropping the last veil, that covered her face, she received Saint John's head on a silver salver which, in Oscar Wilde's play, *Salomé*, she lavishes with a lascivious kiss. ("We are circumveiloped by obscuritads.") With the obvious root of "obscuritads" being "obscure," the obscurantism, that is the deliberate evasiveness, of *Finnegans Wake* is certainly suggested.

clairaudience *FW* 533.31   *n*. 1.seeing or knowing things out of sight or clairvoyance about people gathered to hear or see a performance or an audience. Many a clairvoyant has made a good living through skills of "clairaudience." If the *Wake* expresses Joyce's opinion of clairvoyants, it is not a sympathetic one—"people here who have the phoney habit (it as remarketable) in his clairaudience"—suggesting that they are not only phonies but, rather than being remarkable, are concerned with repeated marketability. Many remember The Amazing Kreskin's "clairaudience" from his many mentalist performances on Johnny Carson's *The Tonight Show*.

cloover *FW* 478.25   *n*. An intelligent or clever use of clover, a low plant of the pea family. St. Patrick, the patron saint of Ireland and a continuous presence in *Finnegans Wake*, beginning with the first page (See **thuartpeatrick**.), makes "cloover" use of the trefoil shamrock to illustrate the Christian concept of the Trinity to the pagan Irish. ("Whur's that inclining and talkin about the messiah so cloover?")

clothse *FW* 148.23   *n*. Apparel or clothes for the body that are tight fitting or close. Joyce, in later age, remarked that he was no longer interested in women's bodies but now only in their clothes. Undergarments were always an interest, and he had a tiny pair of women's drawers made in which he would place two fingers as if they were legs and walk them across the table. ("Did you really never in all our cantalang lives speak clothse to a girl's before?")

cogitabundantly *FW* 88.7-8   *adv*. Full of thought or cogitabund combined with being profusely or abundantly filled results in an excess of thoughts or at least thoughts to a higher power. If any book can be said to be written "cogitabundantly," that book is most certainly *Finnegans Wake*. ("he was only too cognitively conatively cogitabundantly sure of it because, living, loving, breathing and sleeping morphomelosophopancreates")

cohortyard *FW* 455.1 *n.* A space enclosed by walls within or attached to a large building or a courtyard that encloses a group of soldiers or other group or a cohort. ("No petty family squabbles Up There nor homemade hurricanes in our Cohortyard") McHugh references *The House by the Churchyard*, the novel by Le Fanu that makes multiple appearances in many different forms in *Finnegans Wake*. (See **hearseyard**.)

collideorescape *FW* 143.28 *n.* 1. An instrument that creates violent collisions of particles of matter, causing completely new particles to be formed and today known in physics as a particle accelerator. Joyce uses a "collideorescape" in *Finnegans Wake* to cause collisions of words, often of different languages, to create entirely new and previously unknown words. 2. Kaleidoscope is also suggested here as the *Wake* has been seen as one by many scholars, such as William York Tindall's analogy comparing the *Wake* to a kaleidoscope that "framed in a circle, offers endless rearrangements to a few elements." As one turns the pages, an endless variety of continually changing patterns are viewed through the rearrangement of the 26 letters of the alphabet. 3. McHugh provides "collide or (e)scape" as another meaning for "collideorescape." ("then what would that fargazer seem to seemself to seem seeming of, dimm it all? Answer: A collideorscape!")

collupsus *FW* 5.27 *n.* A huge statue or colossus that falls or collapses. The Colossus of Rhodes, one of the seven wonders of the ancient world, was a colossal statue of the Greek god Helios built on the island of Rhodes around 280 B.C.E. It collapsed as the result of an earthquake and was never rebuilt. ("It may have been a misfired brick, as some say, or it mought have been due to a collupsus of his back promises, as others looked at it.")

McHugh gives the Latin *collapsus* for "fallen in." The "collupsus" referred to here is no doubt Tim Finnegan carrying bricks on a hod up a ladder. But the giant Finn MacCool is certainly a "collupsus" whose body lies spread over Dublin, his head at Howth, his trunk the city center, while his feet and toes pop up "well to the west" in Phoenix Park. HCE's fall from grace from some purported sin in the same park figures in as well. Collapses and revivals are the ongoing themes of *Finnegans Wake*, whether on a small scale like HCE's or the overall fall of human civilizations through Vico's cycles.

combarative *FW* 140.33 *adj*. One who likes to fight or is combative regarding how something is alike or different, that is over comparative issues. Political talk shows featuring "combarative" hosts of both liberal and conservative persuasions make for some argumentatively entertaining evenings on television. ("after all the errears and erroriboose of combarative embattled history") (See **erroriboose** & **embattled**.)

comfortumble *FW* 417.14-15 *n*. 1 an easy or comfortable fall, roll, or tumble. Humpty Dumpty and Tim Finnegan each had an uncomfortumble from a wall. See McHugh's *Annotations to "Finnegans Wake"* for the wide variety of references to be found in "sated before his comfortumble phullupsuppy of a plate o'monkynous and a confucion of minthe (for he was a conformed aceticist and aristotaller)."

commendmant *FW* 615.32-33 *n*. Praise, recommendation, or commendation for a law or commandment. The current political frenzy about posting the Ten Commandments in government buildings is certainly a "commendmant" of their value, especially to right-wing Christian fundamentalists. ("it is forbidden by the honorary tenth commendmant to shall not bare full sweetness against a nihgboor's wiles") Three commandments are combined here: Eighth – "Thou shalt not bear false witness;" Ninth – "Thou shalt not covet thy neighbor's wife;"

and Tenth – "Thou shalt not covet thy neighbor's goods."

communicanting *FW* 498.21 *v.* 1. To give information or communicate in an insincere manner or cant, as in the hypocrisy of some religious leaders who preach one thing and practice another. 2. To give information or communicate in a language peculiar to a special group or cant. Irish tinkers are known for "communicanting" in Shelta, a distorted mix of Gaelic and English that appears in the *Wake* as "sheltafocal" and "the shelta of his broguish." *Finnegans Wake* is, as a highly peculiar form of communication, the ultimate example of this definition of "communicanting." ("socializing and communicanting in the deification of his members")

condam *FW* 142.22 *n.* 1. A prophylactic or condom that is condemned or damned *v.* 2. To condemn and damn the use of prophylactics or condoms, as in President George W. Bush's abstinence-only sex education program for the public schools. This program was no doubt condemned and damned by parents of pregnant teenagers. ("condone every evil by practical justification and condam any good to its own gratification") This sentence goes on to mention those "duped and driven by those numen daimons [Latin *in nominee domine* for "in God's name"], the feekeepers at their laws."

condomnation *FW* 362.3 *n.* 1. A declaration of unsoundness or a condemnation of an apartment building in which each unit is individually owned or a condominium. After a series of devastating hurricanes, many Floridians suddenly found their condominium complex had become a "condomnation" complex. For a fictional, though researched, account of such an event, read John D. MacDonald's *Condominium*. 2. A country or nation known for its prophylactics or condoms. With the famous euphemism "French letters," France is the most famous "condomnation." ("in condomnation of his totomptation and for the duration till his repepulation")

confucion *FW* 417.15 *n.* Bewilderment, perplexity, or confusion concerning the ethics of Confucianism. If Confucius himself was ever confused, he might have been said to be suffering from "confucion." If Joyce were to translate Confucius into Wakese, it might read something like this: "sated before his comfortumble phullupsuppy of a plate o'monkynous and a confucion of minthe (for he was a conformed aceticist and aristotaller)."

confusional *FW* 520.12 *n.* An enclosed space where a priest hears the perplexed or confused confessions of sins from church members, most often known as a confessional. Since there are so many sins, both venial and mortal, and since most of us commit so many sins, it's quite understandable, as well as forgivable, we pray, to become confused upon entering the "confusional." Confuse can also mean to make uneasy or embarrass, common feelings among confessing believers. ("tell his holiness the whole goat's throat about the three shillings in the confusional") McHugh reads "goat's throat" as "God's truth." (See **confussed** & **confussion**.)

confussed *FW* 193.21 *v.* 1. Bewildered, perplexed, embarrassed or confused about something admitted or confessed. 2. Confussion confessed. ("And as for she was confussed by pro-Brother Thacolicus.") The word "fuss" contained in "confussed" is no doubt Joyce's belief that that confession, at least in Catholic practice, is a lot of bother about a small matter. But Joyce was somewhat "confussed" about his refusal to honor his dying mother's request that he make his Easter duties (confession and communion) as evidenced by the attention he pays it in *Ulysses*. (See **confusional** & **confussion**.)

confussion *FW* 353.25 *n.* A combination of perplexity or confusion and admission or confession. A confessed confusion and/or a confused confession. ("amidwhiches general uttermosts confussion are perceivable") Finn Fordham finds in "fussion" "a word which brilliantly fuses 'fusion' and 'fission,' words with opposing senses, since one signals the action of splitting, the other of blending, processes that chime strongly with Joyce's manipulation of language." (See **confusional** & **confussed**.)

consciquenchers *FW* 178.3 *n.* The outcome or consequence of putting an end to or quenching one's sense of right and wrong or conscience. We live with the "consciquenchers" of criminals and political leaders every day. ("the consciquenchers of casuality prepestered crusswords in postposition")

contradrinking *FW* 96.3 *v.* To deny, disagree with, or contradictory to the consumption of alcohol or drinking. This gets a little confusing, as what in *Finnegans Wake* doesn't, since "contra" means "against" and "contradicting" means "deny the truth of," so is there the effect of a double negative that really means the contradicting of the contrary or being in disagreement with the denial of drinking that, in effect, supports drinking, which the *Wake* does in no uncertain terms? You can't have "*Hops of Fun at Miliken's Make*" without a drink or two or three. Without whiskey Tim Finnegan would not have fallen from a ladder nor been revived at his wake, thus omitting the central theme of *Finnegans Wake*, fall and resurrection. When I read about the evils of drink, I gave up reading. ("And contradrinking themselves about Lillytrilly law pon hilly")

contrawatchwise *FW* 119.18-19 *n.* 1. Against or contra to the direction of the hands of a clock or watch, or counterclockwise. *v.* 2. Looking or watching for that which is against or contra to that which is smart or wise. ("called after some his hes hecitency Hec, which, moved contrawatchwise, represents his title in sigla") HCE and his stuttering denial to the "cad with a pipe" of any impropriety in Phoenix Park one midnight is certainly present here. The "Cad" had asked for the time, and HCE replied that it was 12:00. With both hands sticking straight up, this was a signal for a homosexual assignation, an action that was "contrawatchwise" to HCE's reputation as an upstanding businessman, husband, and father. But the confusing thing is that it really was 12:00. Joyce developed a system of sigla he used as a sort of shorthand in the notebooks he mined in the writing of *Finnegans Wake*. The siglum for HCE is, quite naturally, an "E" which can be turned in four different directions ("tristurned initials") to represent his various aspects. A drawing of the sigla is found at the bottom of page 299 in the *Wake*.

cooclaim *FW* 129.22 *v.* To announce or proclaim with the soft murmuring sound made by the cooing of doves, especially proclamations of peace. ("seven dovecotes cooclaim to have been pigeonheim to this homer") There may be a suggestion here, as there are hundreds of others, to Finn MacCool (also Cu Chulainn), hero of Irish legends and whose body underlies all of Dublin in *Finnegans Wake*. Adaline Glasheen identifies MacCool as "the heroic and epic avatar of HCE." Whether the dove Noah sent out from the ark to determine if the waters had abated from the land cooed when it returned with an olive leaf as evidence that it had, the Bible doesn't say but, if it did, it could be said to "cooclaim" that the flood was finally finished. Another suggestion here is to the Pigeon House, Dublin's electrical generating station in Joyce's day, the destination of the two truant boys in "An Encounter," a short story from *Dubliners*. Of course any allusion to an encounter suggests HCE's encounter with the "cad with a pipe" in Phoenix Park.

corprulation *FW* 525.6 *n.* Sexual union or copulation stimulated by sight or contact with excrement or copro (Greek: *kopros*). The combining of copulation and coprolagnia. For a multitude of examples of "corprulation," as well as many other sexual unniceties, see the Marquis de Sade's *The 120 Days of Sodom*. ("Tallhell and Barbados wi ye and your Errian coprulation!")

coursets *FW* 236.36 *n.* The progress, advance, or course of a woman's stiff under- garment used to shape her body or corsets. The wasp-waist desired by women in earlier days was achieved by cinching themselves into corsets made with whale bones, instruments of torture that actually reshaped their own bones. Scarlett O'Hara being laced up by Mammy before the Wilkes' barbecue in the film *Gone With the Wind* is a good example. Elastic girdles evolved somewhat later and now, in our new century, no underwear at all is required, as Paris Hilton and Brittany Spears have been kind enough to flash us. On his early dates in Dublin with Nora, Joyce complained of her corset, requesting that she "leave off that breastplate" and compared it to "embracing a letter box." It seems Nora did not comply. ("accourdant to the coursets of things feminite, towooerds him in heliolatry")

corpse *FW* 105.20 *n. & v.* I'll let Philippe Sollers do the honors here with this analysis from his essay "Joyce & Co." in *In the Wake of the* Wake: "CROPSE—*corpse*, *kopros* (waste, shit), *crop up* (appear, come to the surface), *crop* (cut short), and even *croppy* (Irish rebel sympathetic to the French Revolution of 1789). Theme: death and resurrection." ("*Suppotes a Ventriliquorst Merries a Corpse, Lapps for Finns This Funnycoon's Week*") Laplanders and Finland come together to have lots of fun at Finnegan's wake along with ALP concealed in "Lapps."

coughin *FW* 444.14 *n.* A casket or coffin to contain the body of one who died from forcing air from the lungs in a sudden, noisy manner or coughing. ("the dirty old bigger'll be squealing through his coughin")

cropse *FW* 55.8 *n.* In *A Guide Through "Finnegans Wake,"* Edmund Epstein writes that "'corpse' combines with 'crops' to make a wholly new and richly evocative contra-dictory word, 'cropse,' combining the idea of death with resurrection." This is the grand theme of the *Wake*, falling and rising, decline and renewal, death and rebirth. ("on the bunk of our breadwinning lies the cropse of our seedfather") Epstein adds that "'seedfather' does not create a wholly new word, for both elements of 'seedfather' are already existent words, with a double meaning contained in 'seed'; only the combination is novel."

cropulence *FW* 294.22 *n.* A combination of fatness or corpulence and intemperate eating and drinking or crapulence to give at once both the effect and the cause. ("with Mary Owens and Dolly Monks seesidling to edge his cropulence")

crosskisses *FW* 111.17 *n.* xxx's at the end of a letter to signify touches with the lips as a sign of love or kisses. ("must now close it with fondest to the twoinns with four crosskisses for holy paul holey corner holipoli whollyisland pee ess from") These "crosskisses" come at the end of one of a number of versions of the famous letter from Boston that the hen pecks out of the kitchen midden and even appear much later in *Finnegans Wake* with "X.X.X.X." (See **anomorous**.)

cruelfiction *FW* 192.19 *n.* 1. Fiction that delights in causing pain and suffering to to the extent that readers feel they have been put to death by being fastened to a cross, becoming victims of the cruel torture of crucifixion. Most critics have labeled *Finnegans Wake* as a prime example of "cruelfiction." Readers will have their own candidates for this label, usually novels they were assigned to read for a book report in high school. 2. Fiction that's subject is cruelty, such as almost any novel by the Marquis de Sade or short stories and novels that deal honestly with the treatment of Native Americans by the government of the United States. ("O, you were excruciated, in honour bound to the cross of your own cruelfiction!")

crusswords *FW* 178.4 *n.* Words to fill sets of squares in a crossword puzzle and swear or cusswords. Clues to some of the words in a difficult crossword puzzle can cause cussing in the most accomplished of crossword fans. ("the consciquenchers of casuality prepestered cusswords in postposition") Critic John Lehmann described *Finnegans Wake* as a "wanton surrender to the crossword puzzle part of the mind," while the *Wake* describes itself as a "crossmess parzel." The great difficulty presented by the clues to the *Wake*'s puzzles is that they are in a mixture of a multitude of languages.

crydle *FW* 444.13 *n.* A baby bed or cradle in which a child is weeping or crying. A "crydle" often is on rockers so that a crying baby can be soothed into sleep by the gentle, rocking motion. In the classic lullaby, "Rock-a-by Baby" ("hushaby rocker"), if the bough actually does break and the cradle falls, the baby's cradle will instantly become a "crydle." ("when the nice little smellar squalls in his crydle what the dirty old bigger'll be squealing through his coughin")

cryzy *FW* 528.7 *n.* Mad or crazy from and/or for weeping or crying. Joyce anticipated Patsy Cline's hit song "Crazy" years before she was a country-singing star. As two lines from the lyrics go: "I'm crazy for trying and crazy for crying / And I'm crazy for loving you." Joyce's "cryzy" would work much better in these lyrics. ("to go cryzy")

cumulonubulocirrhonimbant *FW* 599.25 *adj.* A combination of cumulus, cirrus, and nimbus clouds appearing in the sky at once or a cloud containing characteristics of all three of these types. ("Cumulonubulocirrhonimbant heaven electing, the dart of desire has gored the heart of secret waters") If you saw the initials of HCE in the first three words of this sentence, you earned extra points.

cunduncing *FW* 310.13 *v.* Leading or contributing to a desirable or favorable outcome or conducing for a stupid person or dunce. Making children wear dunce caps is earlier educational times was not conducing to their learning, while in our more enlightened times we label them "exceptional students" with the same result. ("a meatous conch culpable of conducncing Naul and Santry and the forty routs of Corthy")

cupturing *FW* 371.15 *v.* 1. Catching and keeping or capturing in a handled dish for drinking or a cup. "In one's cups" is slang for being drunk and, as HCE closes down his pub for the night, he drinks the dregs, "cupturing" the contents left by his customers and becomes falling-down drunk. 2. Winning or capturing a trophy or cup given as a prize for a contest, athletic or otherwise. ("emulously concerned to cupturing the last dropes of summour down through their grooves of blarneying") In this case the concern is to capture the last drops of summer, as if they could be contained in a cup. McHugh recalls Thomas Moore's famous song, "'Tis the Last Rose of Summer."

curiositease *FW* 576.24 *n.* Curiosities or an eager desire to know or inquire into as a result of being teased or annoyed by jokes or jests. *Finnegans Wake* itself is a prime example of a "curiositease" on a grand scale. In the Wakean world, if "curiositease" killed the cat, then "sadisfaction" brought him back. ("mirrorminded curiositease and would-to-the-large which bring hills to molehunter")

cynarettes *FW* 236.2 *n.* Cigarettes that are doubtfully or cynically seen as being against the law of God or a sin. Oscar Wilde, a devoted chain smoker who makes many an appearance in *Finnegans Wake*, would have loved Joyce's coinage of "cynarettes." As Wilde proposed in his novel *The Picture of Dorian Gray*, "A cigarette is the perfect type of pleasure; it is exquisite and leaves one unsatisfied." ("Charmeuses chloes, glycering juwells, lydialight fans and puffumed cynarettes.") Cigarettes are puffed and produce fumes, but only smokers enjoy their particular perfume. (See **puffumed**.)

D

daintical *FW* 295.27 *adj.* Exactly alike or identical in delicateness and daintiness or daintily identical. The finest china and crystal can be said to be "daintical." ("And makes us a daintical pair of accomplasses!") (See **accomplasses**.)

damimonds *FW* 134.7 *n.* 1. A precious stone formed of pure carbon in crystals or a diamond that has been cursed or damned. Diamonds mined in a war zone and sold to finance war efforts are referred to as blood diamonds. The United Nations has damned these "damimonds" and has tried to prevent their sale on the world market. Despite this, I doubt even Marilyn Monroe would decline including "damimonds" among her best friends. There's the story of a lady who looks at the diamond ring on the hand of the lady sitting next to her on a plane. "What a beautiful diamond!" she exclaims. "Yes," replies her seatmate, "it's the famous Smith diamond, but it has a curse on it." "What's the curse?" the first lady asks. "Mr. Smith," is the reply. No doubt there are similar damned diamonds worn by many women. 2. In a game of bridge a winning hand strong in diamonds might be cursed by the losers for its "damimonds." ("ace of arts, deuce of damimonds, trouble of clubs, fear of spates")

dantellising *FW* 251.23-24 *v* Tormenting, teasing, or tantalizing by keeping the works of Dante ("Denti Alligator") in sight but not allowing them to be read. "Undante" and "damnty" on later pages of *Finnegans Wake* may refer to "dantellising." While Tantalus of Greek mythology, from whose name "tantalize" is derived, suffered the tantalizing withdrawal of water and fruit each time he reached for them, he should still have had the satisfaction of reading Dante's *Divine Comedy*, especially the *Inferno*. ("Turning up and fingering over the most dantellising peaches in the lingerous longerous book of the dark.") The "lingerous longerous book of the dark" is *Finnegans Wake*, a work that has tormented and teased its readers from the first excerpts of *Work in Progress* right down to this day, tantalizing them with its infinite array of allusions and multitudinous meanings, final solutions for which seem always just out of reach.

dawncing *FW* 513.11 *v.* Moving in rhythm with music or dancing until the beginning of the day or dawn. Late in the evening, when Joyce was in what one of his friends termed a "grape-happy mood," he would perform an exuberant dance with wild "doublejoynted" kicking. In *Finnegans Wake* this is called "Dawncing the kniejinksky," which combines the German *Knie* for "knee" with the Russian ballet star Nijinsky. Since it's impossible to read too much into Joyce, there may be the suggestion of high jinks here as well as a connection with Joyce's daughter Lucia who was a talented dancer and, like Nijinsky, spent her last years in a mental institution. ("Dawncing the kniejinksky choreopiscopally like an easter sun round the colander") (See **doublejoynted**.)

dayagreening *FW* 607.24 *n.* The greening of the day, that is the colors of grass and tree leaves showing with the first light of early morning. McHugh gives the Gaelic *deo-gréine* for "spark of the sun" and the Swedish *daggryning* for "dawn." In Tom Stoppard's play *Arcadia*, a character comments that the dawn is "very beautiful. If only it did not occur so early in the day."

dantellising - decorded | 91

Dawn is one of the 1,700 words that Shakespeare created. ("Dayagreening gains in schlimninging.")

daysends *FW* 610.28 *v.* Sending down or descends during the light of daytime. The sun "daysends" from its zenith at noon toward the horizon. Also, the descending of light and energy to the Earth from the sun during daylight hours. ("By the bright reason which daysends to us from the high.")

dazecrazemazed *FW* 389.27 *v.* Confuse or daze while driving mad or crazy by a labyrinth or maze. The most famous of mazes to daze, craze, and amaze was built by Daedalus in ancient Crete to contain the mythical half-man, half-bull Minotaur ("Minnowaurs"). This "Allmaziful" legendary labyrinth was so successful that even Daedalus had some difficulty finding his way out. If Daedalus suggests Stephen Dedalus, and Stephen as a young man suggests the older James Joyce, then *Finnegans Wake* becomes the maze he designed to daze and craze readers. Joyce said that a few years after writing the *Wake* even he would no longer remember everything he hid in it. Meanwhile, scholars are still searching for that ball of thread that will lead us through and out of the *Wake* with some sure understanding. As readers of the *Wake* discover, when lost in a labyrinth, it is difficult to think outside the box. ("while his deepseepeepers gazed and sazed and dazecrazemazed into her dullokbloon rodolling olosheen eyenbowls") (See **Allmaziful**.)

decorded *FW* 482.35 *v.* To discover a secret meaning or decoding by removing the cords that have bound the secret from view. Alexander the Great "decorded" the supposedly unable-to-be-untied Gordian knot with a swift stroke of his sword. ("What can't be coded can be decorded if an ear aye sieze what no eye ere grieved for.") *Finnegans Wake* has been and continues to be "decorded" by literary scholars in an attempt to reveal its many remaining secret meanings.

deepseepeepers *FW* 389.26 *n.* Eyes, or their slang term "peepers," that are able to observe or see far down or deep into the sea or some deep subject such as *Finnegans Wake*. While cameras enclosed in robotic submarines now allow us to peep into the deepest craters of the seas, scholars continue to give us more detailed viewpoints on the deepest mysteries of the *Wake*. ("while his deepseepeepers gazed and sazed and dazecrazemazed into her dullokbloon rodolling olosheen eyenbowls")

deepunded *FW* 310.5 *v.* Influenced, relied, or depended on a play on words or a pun. *Finnegans Wake*, like no other book, deeply depends on puns, especially deep puns that take readers off the deep end, way over their literary heads. Morley Callaghan writes of Joyce: "His humor depended on puns. Even in little snips of conversation, he played with words lightly." Seen in its Wakean context—"lackslipping along as if their liffing deepunded on it"—this phrase could be read "as if their living depended on puns." A play on the river Liffey, "liffing" is the lifeblood of Dublin, and its personification as Anna Livia Plurabelle or ALP. (See **thuartpeatrick, punical, Punman, punplays, punsil, puntomine,** & **spunish.**)

defecalties *FW* 366.20-21 *n.* Troubles or difficulties regarding the stealing or misuse of monies or defalcations. ("e'en tho' Jambuwel's defecalties is Terry Shimmyrag's uppperturnity, if that is grace for the grass what is balm for the bramblers") McHugh gives a reference here to the phrase "England's difficulty is Ireland's opportunity." The Irish certainly had more than their share of "defecalties" during the long and oppressive English occupation of their country. Tucked neatly in this passage he finds the Irish *Tír na Simearóig* for "Land of the Shamrock." Also found is "What is sauce for the goose is sauce for the gander," an old phrase appearing in various guises throughout *Finnegans Wake*.

deluscious *FW* 148.1 *adj.* 1. Delighting the senses or delicious with the added emphasis of being richly sweet or luscious. The lyrics of the old song could be amended to "It's delovely, it's delightful, it's 'deluscious.'" ("Is it not divinely deluscious?") 2. Deceptive or delusive and delighting the senses or delicious. It was a "deluscious" apple that Eve and Adam shared in the Garden of Eden after the serpent deceived them into believing that one delicious bite would lift life's delusions from their eyes and that they would, like God, possess the knowledge of good and evil.

demosthrenated *FW* 542.18 *v.* Shown, proven clearly, or demonstrated in the manner of the ancient Athenian orator and statesman Demosthenes, famed for his ability to speak clearly and convincingly. Those who have "demosthrenated" their point in a debate or argument are most likely to win. Unfortunately, HCE was never quite able to demosthrenate innocence of any wrongdoing in Phoenix Park during his trials. ("in Forum Foster I demosthrenated my folksfiendship")

deparkment *FW* 364.7 *n.* A special division or department to deal with all issues related to land set aside for recreation and/or ornamentation or parks. ("the post puzzles deparkment with larch parchels' of presents for future branch offercings") This is a "deepunded" phrase in the true Wakean tradition.

deplurabel *FW* 224.10 *adj.* Something that is lamentable or deplorable for more than one or plural reasons. George W. Bush's presidency was quite "deplurabel." Also suggested are the multiple or plural manifestations of Anna Livia Plurabelle, both as various segments of the river Liffey and as a young girl, matron, and elderly woman. ("It was so said of him about of his old fontmouther. Truly deplurabel! A dire, O dire!") In Book One, Chapter Eight of *Finnegans Wake*, known as the Anna Livia Plurabelle chapter and considered the most beautiful of all, two Irish washerwomen working on opposite banks of the Liffey gossip about the "deplurabel" behavior of ALP: "She must have been a gadabout in her day, so must, more than most ... She had a flewmen of her owen ... Casting her perils before our swains."

Her husband HCE comes in for his share of condemnation for "deplurabel" conduct as well.

desception *FW* 270.fn.4 *n.* A misleading or deceptive account of or a description. "Unreadable" is a "desception" of *Finnegans Wake* made by many critics. What at first glance appears to have no meaning is finally found to have meanings almost beyond measure, both meaningful and meaning full. ("He is my all menkind of every desception.")

deturbaned *FW* 353.6 *adj.* Resolved or determined to trouble or disturb by taking away or removing a scarf wound around the head or a turban. ("*apoxyomenously deturbaned but thems bleachin banes will be after making a bashman's haloday*") The determined, disturbing removal of the turban here seems to have occurred during a busman's holiday.

devoused *FW* 340.22 *v.* To eat, consume, destroy, or devour that which is planned, invented, or devised. The range here is wide, from cooks who eat their culinary creations to animals that eat their young. ("For he devoused the lelias on the fined") The thing "devoused" here seems to be the lilies of the field, though McHugh makes reference to the Bible's "De . . . lilah" and to Lilias Walsingham, the heroine of the novel *The House by the Churchyard* that appears in the *Wake* as "the church by the hearseyard." (See **hearseyard**.)

dhrone *FW* 417.11 *n.* A chair for a person of high rank or a throne for a loafer, idler, or drone. ("Behailed His Gross the Ondt, prostrandvorous upon his dhrone, in his Paplyonian babooshkees, smolking a spatial brunt of Hosana cigals, with unshrinkables farfalling from his unthinkables, swarming of himself in his sunnyroom") In the *Wake*'s take on Aesop's fable ("esiop's foible") of the Ant and the Grasshopper, the "Ondt and the Gracehoper," the "Ondt," having worked hard and saved for the winter, is able to relax on his "dhrone" smoking a

desception - dirtiment | 95

special brand of Havana cigars while the improvident "Gracehoper" goes begging, wishing he had a "dhrone" as well. If you are wise to Wakean ways, you will have spotted Oscar Wilde's witty comment on foxhunting in this passage: "the unspeakable in full pursuit of the uneatable."

diasporation *FW* 257.25 *n*. Amusement, play, or disport in the transportation of those being dispersed in a diaspora. ("in deesperation of deispiration at the diasporation of his diesparation")

dimb *FW* 53.2 & 237.8 *adj*. At once dull or dim and stupid or dumb. ("It scenes like a landscape from Wildu Picturescu or some seem on some dimb Arras, dumb as Mum's mutyness") & ("dewyfully as dimb dumbelles, all alisten to his elixir") Dumbbell is slang for a very stupid person and combined here with very pretty girls or belles gives pretty girls who are stupid and dim. (See **dumbelles**.) McHugh hears the nursery rhyme "Ding Dong Bell" in the second quote.

dimentioned *FW* 299.6 *v*. Spoken of, referred to, or mentioned regarding the size, scope of, or dimension of an object or project. When Jesus "dimentioned" that in his Father's house there were many mansions, he imparted the extreme extent of Heaven. ("I don't know is it your spictre or my omination but I'm glad you dimentioned it!")

dinnerchime *FW* 26.28 *n*. A set of tuned bells or a chime used to signal the time for the main meal of the day or dinner. ("The horn for breakfast, one o'gong for lunch and dinnerchime.") In English country houses the butler would sound a gong to announce that it was time to dress for dinner.

dirtiment *FW* 353.4 *n*. Uncleanness, foulness, or dirt that causes harm, damage, or detriment to a person or thing. A hard game of soccer is a "dirtiment" to the players' uniforms, and HCE's encounter with the Cad in Phoenix Park was not without "dirtiment" to his reputation. ("And to the dirtiment of the curtailment of his all of man?")

disappainted *FW* 90.16 *v.* Failure to please or disappointed by a picture or a painting. Most new art forms, abstract art as one example, leave first-time viewers "disappainted." ("The devoted couple was or were only two disappainted solicitresses on the job of the unfortunate class on Saturn's mountain fort?") Portrait painters especially must please their patrons for, if their subjects are "disappainted," the artists will lose commissions and possibly starve.

disemvowelled *FW* 515.12 *v.* Eviscerated or disemboweled by the removal of a word's essential vowels, *a, e, i, o, u*, and sometimes *y*, letters which are necessary to its existence as a word. In the popular television game show *Wheel of Fortune*, contestants may buy vowels, the addition of which can provide vital clues to the identification of the words. ("Secret speech Hazelton and obviously disemvowelled.") Examples of words that have been "disemvowelled" are to be seen on 515.5 & 6: "— Nnn ttt wrd?" and "—Dmn ttt thg." McHugh translates these as "not a word." and "damn the thing." McHugh also clues us in to the contextual meaning of "disemvowelled" in its Wakean sentence—"W.G. 'Single Speech' Hamilton: Ir. M.P.; made brilliant maiden speech; said never to have spoken again"

disselving *FW* 608.5 *v.* Fading away or dissolving of one's nature or self. Various forms of meditation are designed for the "disselving" of our human nature into the grander scheme of things, such as some spiritual cosmos, through the contemplation of God, the recitation of a special mantra, or simply staring at a lighted candle. Within *Finnegans Wake* we find Saint Kevin digging a hole on an island, filling the hole with water, placing a bathtub ("tubbathalter") filled with water in the waterhole, and then sitting in the tub of water to meditate on "baptism or the regeneration of all man by affusion of water" or, in a sense, "disselving" himself. With "as in pure (what bunkum!) essenesse, there have been disselving forenenst you," the *Wake* doesn't put much stock in the idea of meditation through "disselving."

dissentant   *FW* 313.33   *n.* Offspring of parents, grandparents, etc. or a descendant in disagreement with some issue, political, religious, etc., or a dissident. Dissonant or out of harmony with others may be distantly suggested. HCE as a Scandinavian Protestant in predominantly Catholic Ireland is certainly a "dissentant." (should he be himpself namesakely a foully fallen dissentant from the peripulator")

divorsion   *FW* 9.35   *n.* The legal end to a marriage or divorce that provides entertainment, amusement, or diversion. A quick scan of the front pages of the many "newspapers" at any supermarket checkout line reveals "divorsion" to be a major selling feature. Some stars go beyond the call of duty providing "divorsion," as have Elizabeth Taylor or Za Za Gabor. ("Sophy-Key-Po for his royal divorsion on the rinnaway jinnies.") McHugh gives a reference to W. G. Wills' play about Napoleon's divorce from Josephine, *A Royal Divorce*.

doaters   *FW* 526.35   *n.* Those who are overly fond of or doters of female descendants or daughters. Joyce could be said to dote on his daughter Lucia, once giving her a fur coat in the belief it would improve her mental outlook. ("Nircississies are the doaters of inversion.") The old maxim, "Necessity is the mother of invention," is seen along with an old term for homosexuality, "inversion."

doctator   *FW* 170.22   *n.* A physician or doctor with absolute authority or a dictator. In a hospital, doctor's orders come near to being dictatorial. But the best real-life example has to be Francois "Papa Doc" Duvalier, longtime "doctator" of Haiti. His deposed son, known as "Baby Doc," evidently didn't have his dad's graveside manner. ("All were wrong, so Shem himself, the doctator, took the cake, the correct solution being") As a "doctator," "Papa Doc" not only took the cake but everything else he could get his hands on, as did "Baby Doc."

doffensive *FW* 78.30 *adj.* At once protective or defensive and combative or offensive. It's often said that the best defense is a good offensive. With the War of Southern Secession, Lincoln saw himself as defending the Union by taking the offensive against the Confederacy. ("on the purely doffensive since the eternals were owlwise on their side every time")

doublejoynted *FW* 27.2 *adj.* Having joints that bend easily in a joyful way or overjoyed to be double-jointed. Joyce was said to be "doublejoynted" when, well lubricated with wine or whiskey, he would dance for joy in the early morning hours, what the *Wake* describes as "Dawncing the kniejinksky" after the fanciful movements of the Russian ballet star Nijinsky. ("You were the doublejoynted janitor the morning they were delivered") (See **Dawncing**.)

dreamadoory *FW* 377.2 *n.* 1. A camel with one hump trained for riding or a dromedary formed as a mental image during sleep or a dream. 2. A building with sleeping rooms or a dormitory for camels or dromedaries. ("The keykeeper of the keys of the seven doors of the dreamadoory in the house of the household of Hecech saysaith.") McHugh identifies this sentence as a frequent introduction in *The Egyptian Book of the Dead*: "The overseer of the house of the overseer of the seal, Nu, triumphant, saith." McHugh also references the sentence to the Irish legend of Diarmaid who built an enclosure with seven doors while eloping with Grania, the wife-to-be of Finn MacCool, a story thought to be a spin-off of the Tristram and Iseult saga. While "Hecech" has the look of an ancient Egyptian word, it is a double image of the ever-present Humphrey Chimpden Earwicker's initials, HCE.

doffensive - druidful | 99

dreamskwindel *FW* 426.27   *n*. In *Scandinavian Elements of "Finnegans Wake,"* Dounia Bunis Christiani writes: "By setting the Danish adjective suffix *–sk* in the middle of this trope, Joyce manages to convey three images: A dreamy whorl or spiral: *drømsk vindel*. A dream giddiness or vertigo: *svindel* (Swedish, archaic Danish). A dream swindle: *svindel.*" Any or all of the three might be used to describe the *Wake*, depending on readers' viewpoints.

dredgerous *FW* 197.22 *adj*. An unsafe, risky, or dangerous activity or situation that brings a feeling of great uneasiness, terror, or dread. Nothing is inherently "dredgerous," as what is dreadful to one may be a lark to another. ("by dredgerous lands and devious delts, playing catched and mythed with the gleam of her shadda") McHugh reads "dredgerous" as "treacherous," and treachery is without a "shadda" of a doubt something to be dreaded and dangerous to one betrayed.

drema *FW* 69.14 *n*. A drama in a dream and/or a dream in a drama, that is, a dream with theatrical features and/or exciting real-life elements and/or a theatrical production having a dream-like style or features and/or dealing with dreams. Shakespeare's *A Midsummer Night's Dream* is one of many examples. The Russian for somnolence is *drema*. ("In the drema of Sorestost Areas, Diseased.") *Finnegans Wake* is a dream with many dramas, though the identity of the dreamer(s) is hotly debated in academic circles. When Nathaniel Hawthorne wrote of an idea for a story in his Salem notebook—"To write a dream which shall resemble the real course of a dream, with all its inconsistency, its strange transformation . . . with nevertheless a leading idea running through the whole. Up to this old age of the world, no such thing has ever been written."—he didn't realize a story like this would have to wait more than 100 years for a man of Joyce's genius to write it.

druidful *FW* 347.16 & 609.35 *adj*. Terribly fearful or dreadful of members of the Celtic religious order known as Druids. While many Irish did fear the power of the Druids, Saint Patrick stood up to them and overpowered their rites with Christianity. Patrick's lighting of the paschal fire at Slane and his challenge to the Druids' authority at Tara are recounted in numerous ways in *Finnegans Wake*. ("the great day and the druidful day come San Patrisky and the grand day" & "An I would uncertain in druidful scatterings one piece tall chap he stand one piece same place?")

dumbbbawls *FW* 284.19 *v.* To stupidly or dumbly cry out loudly or bawl. The electorate is often subjected to "dumbbawls" during a presidential election, and even on the floor of Congress when "You lie!" was yelled at President Obama. ("Imagine the twelve deaferended dumbbawls of the whowl abovebeugled to be the continuation through regeneration of the urutteration of the word in pregross.") Here is yet another reference to the *Wake*'s working title, "Work in Progress."

dumbelles *FW* 237.8 *n.* Stupid or dumb though beautiful and charming young women or belles. No doubt Shaun sees his sister Issy and her 28 rainbow girls as "dumbelles." ("dewyfully as dimb dumbelles, all alisten to his elixir. Lovelyt!") (See **dimb**.)

dumbestic *FW* 38.11 *n.* A stupid or dumb household servant or domestic. Kate ("Kothereen the Slop" among many others) and Sackerson ("be he . . . Comestipple Sacksoun" with even more variations than Kate) are the two servants in the Earwicker's pub and household and, while each at times appears to be a "dumbestic," they are much more wily and clever than we are first led to believe. In this case it's the "Cad's" wife who appears as "Our cad's bit of strife (knee Bareniece Maxwelton) with a quick ear for spittoons (as the aftertale hath it) glaned up as usual with dumbestic husbandry."

dumbfounder *FW* 121.27 *n.* An amazed or dumfounded establisher or founder. Jonathan Sawyer who founded the town of

Dublin, Georgia, would have been dumfounded to know that 132 years later he would appear on the first page of *Finnegans Wake* ("topsawyer's") and even more dumfounded to find that Joyce mistakenly identified him as Peter Sawyer ("Peter's sawyery") through an error made in the 1907 centennial issue of Dublin's newspaper. Joyce was also led to believe that Mr. Sawyer named his new city after his birthplace, Dublin, Ireland, but the closest connection with Ireland seems to be through some of Mrs. Sawyer's ancestors. ("as blackartful as a *podatus* and dumbfounder oh ho oaproariose as ten cannons in skelterfugue")

duskcended *FW* 222.35 *v.* Came down or descended just before dark or dusk. Nocturnal animals that found protection in trees during daylight hours "duskcended" and searched for food under the cover of night. ("naughtily all the duskcended airs and shylit beaconings from shehind hims back")

duskguise *FW* 532.27 *v.* Conceal identity or disguise through the limited vision that comes just before dark or dusk. ("I should her have awristed under my duskguise of whippers through toombs and deempeys") Many robbers "duskguise" their crimes by waiting until nightfall to go to work.

dustiny *FW* 162.3 *n.* The fate or destiny of human lives and their achievements is to return to the earth or dust from which all arose or, as the Bible reminds us, "ashes to ashes, dust to dust," especially at funeral ceremonies. *The Rubaiyat of Omar Khayyam* ("quatrain of rubyjets") as translated by Edward Fitzgerald contains a poetic portrait of our "dustiny:"

> Ah, make the most of what we yet may spend,
> Before we too into the Dust descend;
> Dust into Dust, and under Dust, to lie,
> Sans wine, sans song, sans Singer and—sans End!

("the compositor of the farce of dustiny however makes a thunpledrum mistake") Throughout the *Rubaiyat* our limited lives are seen as the *Wake* sees them here, a farce of destiny. Joyce saw life as a joke that might as well be enjoyed and, as did Khayyam, sought solace in wine. McHugh gives the reference here as the composer Verdi's *La Forza del Destino*.

E

eaden *FW* 597.35 *v.* Chewed and swallowed or eaten in the garden where Adam and Eve first lived or Eden. The "forebitten" fruit "eaden" in the Garden of Eden by Eve and Adam resulted in their banishment east of Eden. The Bible does not specify the type of fruit that was "eaden," though an apple has become the popular culprit. The last sentence of the *Wake*'s first page mentions oranges, of which McHugh writes: "Basque word for orange etymologised 'the fruit which was first eaten.'" ("You have eaden fruit. Say whuit.")

earopean *FW* 598.15 *adj.* Having to the ear the sound of something European. With his knowledge of so many European languages, Joyce certainly had an "earopean" sensibility and, while *Finnegans Wake* draws on many of the world's languages, it has an overall "earopean" tone to it. ("In that earopean end meets Ind.")

earsighted *FW* 143.9-10 *adj.* Able to hear a sound distinctly at a short distance only, in the same sense that the nearsighted can see distinctly at a short distance only. Generally, a sound that can be heard distinctly by the "earsighted" is close enough to to be seen distinctly by the nearsighted. ("with an earsighted view of old hopeinhaven") While Joyce's hearing was excellent, almost everything, both far and near, was out of sight for him. He did stress quite firmly that the best way to understand *Finnegans Wake* is to read it out loud or, as the *Wake* puts it, to see with "our ears, eyes of the darkness." We actually need to both see and hear at the same time, as relying on only one sense can be misleading. The present word is a case in point for, if only heard, "earsighted" could easily be mistaken for "nearsighted."

earwitness *FW* 5.14 *n*. As an eyewitness is someone who has actually seen some act or object and can testify concerning it, an "earwitness" is someone who has actually heard some sound or occurrence and can testify regarding it. Eyewitness testimony in a court of law is often found to be unreliable, and there is no reason to believe that the testimony of an "earwitness" is any more reliable. Joyce enjoyed playing the game of Gossip in which some bit of information is passed secretly from person to person, and the fun comes from finding how far off the original message is from what is heard by the final player. This very thing occurs when the information the "cad with a pipe" shares with his wife concerning his midnight encounter with HCE in Phoenix Part is passed by her to her priest who shares it with a friend until the final "earwitness" turns the story into a song, "The Ballad of Persse O'Reilly," that is sung all over Dublin, much to the discredit of HCE. (See **contrawatchwise**.) ("Our cubehouse still rocks as earwitness to the thunder of his arafatas") McHugh identifies "cubehouse" as the literal translation of Ka'aba, centre of Islam, and "arafatas" as "Our Father" from the Lord's Prayer. The sound the "earwitness" hears is Vico's thunder, signaling a ricorso and, naturally, any word in the *Wake* with "ear" in it brings H. C. Earwicker immediately to mind. (See **eyewitless**.)

easger *FW* 340.18 *adj*. Ardent or eager if without difficulty or easy. In *Finnegans Wake*, Shaun is eager to be thought well of and to be a leader as long as he doesn't have to exert much effort. ("Bernesson Mac Mahahon from Osro bearing nose easger for sweeth prolettas on his swooth prowl!") *Finnegans Wake* is most certainly not a book for the "easger" student of literature.

Eatsoup *FW* 246.31 *n.* The Wakean version of Esau whose twin brother Jacob duped his famished older brother into trading his birthright for a mess of pottage or a bowl of lentil soup. ("that dark deed doer, this wellwilled wooer, Jerkoff and Eatsoup, Yem or Yan") These famous twins mirror the Earwicker twins Shem and Shaun whose rivalry flows through *Finnegans Wake*. They appear first on the first page as "Jhem or Shen," one among many of the sets of names they assume. Jacob appears two lines above the twins as the "kidscad" or younger son who proved a cad when he tricked his blind old dad, "a bland old isaac," into believing he, Jacob, was the hairy Esau by wearing the skin of a goat or kid on his arms. "Yem or Yan" may also be the negative and positive elements in Chinese dualistic philosophy, Yin and Yang.

Eatster *FW* 623.8 *n.* Christian festival celebrating Christ's resurrection or Easter with an emphasis on the special foods prepared for eating during this holiday, colored eggs being the most ubiquitous. ("You invoiced him last Eatster so he ought to give us hockockles and everything.") McHugh identifies "hockockles" as "hot cockles," edible saltwater mollusks that have heart-shaped shells.

eggtenticdal *FW* 16.36 *adj.* The same or identical to an egg. ("He was poached on in that eggtenticdal spot.") This may be the identical spot that Humpty Dumpty fell from the wall. If the pavement was hot enough to fry an egg, he might also have been poached. Humpty elicits thoughts of the Norwegian captain and HCE who each had a hump on his back and, like ALP, he appears on the *Wake*'s first and last page as well as making s(c/h)attered appearances throughout the book.

embottled *FW* 140.33 *v.* Fortified for a violent struggle or embattled by means of liquor from a bottle. In the massed warfare of past centuries, it's said that most of the soldiers were heavily fortified by booze ("liquid courage") or "embottled" before the fighting began, and who can blame them. In *George Washington's Expense Account*, Marvin Kitman reports the large sums spent on alcohol by Washington during the Revolutionary War. "Washington never drank more than a bottle of Madeira a night," Kitman writes, "as all historians say, besides rum, punch and beer," and he "often drank cider, champagne and brandy, especially after the French alliance when surplus wine flowed into this country." Kitman sums up with: "Much of Washington's continuing good cheer and famed fortitude during the long years of the war, caused to some extent by his overly cautious military tactics, may have come from the bottle." Drinking by revolutionary soldiers was limited only by available supplies and, not being on expense accounts, by what they could afford. In the first stanza of "Concord Hymn" by Ralph Waldo Emerson—By the rude bridge that arched the flood, Their flag to April's breeze unfurled, Here once the embattled farmers stood, And fired the shot heard round the world. —one might well wonder if Joyce's "embottled" might more accurately be substituted for Emerson's "embattled." ("after all the errears and erroriboose of combarative embottled history") (See **erroriboose**.)

emporialist *FW* 589.10 *n.* An imperialist as one favoring the establishment of authority or control over another country's markets, trade, or emporium. The government of China is presently imperialist and "emporialist," supplanting America's once dominant role in both of these areas. ("making party capital out of landed self-interest, light on slavey but weighty on the bourse, our hugest commercial emporialist") HCE makes another appearance here.

encestor *FW* 96.34 *n.* A forefather or ancestor who had sexual relations with a family member proscribed because of close blood ties or incest. *Finnegans Wake* is filled with incestuous suggestions, primarily from HCE's thoughts of his daughter Issy, who is also incestuously viewed by her twin brothers, Shem and Shaun. ("that by such playing possum our hagious curious encestor bestly saved his brush with his posterity") Together with the adjectives describing "encestor," we find the ever-recurring initials HCE.

enchainted *FW* 237.11 *v.* 1. A combination of enchain and enchant. To restrain with a chain or enchain while using magic or a spell to enchant. 2. To attract and hold one's attention or emotions by delighting, charming, or captivating. ("—Enchainted, dear sweet Stainusless, young confessor, dearer, dearest") Joyce's younger brother Stanislaus appears here as being useless, though in fact he saved the Joyce's financially time after time. While Stanislaus recognized his brother's literary genius, he thought *Finnegans Wake* went too far, describing it as "the witless wandering of literature before its final extinction," and he refused the copy Joyce sent him. To say that Stanislaus was not "enchainted" by the *Wake* requires no further evidence.

enemay *FW* 352.10 *n.* A foe or enemy and a flushing of the bowels or enema. Even for *Finnegans Wake* this seems a bizarre combination, but a close look at its context gives a few clues. ("bung goes the enemay the Percy rally got me") With bung hole as slang for the anus, enema makes a perfect fit here. McHugh reads this as "how goes the enemy?: what time is it?" This relates to the question the "cad with a pipe" asked HCE one night in Phoenix Park, an incident that leads to accusations of sexual perversity against the *Wake*'s main male protagonist. This is reinforced by "Percy rally got me," a reference to the salacious song, "The Ballad of Persse O'Reilly," that maligns HCE and that all Dublin is singing. The French *perce-oreille* means "earwig." (See **gossipaceous**.)

enouch *FW* 535.21 *interj.* An exclamation combining enough and ouch to indicate that one has had a sufficiency of sudden pain and wants no more. ("Hole affair is rotten muckswinish porcupig's draff. Enouch!") McHugh references "Enoch," the first city built by Cain. Cain named the city after the son he had with his wife, but where she and all the other inhabitants came from is unexplained. If they were all produced by Adam and Eve as the Bible implies, I can hear Eve shouting at Adam, "Enouch!" as pain in childbirth was one of the penalties for eating the Eden apple.

enterruption *FW* 332.36 *n.* A hindrance, break in some action, or interruption caused by coming into or entering. The most famous "enterruption" related to *Finnegans Wake* is the story of Joyce dictating part of the *Wake* to Samuel Beckett. As Richard Ellmann tells it, "there was a knock at the door that Beckett didn't hear. Joyce said, 'Come in,' and Beckett wrote it down. Afterwards he read back what he had written and Joyce said, 'What's that Come in?' 'Yes, you said that,' said Beckett. Joyce thought for a moment, then said, 'Let it stand.'" While I haven't been able to find "Come in" in my readings of the *Wake*, I have found "Come-Inn," "Come indoor," and "common inn," each of which could refer to Beckett's account of this literary "enterruption." Farther afield, another possibility is "kemin in" with the Danish *Kime* for "to chime," giving "chime in." This incident corresponds to a comment Joyce made about his construction of *Finnegans Wake*: "It is not I who am writing this crazy book. It is you, and you, and you and that man over there and that girl at the next table." He carried a small notebook and pencil with him to write down snippets from the conversations of people around him. ("Enterruption. Check or slowback. Dvershen.")

entertrainer *FW* 106.9 *n.* One who teaches or trains one who performs or an entertainer. An acting or voice coach can be considered an "entertrainer." ("*The Great Polynesional Entertrainer Exhibits Ballantine Brautchers with the Link of Natures*")

enouch - epistlemadethemology | 109

To update an old saying, "Those who can, do. Those who can't, become an 'entertrainer.'"

enthreateningly *FW* 246.6 *adv*. Earnestly ask or entreat with a warning of harm and punishment or threateningly. ("Housefather calls enthreateningly.") This is one of the numerous ways Humphrey Chimpden Earwicker's initials are interwoven in the text. But this sentence may also refer to God the Father's threats of punishment for sin accompanied by the sound of thunder echoed in the *Wake*'s ten very, very, very, long thunder words.

entowerly *FW* 4.36 *adv*. Completely or entirely a high structure either standing alone or attached to another building or a tower. The Leaning Tower of Pisa stands "entowerly" and is not part of a larger structure. The Tower of Babel, at least as far as artists' imaginations go, was built "entowerly." *Finnegans Wake*, written entirely with words selected from and/or assembled from a multitude of the world's languages, is Joyce's attempt at rebuilding The Tower of Babel in one book. ("a skyerscape of most eyeful hoyth entowerly, erigenating from next to nothing and celescalating the himals and all, hierarchitectitiptitoploftical, with a burning bush abob off its baubletop") The references here to a skyscraper, a tower, heaven (German: *Himmel*), God speaking from a burning bush on a "baubletop" (top of the Tower of Babel), make "entowerly" clear the structure readers are meant to picture.

eolders *FW* 372.34 *n*. Senior in years, earliest, or elders who are aged or older than their fellows or the oldest of the elders. Since some church officers are given the title "Elder" even though they may be teenagers, the age difference among some elders and their "eolders" can be quite great. ("The for eolders were aspolootly at their wetsend in the mailing waters, trying to. Hide! Seek! Hide! Seek!")

epistlemadethemology *FW* 374.17 *n*. An epistle or letter made

110 | A *Finnegans Wake* Lextionary

to explain the philosophical nature, origin, and boundaries of knowledge or epistemology of God, religious ideas, and beliefs or theology. Beckman writes of this word: "Authority provides factitious epistemological certainties as did Paul's authoritative epistles" and sees *Finnegans Wake* as "a burlesque expressing skepticism of all totalizing systems and all insistence on invisible realities such as good things stored up in futurity with life after death to clinch the deal: 'Postmartem is the goods.'" ("Wait till we hear the Boy of Biskop reeling around your postoral lector! Epistlemadethemology for deep dorfy doubtings.") The last three words here are one of the many allusions to Lady Morgan's comment on Ireland's capital, "Dear dirty Dublin."

eroscope *FW* 431.14 *n*. An instrument providing the means to view or observe Eros, the Greek god of love and, by extension, acts of sexual or erotic activity. With the profusion of pornographic sites on the internet, the computer has become the modern world's most popular "eroscope." ("Juan, after those few prelimbs made out through his eroscope the apparition of his fond sister Issy for he knew his love by her waves of splabashing and she showed him proof by her way of blabushing nor could he forget her so tarnelly easy as all that since he was brotherbesides her") Here is yet another instance of the incest theme within *Finnegans Wake*. Shaun appears as Juan, with a hint of Don Juan.

errears *FW* 140.32 *n*. Mistakes or errors in an unpaid debt or unfinished work that is in arrears. (" after all the errears and erroriboose of combarative embottled history") A scrambled version of HCE is found in this phrase.

erronymously *FW* 617.30 *adv*. At once incorrectly or erroneously and namelessly or anonymously, such as an error of unknown authorship. ("Well, here's lettering you erronymously anent other clerical fands allieged herewith.") The infamous letter written by Pigott to implicate Parnell in the Phoenix Park murders was shown to be a forgery when it was revealed in court that Pigott's misspelling of "hesitancy" as "hesitency" matched the misspelling in the letter. So the author of what was meant to be an anonymous letter was revealed through his error, making it "erronymously" written. Pigott should be used as an example for children who don't study their spelling words in school. (See **Anoymany's, hasitte, & hazeydency.**)

erroriboose *FW* 140.33 *n.* A mistake or error caused by the consumption of any intoxicating liquor that is commonly called booze. ("after all the errears and erroriboose of combarative embottled history") Any comparative study of combative history will reveal all the errors embattled with alcohol. (See **combarative** and **embottled.**) Oscar Wilde revealed his discovery that "alcohol, when taken in sufficient quantities, produces all the effects of intoxication."

Errorland *FW* 62.25 *n.* Ireland, a land of many wrongs or errors (family, church, and state), from which Joyce felt he had to exile himself in order to write. His weapons to combat these errors were "silence, exile, and cunning." With *Finnegans Wake*, Joyce changed these to silence, exile, and punning. ("the Man we wot of took little short of fighting chances but for all that he or his or his care were subjected to the horrors of the premier terror of Errorland.")

essenesse *FW* 608.4 *n.* The necessary part that makes something what it is or the essence of the monastic sect of Jews in Palestine known as the Essenes. Today the "essenesse" of the Essenes is the *Dead Sea Scrolls* found during the 1940-50's in caves where these men lived before, during, and after the time and teachings of Jesus. Some scholars believe Jesus' "lost years" were spent in study with the Essenes where he received the "essenesse" of his teachings. McHugh gives *esse* as the Latin for "to be." Whatever is of "essenesse" in *Finnegans Wake*, "mentioning of it under the breath, as in pure (what bunkum!) essenesse," it appears to be pure bunk or nonsense.

ethiquethical *FW* 109.21 *adj.* What is both morally right or ethical and correct conduct or etiquette. ("preferring to close his blinkhard's eyes to the ethiquethical fact that she was, after all, wearing for the space of the time being some definite articles of evolutionary clothing") In *The Picture of Dorian Gray*, Oscar Wilde weighs in on the subject of the "ethiquethical:" "Civilized society feels that manners are of more importance than morals, and the highest respectability is of less value than the possession of a good chef. Even the cardinal virtues cannot atone for cold entrées, nor an irreproachable private life for a bad dinner and poor wines."

eunique *FW* 562.33 *adj.* A castrated man or eunuch who is one of a kind or unique. In the Orient, a man placed in charge of the ruler's harem was castrated to keep him from sampling the wares, so to speak. Among all the men in service within the palace, he was, without question, "eunique." ("He is too audorable really, eunique!")

Europasianised *FW* 191.4 *v.* To mix European and Asian influences. East may be east and west may be west, yet the twain not only meet but mingle once *Finnegans Wake* has "Europasianised" them. With the *Wake*'s, "you (thanks, I think that describes you) Europasianised Afferyank," the Latin *afer* for "African" tosses in the middle ground between east and west. HCE as the dead hero Finn MacCool interred in the Dublin landscape, with his "humptyhillhead" in the east at "Howth Castle and Environs" connected to his "tumptytumtoes" "well to the west" in Phoenix Park, appears in the first and last sentences on the *Wake*'s first page, a meeting of east and west.

everintermutuomergent *FW* 55.11-12 *adj.* Everything forever together mutating, merging, shifting, and changing. This word aptly describes most of the people and places, themes and motifs of *Finnegans Wake*. The more they change the more they stay the same. ("The scene, refreshed, reroused, was never to be forgotten, the hen and crusader everintermutuomergent, for later in the century on of that puisne band of factferreters") Here's yet another appearance of HCE's initials.

exaspirated *FW* 251.31 *v.* 1. Made angry or exasperated by someone's harshness, severity, or asperity. 2. Made angry or exasperated by someone's ambition or aspiration. 3. Made angry or exasperated by someone's use of a breathing sound in pronunciation or aspirating. ("with man's mischief in his mind whilst her pupils swimmed too heavenlies, let his be exaspirated, letters be blowed")

excits *FW* 368.19 *n.* A way out or exit that stirs up strong feelings or excites. It would seem that within its context of brothels the *Wake* is referring to anal sex, though there may be other exits that could prove exciting. The sight of Marilyn Monroe's posterior as she ascends the staircase to her apartment in *The Seven Year Itch* is a fine example of "excits." ("yesayenolly about the back excits. Never to weaken up in place of the broths")

expercatered *FW* 219.6 *v.* To make clear, explain, or explicate exactly what objectionable or offensive words or passages are to be removed, excised, or expurgated from a book or any written work. Joyce delayed publication of *Dubliners* for many years by his refusal to agree to what was "expercatered" by his publisher. ("By arraignment, childream's hours, expercatered.")

explodotonates *FW* 353.23-24 *v.* To burst with a loud noise or explode as when a device detonates substances such as dynamite, nitroglycerin, or nuclear materials. ("The abnihilisation of the etym by the grisning of the grosing of the grinder of the grunder of the first lord of Hurtreford explodotonates through Parsuralia with an ivanmorinthorrumble") It's evident that the detonating and exploding here comes from the

114 | A *Finnegans Wake* Lextionary

splitting of an atom, something first accomplished by Lord Rutherford in 1919. Joyce predicts the coming horror of atomic war with "Whatthough for all appentices it had a mushroom on it . . . nogeysokey first" and "hriosmas, whereas take notice be the relics of the bones." This was published in 1939, years before the United States "explodotonates" two atomic bombs over Japan. The other thing annihilated here is etymology or existing words, something *Finnegans Wake* does effectively. Joyce, writes Paul Strathern, "split the atom of the word, thus releasing all the vast energy of its different syllabic meanings and associations." McHugh references "Hurtreford" with Dublin as it was earlier known as "The Town of the Ford of the Hurdles." The sound of the explosion in this passage is more terrible than the rage of the infamous Russian Czar Ivan or the rumble of the Scandinavian god Thor's thunderbolt hammer.

exqueezit *FW* 412.8 *adj*. Lovely, delicate, or exquisite to compress or squeeze. Many "exqueezit" things come immediately to mind, from voluptuous ladies to that old television ad for toilet paper in which the supermarket manger is constantly telling the customers, "Please don't squeeze the Charmin." ("How mielodorous is thy bel chant, O songbird, and how exqueezit thine after draught!")

eyewitless *FW* 515.30 *n*. A stupid or witless firsthand observer or eyewitness. The unreliability of testimony from those who have seen something firsthand is legendary, with different accounts coming from different observers of the same scene or action. In *Finnegans Wake* HCE suffers from accusations of impropriety in Phoenix Park made by two girls and three soldiers. Their various versions of what occurred are "dandymount to a clearobscure" and, despite several trials, the varying accounts of HCE's alleged crime are never resolved. Of course everyone still believes HCE must have done something improper since five people were "eyewitless" at the scene. ("—Ah, sure, I eyewitless foggus. 'Tis all around me bebattersbid hat.") "Fog" in "foggus" may suggest why the eyewitness's testimony is witless. The strong belief of an eyewitness account is found in *FW* 247.32: "He knows for he's seen it in black and white through his eyetrompit." (See **earwitness**.)

F

factferreters *FW* 55.13 *n.* To hunt out of a place of hiding, to search for through clever questioning, to rummage about, or to ferret out the truth or facts, in short, exactly the skills required to tackle *Finnegans Wake*. A small army of "factferreters" has been diligently at work since 1939 in digging and sifting, tracking down and beating the bushes, leaving no stone unturned while looking high and low to ferret out the facts, meanings, and allusions found in Joyce's final work, his book of the dark. ("for later in the century one of that puisne band of factferreters")

fadograph *FW* 7.15 *n.* 1. A picture taken by a camera or a photograph that is losing its color or a faded photograph. ("Only a fadograph of a yestern scene.") In this Wakean context we find a fading photograph of a western scene of yesterday. 2. A photograph of the latest craze, rage, or fad. A photo of children playing with a Hoola Hoop is a "fadograph."

fainfully *FW* 124.32 *adv.* Being full of gladness, willingness, or the archaic "fain." In its Wakean context, faithfully is suggested but with the addition of the positive attributions above. There is often a touch of obligation that tempers this willingness.

("With acknowledgment of our fervour of the first instant he remains years most fainfully."

fairescapading *FW* 388.3   *v.* There are so many meanings attached to "fair" that it's difficult to know where to start. And the second half of the word is complicated as well. Our minds latch on to the most familiar reference, in this case fire escape, a ladder or staircase on the outside of a building to use in case of fire. So "fair" in this sense would refer to escaping safely or with a promise of success. The meaning of "escaping" is easier as it usually implies getting away, getting free, or fleeing. Yet a closer look reveals not "escaping" but an "escapade," that brings in some sort of prank or adventure, and one that generally raises a few eyebrows. In its Wakean context we read "fairescapading in his natsirt." With McHugh's provision of the Danish *nat* for "night," a long, loose shirt worn by males in bed or a nightshirt appears. As to what male is escaping in a nightshirt by means of a fire escape, it's Charles Stewart Parnell who pops up in *Finnegans Wake* from the first page on. He was the popular Irish leader and member of Parliament who was just on the verge of achieving Home Rule for his country when Captain O'Shea, one of his lieutenants and the husband of Parnell's mistress, Kitty O'Shea, decided to stop turning a blind eye on the affair and sued for divorce. It seems that, during the trial, a reporter misunderstood some evidence and wrote a story indicating that a nightshirt-clad Parnell had escaped from Mrs. O'Shea's bedroom by way of a fire escape to avoid detection by the Captain. In a sense, Parnell was fairly escaping from the escapade of his affair. Though Joyce, by way of this father, idolized Parnell (See the heated Christmas dinner political firestorm in *A Portrait of the Artist as a Young Man*.), he was not averse to including this amusing incident in his last work. It's fair to say the escapade of the affair destroyed Parnell, his political power, and any immediate hope for Ireland to escape the clutches of England. Though he married Mrs. O'Shea shortly after her divorce, Parnell died a few months later, a broken man.

fairwell *FW* 225.30   *n.* Good wishes upon parting or farewell to someone going or traveling (*fare* is archaic for "go" or "travel") with the additional wish for pleasant or fair weather during the trip. "Fairwell" may also play on the various meanings of "fair," such as the parting wish for a trip that is neither good nor bad but just fair ("Foreweal! Ring we round, Chuff! Fairwell!") Lord Byron's poetic lines come to mind here: "Fare thee well and if forever, / Still forever, fare thee well."

farmament *FW* 494.3   *n.* The arch of the sky, the heavens, or firmament with an unequivocal indication that it is distant or far away. ("that skew arch of chrome sweet home, floodlit up above the flabberghosted farmament")

farst *FW* 340.35 & 356.12   *n.* The earliest or first absurd or ridiculous play or farce. The film *Animal House* was National Lampoon's "farst." ("as my farst is near to hear and my sackend is meet to sedon while my whole's a peer's aureolies" & "the farst wriggle of the ubivence, whereom is man, that old offender, nother man, wheile he is asame") This last passage is one of several plays on the *Wake*'s "first riddle of the universe: asking, when is a man not a man?" The answer is, "When he is a . . . Sham." Could "farst" mean first fart, ala Bloom in *Ulysses*? Sure, if you want it to. ("See **farternoiser.**)

farternoiser *FW* 530.36   *n.* One who makes the sound or noise of expelling gas or farting. This suggests the Our Father or Pater Noster. In *Finnegans Wake*, God's voice through thunder can come across as a farting sound. ("A farternoiser for his tuckish armenities.") The next sentence begins, "Ouhr Former who erred in having," that brings in the *Wake*'s contention that God messed up big time when he created the heavens and the earth, what Joyce believed was the real Original Sin. In *Ulysses*, Joyce created the noise of Bloom's fart on the sidewalk with "Kraaaaaa . . . Pprrpffrrppfff," a hint of many more literary inventions to come within *Finnegans Wake*. This fart is famous as the place where a disgusted Virginia Woolf finally abandoned her reading of Joyce's banned book.

farwailed *FW* 590.16 *v.* 1. To mournfully cry or wail at parting, making a sad goodbye or farewell. The Irish cry of "Ochon" (this cry is suggested on the *Wake*'s first page with "Oconee.") for "woe is me" is an example of a "farwailed" good-bye. 2. To mournfully cry or wail at a distant or far away place. Irish men and women sailing for America were often given "American wakes" because they were going so far away that they would probably never be seen again by their families and friends. Wails of "Ochon" were no doubt heard long after these "wakes." (See **woice**.) ("At folkmood hailed, at part farwailed") This suggests the Latin *ave et vale* for "hail and farewell."

faturity *FW* 292.19 *n.* The silliness and stupidity or fatuity of what is to come or futurity. ("search lighting, beached, bashed and beaushelled *à la Mer* pharahead into faturity") McHugh translates these last three words as "far ahead into futurity." Given my definition of "faturity" and "pharahead" (See **pharahead**.), this may mean seeing through the use of a very strong light the silliness and stupidity awaiting us down the road to the future. Given all the silliness and stupidity of the past and present, this look far ahead should come as no surprise.

faullt *FW* 558.8 *n.* Drop down or fall and mistake, error, or fault. The "faullt" of Tim Finnegan's fall from the ladder was from his over-consumption of alcohol. ("so prays of his faullt you would make obliteration but from our friend behind bars") In today's litigious climate, Tim's widow could sue if the distillery hadn't put a warning label on their bottles to the effect that drinking whiskey before carrying a brick-loaded hod up a ladder could be injurious to one's health.

faustive *FW* 74.9 *adj.* Joyous or festive in the spirit of Faust, the hero of a play by Goethe, who sells his soul to the Devil. After a wonderful life, the Devil collects on his debt, but Faust's soul is saved in the last act, a "faustive" event if ever there was one. ("Silence was in thy faustive halls") McHugh references a song by Irishman Thomas Moore: "Silence Is in Our Festive Halls [The Green Woods of Truiga]."

femaline *FW* 251.31 *adj.* Having the womanly or feminine features of a cat or feline. ("I is a femaline person. O, of provocative gender.") The fictional character Cat Woman of OC Comic's *Batman* franchise is a case in point.

feminiairity *FW* 606.22 *n.* Close knowledge or familiarity with the nature of women or femininity. On reading Molly Bloom's closing soliloquy in *Ulysses*, Jung wrote Joyce, "I suppose the devil's grandmother knows so much about the real psychology of a woman, I didn't." Joyce's wife Nora took an opposite view, saying, "He knows nothing at all about women." Thus, Joyce's "feminiairity" is in dispute. ("Their design is a whosold word and the charming details of light in dark are freshed from the feminiairity which breathes content.") The famous phrase, "Familiarity breeds contempt," is here as well, though Warren Beatty personally proved that familiarity with femininity brings content.

feminite *FW* 237.1 *adj.* Having close or intimate and endless or infinite womanly or feminine qualities. In *Finnegans Wake* ALP, in her role of all women of all stages and ages from the ancient Earth Mother on, is the eternal, all-pervading "feminite" fixture of the universe. ("she is tournesoled straightcut or sidewaist, accourdant to the coursets of things feminite, towooerds him in heliolatry") The feminine undergarment called a corset, to which Joyce was decidedly adverse, appears here. (See **coursets**.)

fiancy *FW* 226.14 *n.* The power to imagine or fancy an engagement to be married to someone or to be one's fiancé or fiancée. ("And among the shades that Eve's now wearing she'll meet anew fiancy, tryst and trow.")

122 | A *Finnegans Wake* Lextionary

figuratleavely *FW* 296.31 *adv.* Symbolically or figuratively combined with the leaf of a fig tree. Adam and Eve "figuratleavely" clothed themselves with fig leaves after a bit of apple opened their eyes to the shocking sight of their nakedness. It's ironic that God later clothed the first couple in animal skins before kicking them out of the Garden of Eden, while today members of PETA take off all their clothes to protest God's original glad rags. As an aside, if you closely observe a fig leaf, you'll find it is "figuratleavely" shaped like that part of the male anatomy it was used to conceal. ("I'll make you to see figuratleavely the whome of your eternal geomater.") This comes in the lessons chapter where Shaun instructs his bother Shem on their mother's sexual geometry, the symbol of the womb or ALP's siglum as the triangular delta of a river.

fingures *FW* 282.11 *n.* Numbers or figures calculated on one or more fingers. It is not uncommon for even the most mathematically astute to figure with the fingers in solving a simple numerical problem. Most people generally turn to a calculator for numbers above ten. ("why his fingures were giving him whatfor to fife with")

flightening *FW* 626.16 *adj.* Something that causes fleeing or flight from terror or fright. ("I'm sure he squirted juice in his eyes to make them flash for flightening me.") In Vico's circular scheme of history, at the end of the third or human age, God's lightning and thunder has a "flightening" effect that drives humans back into caves where, praying for God's mercy, the first or divine age begins the cycle anew.

foamous *FW* 7.12 *adj.* Well-known or famous masses of bubbles or foam. There are many types of foam that are famous, from shaving cream to bubble baths, but in this particular instance it's "A glass of Danu U'Dunnell's foamous olde Dobbelin ayle." This translates into the "foamous" O'Connell Ale from a brewery in Phoenix Park owned by the son of the famous and Irish political leader known as The Liberator, Daniel O'Connell. But I can't forget that "foamous" film scene of Jane Mansfield taking a bubble bath.

fokloire *FW* 419.12   *n*. With the Irish *foclóir* for "vocabulary," we have a legend or folklore told in Irish about the French river Loire. Since Joyce was writing *Finnegans Wake* in France, the Loire could substitute for the Liffey. ("How farflung is your fokloire and how velktingeling your volupkabulary!") (See **volupkabulary**.)

folksfiendship *FW* 542.18   *n*. A condition between people who like one another or the friendship of an evil person or fiend for a group of people or folks. A fiendish friendship is in truth no friendship at all. ("I demosthrenated my folksfiendship, enmy pupuls felt my burk was no worse than their brite") McHugh references Ibsen's play *En folkefiende* (*An Enemy of the People*) and the old saying, "his bark is worse than his bite." Adolf Hitler's professed friendship for the German folk (Volk) was indeed a "folksfiendship" with terrible consequences. His slogan was "ein Volk, ein Reich, ein Furher" or "one folk, one realm, one leader." Hitler and his "sohns of a blitzh" appear in *Finnegans Wake* as "heal helper! One gob, one gap, one gulp and gorger of all," and the Holocaust ("haul it cost") was foreseen. As Joyce predicted to Miss Weaver, Europe "is where the gas is really going to be turned on." Joyce commented that the Germans should "leave Poland in peace and occupy themselves with *Finnegans Wake*." His suggestion is not as farfetched as it seems, since an ample supply of German words or *Wake* words created from German enabled Helmut Bonheim to write an excellent reference book, *A Lexicon of the German in "Finnegans Wake."*

forebeer *FW* 84.36   *n*. An ancestor or forebear who brewed and/or consumed beer. This word is particularly pertinent for me as my first American forefather was an indentured servant to a brewer and dyer in Oglethorpe's first Georgia colony. Since in one Wakean scene Shaun floats away on the Liffey in a Guinness Stout barrel, "pursuits of our forebeer, El Don De Dunelli, (may his ship thicked stick in the bottol of the river and all his crewsers stock locked in the burral of the seas!)" may refer to this strange incident. Like the English clergyman who thanked God he was not born before tea, many of us are thankful we were not born before beer.

forebitten *FW* 303.16-17   *adj.* To prohibit or forbid something being bitten in advance or before it's being bitten. God's command that Eve and Adam not eat of the Tree of the Knowledge of Good and Evil in the Garden of Eden is a prime example. (See **applegate**.) ("that Jacoby feeling again for forebitten fruit")

fornicular *FW* 319.28   *n.* With the Latin *fornix* for "brothel," "fornicular" suggests, without actually saying so, the informal, everyday, or in particular, the vernacular for fornicate that, for decency's sake, often appears in print as "f**k." ("he sagd in the fornicular, and, at weare or not at weare, I'm sigen no stretcher")

fostard *FW* 603.34 *n.* A child whose parents were not legally married and who is brought up by persons other than his parents or a foster bastard. ("But what does Coemghem, the fostard?")

foully *FW* 113.13 & 313.33   *adv.* Completely, entirely, or fully dirty, filthy, or foul. Readers who found *Ulysses* "foully" written would have been even more shocked by certain passages in *Finnegans Wake* had they taken the time to decipher them. ("He had to see life foully the plak and the smut" & "should he be himself namesakely a foully fallen dissentant from the peripulator") This is a long shot, but since the dump or midden from which the hen pecks out the letter or "litter" is fully foul, then we might say that the "litter" was finally, fowlly found "foully."

foundingpen *FW* 563.6   *n.* With a fountain pen as a metaphor for penis, and the ink that flows from it as a metaphor for semen, a founding father is founding a new life. ("And he has pipettishly bespilled himself from his foundingpen as illspent from inkinghorn.")

fraudstuff *FW* 7.13 *n.* 1. Meant to deceive or fraudulent and material for food or foodstuff. Most of the fattening snacks and desserts on supermarket shelves are so full of empty calories, artificial flavorings, and preservatives, that they should be labeled "fraudstuff." Other foods are so far removed from the real thing, such as canned corn compared to freshly picked corn, that they become fraudulent foodstuffs. In *Finnegans Wake*, "fraudstuff" is specific to the Eucharist, which in Catholic theology is the actual presence of God, a concept Joyce considered a fraud. ("But, lo, as you wold quaffoff his fraudstuff and sink teeth through that pyth of a flowerwhite bodey behold of him as behemoth for he is noewhemoe.") With "quaffoff," the wine or blood of Jesus is suggested while "a flowerwhite bodey" refers to bread or His body. 2. A stretch, I confess, but I find something of Sir John Falstaff ("Fall stuff") from Shakespeare's *Henry IV*, parts 1 and 2 here. This "lying tub of lard," as *Wikipedia* describes him, is something of a fraud and certainly stuffs himself with food and drink. The pun-loving Joyce would have enjoyed the internet encyclopedia Wikipedia's comment that the name Falstaff "invites humor, as it is a sort of pun on impotence, brought on by the character's excessive consumption of alcohol."

freudful *FW* 411.35-36 *adj.* Alarming, shocking, or frightful of the Austrian doctor who developed psychoanalysis, Dr. Freud. Joyce was, as we read in the *Wake*, "not yung and easily freudened" of Freud, though he did send his daughter Lucia to Jung for treatment. ("You never made a more freudful mistake, excuse yourself!") "Written in Lappish language" is the *Wake*'s comment on itself that suggests the Latin *lapsua linguae* for "slips of the tongue," a suggestion of Freudian slips where you say one thing and mean your mother.

fuchu *FW* 466.4 *interj.* With Joyce's reputation for salacious, sexual stuff in *Ulysses* that caused it to be banned from English-speaking countries for well over a decade, and with the *Wake*'s steamy scenes escaping the censor's wrath only from their apparent unintelligibility, it's only natural to expect the "F" word to make a full frontal appearance at some point in the text. The fact that it doesn't is, to quote an alleged remark of Presidential candidate Hillary Clinton's reported by John Heilemann and Mark Halperin, "Unfuckingbelievable!" But it does appear in a distorted form if you are wise to the *Wake*'s way with words. ("Lets have a fuchu all round, courting cousins!") One would, on the basis of this sentence alone, be on somewhat unstable ground to read "fuchu" as "fuck you," but read in context it becomes quite clear. The sentence preceding this—"Can you reverse positions?"—sets up a sexual situation and, with "love potients" appearing two lines down, it's clearer still. All this comes in a description of Tristram and Iseult's passionate shipboard lovemaking as seen by those four dirty old men, "Mamalujo." (See **amotion, inthrusted,** & **throust.**) If the young couple had known they were being spied upon, no doubt they would have given those four voyaging voyeurs the finger and said, "fuchu."

funantics *FW* 450.27 *n.* 1. One who has amusement or fun being excessively enthusiastic or fanatical 2. One who has fun performing silly tricks or antics. The *Wake* recognizes its funny antics with: "And the lark that I let fly (olala!) is as cockful of funantics as it's tune to my fork." Those *Finnegans Wake* fanatics, known as Wakeans, find a great deal of fun exploring the multitudinous meanings among the fantastic literary antics of Joyce's one-of-a-kind or *novel* novel.

funferall *FW* 111.15 *n.* A service for the dead or a funeral that is amusing or fun for everyone or all those attending. Irish wakes were one part mourning for one who is dead and another part celebrating that one who was alive no longer has to suffer the pains and toils of the living. Tim Finnegan's wake also became a free for all as the watchers at his wake got into a fight where "Shillelagh law did all engage, / And a row and a ruction soon began." Some find a wake without a good old-fashioned knock down, drag out lacking, and with plenty of whiskey punch and beer on hand, Tim's wake was well fueled to provide fun and fighting for all. ("with grand funferall of poor Father Michael don't forget unto life's")

funnaminal *FW* 244.13 *adj.* An extraordinary, rare, unique, or phenomenally humorous or funny animal. Kangaroos must have appeared "funnaminal" to the first English settlers in Australia. With "darkle" meaning "grow dark," the nighttime land of *Finnegans Wake* could be described with: "It darkles, (tinct, tint) all this our funnaminal world." Looking at a photograph in the *Irish Times* of a tramp in the same pose as O'Connell's statue in Dublin, Joyce's expressed his delight to Jacques Mercanton: "Altogether the meaning of 'Work in Progress': history repeats itself comically; this is our funnaminal world."

funpowtherplother *FW* 142.11 *n.* One who has an amusing time or fun organizing a secret plan or plot involving an explosive material such as gunpowder. Guy Fawkes, in his attempt to blow up the English parliament with gunpowder, could be considered a "funpowtherplother." (See **novembrance**.) Given the centuries of systematic mistreatment of Ireland by England, the Irish might rightly see Fawkes's gunpowder plot as just a bit of fun. ("the bleakablue tramp, the funpowtherplother, the christymansboxer") Fawkes and his plot pop up often in *Finnegans Wake*, with "*How a Guy Finks and Fawkes When He Is Going Batty*" as one of many examples.

funtasy *FW* 493.18 *n.* An amusing or funny illusory image, phantasm, or fantasy. At times the reading of *Finnegans Wake* feels like a "funtasy." ("Fantasy! funtasy on fantasy, amnaes fintasies!") McHugh references the Bible's "vanity of vanities, all is vanity," which is referred to on the *Wake*'s first page with "vanessy."

furbear *FW* 132.32 *n.* An ancestor or forebear so ancient that the skin of this early form of man is covered with fur akin to a bear. Another take on this could be our forefather as furfather. ("our family furbear, our tribal tarnpike") HCE's middle name, Chimpden, may be an allusion to Darwin and our close genetic relationship to the chimpanzee, a cute, furbearing animal.

furrowards *FW* 18.32 *adj.* Onward or forward in the line of direction of a trench or furrow made by a plow. It is always easier to move "furrowards" or parallel rather than perpendicular to furrows. An overseer's command to farmhands preparing to pick a crop such as strawberries might be "furrowards," march. ("the pourquose of which was to cassay the earthcrust at all of hours, furrowards, bagawards, like yoxen at the turnpaht")

G

gattling *FW* 377.6 *v.* Obtaining or getting that's infused with Richard J. Gatling's invention of an early machine gun, known as a Gatling gun. In other words, getting that involves an extreme use of force. Machine Gun Kelly could have been charged with "gattling" money from banks. ("The groom is in the greenhouse, gattling out his. Gun!") In *Finnegans Wake* this is a play on the line from a nursery rhyme: "The king was in his countinghouse, counting out his money."

genderous *FW* 268.25 *adj.* Willing to share or generous based on sex or gender. Women, said to come from Venus, are often thought to be more "genderous" than men, said to come from Mars. ("so spake gramma on the impetus of her imperative, only mind your genderous towards his reflexives such that I was to your grappa")

genitalmen *FW* 569.31 *n.* Men of good breeding and manner or gentlemen, with an emphasis on the strongly sexual side of man's nature dominated by his genitals. *Finnegans Wake* transforms the gentle reader into a genital reader through its sensuous, salacious sexual references. Since most of these references are written in the *Wake*'s tortuous, baffling, roundabout way with words, perhaps no real harm may be done, but studious, analytical, and inquisitive minds may be in moral danger. ("as they're two genitalmen of Veruno") This passage exposes Shakespeare's play *Two Gentlemen of Verona*. *Finnegans Wake* is filled with slang for the male genitals, beginning on the first page with "his penisolate war," one meaning of which is the late war of the penis that Tristram fought with his uncle King Mark for the love of Iseult, and "topsawyer's rocks" which can refer to testicles. Genitals are hidden in "little rude hiding rod," "penisills," and the middle line in the siglum of HCE which is a capital "E." This last reference is explained by "wick" which is slang for "penis" and the fact that it's the middle syllable in "Earwicker." The siglum for HCE's son Shem is a capital "E," but missing the middle line, indicative of his impotency.

gentilemen *FW* 573.35 *n.* Men of good breeding and manners or gentlemen who are also gentiles, that is, depending on who is making the distinction, pagans or heathens or not Jewish or Mormon. Additionally, Richard Beckman comments that "The incompatibility of gentleman and Jew is condensed in the pun 'gentilemen.'" ("This, lay readers and gentilemen, is perhaps the commonest of all cases arising out of umbrella history in connection with the wood industries in our courts of litigation.")

gentlehomme's *FW* 106.12 *n.* A place where one lives or a home belonging to a well-bred man or a gentleman. This is one of the many *Wake* words that combine two languages, the English word *gentle* and the French *homme* for "man," with *homme* suggesting "home" to readers of English. This is one of Joyce's easier constructions to be found in *Finnegans Wake*. ("Siegfield Follies and or a Gentlehomme's Faux Pas")

ghast *FW* 349.19 *n.* A shocking, horrible, or ghastly spirit of the dead or a ghost. One is generally aghast when confronted with a ghost. The comic character Casper the Friendly Ghost is an exception to the concept of "ghast." ("*the figure of a fellowchap in the wohly ghast*") The third member of the Trinity, the Holy Ghost, becomes "*the wohly ghast*" here. (See **wohly**.)

gianerant *FW* 368.8 *n*. 1. A high ranking military officer or general who has great power and importance or a giant. ("bungley well chute the rising gianerant") *Finnegans Wake* recounts and often refers to a story Joyce heard from his father about how Buckley shot the Russian general. It seems that during the Crimean War an Irish sharpshooter named Buckley had an opportunity to shoot a Russian general but, awed by the elaborate uniform, hesitated. As Buckley took aim once more, the general dropped his pants to defecate. Unable to shoot a man in such a position, Buckley hesitated once more. But when the general picked up a piece of sod (Ireland was called "Old Sod.") to wipe himself, Buckley fired. Samuel Beckett's response to Joyce's story was, "Another insult to Ireland." ("bulkily he shat the Ructions gunorrhal" & "instullt to Igorladns!" with the Russian *igo* for "suppression" are two of many references to Joyce's story and Beckett's response) Joyce's father was a famed raconteur and undoubtedly made quite a production of this tale. 2. A general fact, idea, or principle that is of great or gigantic importance. $E=mc^2$ is a "gianerant" of the 20th Century.

glaciator *FW* 232.32 *n*. A captive or paid fighter or gladiator with cold, crushing or glacial characteristics. Dolph Lundgren as the Russian boxer Drago in the film *Rocky IV* is the perfect example of a "glaciator." ("in appreciable less time than it takes a glaciator to submerger an Atlangthis") The ill-fated Titanic's unequal contest with an iceberg, the offspring of a glacier, submerged the ship in the Atlantic in appreciably less time than was ever imagined.

glistery *FW* 403.24 *adj*. Sparkle or glister combined with shinning with a bright, sparkling light or glittering, giving twice the brilliancy and brightness of either word on its own. The refraction of sunlight on the rippling water of Dublin Bay would give it a "glistery gleam." ("Irish objects nonviewable to human watchers save 'twere perchance anon some glistery gleam darkling adown surface of affuvial flowandflow")

goddinpotty *FW* 59.12 n. The Creator or God combined with commode or potty. The reference here is to the garden party in the Garden of Eden from which Eve and Adam were expelled or crapped out. ("the sprangflowers of his burstday which was a viridable goddinpotty for the reinworms") McHugh finds Abel in "viridable," further evidence of a link to Eden. Joyce was obviously thinking ahead to Rick Nelson's hit song, "Garden Party," that he wrote after his potty bad reception at Madison Square Garden.

goodbark *FW* 382.28-29 n. A special form of farewell or goodbye to one embarking on a voyage by ship or, in archaic and poetic terms, bark or barque. It appears in the *Wake* as: "So sailed the stout ship *Nansy Hans*. From Liff [Dublin's River Liffey] away. For Nattenlaender [*natten land* is Norwegian for "land of night"]. As who has come returns. Farvel [Danish for "farewell"], farerne! Goodbark, goodbye!" The term "land of night" may suggest sleep, with a wish for a restful night of good dreams, since *Finnegans Wake* represents a dream and dream language. There is also the implication that the ship should be good or sound and safe for the voyage. "Nancy Hand's," the local name for a pub near Dublin's Phoenix Park and stout, such as the Dublin-brewed Guinness Stout, a strong, heavy, almost black beer, together suggest a beverage served in a pub and a ship that is strongly built.

gossipaceous *FW* 195.4 adj. Idle, often untrue, talk about others or gossip that is large in scope or spacious. HCE and his entire life become the subject of "gossipaceous" Dubliners after his encounter with the "Cad" at midnight in Phoenix Park. Like the game of Gossip that Joyce enjoyed playing, each retelling caused

HCE's purported crime(s) to become worse, worser, worsest. "The Ballad of Persse O'Reilly" that is sung all over town is filled with "gossipaceous" slander and ends with: "And not all the king's men nor his horses / Will resurrect his corpus." ALP bravely comes to his defense using the "litter" the hen pecks out of the dump as evidence of his innocence. ("babbling, bubbling, chattering to herself, deloothering the fields on their elbows leaning with the sloothering slide of her, giddygaddy, grannyma, gossipaceous Anna Livia") In a "gossipaceous" vein, the Duchess of Windsor had an embroidered pillow on one of her sofas that read, "If you have nothing good to say, come sit my me."

gossiple *FW* 38.23 *n.* Teachings believed to be the absolute truth and guide to action or the gospel that are possibly based on idle, often untrue, talk or gossip. Joyce may be suggesting that the Gospels of Matthew, Mark, Luke, and John, the Apostles who appear as the four old men, Mamalujo, in *Finnegans Wake* are more likely "gossiple" than gospel. ("that the gossiple so delivered in his epistolear, buried teatoastally in their Irish stew would go no further than his jesuit's cloth")

gossipocracy *FW* 476.4 *n.* Idle, often untrue, talk about others or gossip and a pretense to goodness or hypocrisy. Those who gossip about alleged misdeeds of others, such as the gossip about HCE's supposed sexual perversion in Phoenix Park, usually pretend to be better than they actually are or gossipcrites. ("godsons' goddestfar, deputising for gossipocracy") McHugh gives the Danish *bedstefar* for godfather and *gossip* as archaic for godfather.

grandfallar *FW* 29.7 *n.* 1. A forefather or grandfather who has dropped or fallen. With falling, as well as resurrection, dominant themes in *Finnegans Wake*, the first forefather to fall is Adam in the *Wake*'s opening sentence. They keep falling right up to the book's primary protagonist, HCE. 2. A large or great number, as well as important or great fallers, make up the falling scenarios of the *Wake*. Tim Finnegan's fall from a ladder, as signaled in the title, starts the falls' ball rolling. ("humphing his share of the showthers is senken on him he's such a grandfallar") The word "humphing" is a reference to HCE's first name, Humphrey, to the hump on his back, and possibly to his humping not only his wife but to his purported sin in Phoenix Park. Humpty Dumpty was also a "grandfallar" from the magazine wall in that same park. 3. To continue the quote above, "he's such a grandfallar, with a pocked wife in pickle that's a flyfire and three lice nettle clinkers, two twilling bugs and one midget pucelle," HCE appears as a grand fellow with a wife and three children, twin boys and a girl.

greeding *FW* 377.1 & **greedings** *FW* 308.17 *n*. An avaricious or greedy salutation or greeting. The greediness within such a greeting is usually well concealed until it is too late to escape the request that follows the smile and well wishes. A panhandler on the streets is a master of a friendly "greeding." ("With easter greeding. Angus! Angus! Angus!" & "With our best youlldied greedings to Pep and Memmy and the old folkers below") Christmas or Yuletide greetings often have an element of greed in them as this second quote makes clear. Stephen Foster's famous song "Old Folks at Home" also appears here and on other pages in the *Wake* ("weights downupon the Swanny"), and the immensely popular American blackface group, Christy's Minstrels, who were said to have paid Foster $15,000 for the exclusive rights to the song, appear on the *Wake*'s first page as "christian minstrelsy."

groupography *FW* 476.33 *n*. The geography of a number of persons, animals, or things together or a group. Just as geography is the science of the Earth that studies and describes its physical features, "groupography" studies and describes the nature and features of a group. ("the map of the souls' groupography rose in relief") There is so much shifting and merging of groups in *Finnegans Wake* as to make "groupography" inherently difficult.

Adaline Glasheen recognized this when she asked her famous, oft-quoted question, "Who is who when everybody is somebody else?"

grumpapar *FW* 65.12 & 65.19 *n.* A surly, gruff, or grumpy grandfather or grandpapa. ("For dear old grumpapar, he's gone on the razzledar, through gazing and crazing and blazing at stars." & "half the gels in town has got their bottom drars while grumpapar he's trying to hitch his braces on to his trars") The addition of an 'r' at the end of this word suggests "oldparr" from the *Wake*'s first page, a reference to an Englishman known as Old Parr who supposedly lived 152 years. He first married at 80 and fathered an illegitimate child at 100. He appears in *Finnegans Wake* as "Old Party," "old pairs," "We're parring," as a small sample, and he begins the eighth 100-letter thunder word with "Pappappapparr..." He is one among a number of examples of the old-man, young-girl motif in the *Wake*. The quotes for "grumpapar" above refer more specifically to Peaches and Daddy Browning, a scandalous American couple fitting the motif above who made the tabloids in the 1920's. And then there's HCE's "sin" in Phoenix Park that may have involved two young girls.

guardiance *FW* 258.33 *n.* Leadership or guidance that protects or guards. A seeing-eye dog offers "guardiance" to one who is blind. ("err not in the darkness which is the afterthought of thy nomatter by the guardiance of those guards which are thy bodemen")

gunne *FW* 625.32 *adj.* 1. Left or gone with a firearm or gun. The old TV western *Have Gun, Will Travel* could be shortened to *Have "Gunne."* 2. Deceased or dead and gone as a result of being shot by a firearm or gun. This old phrase can be updated to "dead and 'gunne.'" ("All them that's gunne.") McHugh references Michael Gunne, manager of the Gaiety Theatre in Dublin, who makes many cameo appearances in *Finnegans Wake*.

gynecollege *FW* 389.9 *n.* A degree-giving institution of higher learning or a college for the study of the functions and diseases of the female reproductive system or gynecology. ("Those were the grandest gynecollege histories") Hysterectomies could be suggested here with "histories."

H

hagiohygiecynicism *FW* 353.8 *n*. In *Lots of Fun at "Finnegans Wake,"* Finn Fordham describes this strange looking and sounding word as one "which shunts the Greek words for 'holy' and for 'health' or 'sanitation' (Hygeia is the goddess of medicine) onto the philosophy of the Cynics, with its fault-finding contempt for the enjoyments of life. Righteous cleansing disdain for life is part of a purism that Joyce's writings seem continually to militate against." (*"the euphorious hagiohygiecynicism of his die and be deademmed"*) As to the adjective "*euphorious*" that describes this word, Fordham finds it "a portmanteau of euphoric (fecund, healthy, cheerful, and optimistic) and euphonious (pleasant sounding)." Both words together, he writes, "seem like a contradiction in terms: 'cheerful contempt,'" and "suggest that the clash of words represents a clash of ideologies, classical Greek encountering the Christian Orthodox Greek.

haloday *FW* 353.7 *n*. A holy day or holiday in honor of saints or those who have a circle of light or a halo over their heads. (*"thems bleachin banes will be after making a bashman's holoday"*) A "busman's holiday" is suggested here.

hamd *FW* 464.25 *n.* The end of the arm below the wrist or a hand with the appearance of the meat from a hog's hind leg or a ham. A person with such a hand has been referred to as hamfisted. Generally, if someone with a "hamd" asks for something, it's wise to hand it to them. ("I met with dapper dandy and he shocked me big the hamd.") McHugh gives the reference here to the "The Wearing of the Green," a song in John McCormack's repertoire with the line, "I met with Napper Tandy & he took me by the hand."

harrobrew *FW* 419.27 *adj.* In his article "The Jew's Text: 'Shem The Penman' and 'Shaun The Post,'" in the Winter 2008 issue of the *James Joyce Quarterly*, Maren Linett writes: "Shaun also describes Shem's writing as 'harrobrew bad on the corns and calloused' (*FW* 419.27), mixing 'Hebrew' with 'horribly' and 'harrowing.' These references quietly remind us of Shem's Jewish identity, which is established more strongly throughout the two chapters in passages never far—in theme or distance—from the attacks on Shem's writing." The allusions, intended or not, in *Finnegans Wake* are unlimited and, as often as not, unique to each reader. The poetry of Lord Byron was my first literary enthusiasm, and I was pleased to find I shared this enthusiasm with the young James Joyce who was once beaten by some school friends for maintaining that Byron was the best poet despite his questionable morals. Anyway, I see in "harrobrew" not only Hebrew as discussed above but also Harrow, the public school Bryon attended as a young boy. Combining Harrow and Hebrew immediately brought to mind the collection of Byron's poems published under the title *Hebrew Melodies*. After all, it was at Harrow that Byron would have heard read in chapel many of the Biblical stories these poems were based on.

harse *FW* 8.17, 8.21, 10.2, 10.11, 10.13, & 10.21 *n.* A horse combined with a stupid, stubborn person derogatorily referred to as an ass and, also, with the buttocks or ass, arse for the British, resulting a dingbat who is a real pain in the butt. The Duke of Wellington rode a big white horse named Copenhagen that in *Finnegans Wake* becomes "This is Willingdone on his same white harse, the Cokenshape," "This is his big wide harse," "Wellingdone from his big white harse, The Capinhope," "the buckside of his big white harse," "This is the same white harse of the Willingdone, Culpenhelp," & "the tail on the back of his big wide harse." The Irish-born Wellington might be considered something of a "harse" himself for his remark that being born in Ireland didn't make him Irish anymore than a man born in a stable was a horse, which the *Wake* refers to with "This is Willingdone, bornstable ghentleman." The construction of Wellington's monument in Dublin's Phoenix Park was delayed for many years thanks in part to the duke's anti-Irish attitude.

hasitate *FW* 149.16 *v.* To fail to hold back or hesitate long enough, thus still acting in too great a hurry or in a hasty manner. In his efforts to incriminate Parnell in the Phoenix Park murders, Pigott was too hasty to spell check his forged letter, thus incriminating himself by misspelling "hesitancy" as "hesitency." The "a" in "hasitate" points out Pigott's error. When found out, Pigott did not hesitate to put a bullet through his head. ("it would be far fitter for you, if you dare! To hasitate to consult with") (See **hazeydency, anonymay's,** & **erronymously.**)

hauhauhauhaudibble *FW* 16.18 *adj* A hesitancy in speech or stammer that is terrible or horrible to be heard or audible. Stuttering throughout *Finnegans Wake* is a sure sign of guilt and is most often heard from the lips of HCE. Whether his stammer comes from guilt or nerves is never quite determined. The most horrible of the audible stuttering comes from the sound of thunder as heard in the 1,001 letters of the ten thunder words. Thunder was one of Joyce's great fears. (See **bababadalgharaghtakamminarronnkonnbronntonnerronntuonnthunntrovarrhounawnskawntoohoohoordenenthurnuk!, thuthunder,** & **unpeppeppediment.**) ("Mutt.—I became a stun a stummer. Jute.—What a hauhauhauhaudibble thing, to be cause! How,

Mutt?") McHugh gives the German *Stummer* for "mute person." A person with a stammer may sometimes appear mute from a disinclination to speak because of its great difficulty.

hazeydency *FW* 305.4 *n.* Unclear, indistinct, or hazy concerning indecision, wavering, or hesitancy. Haziness creates the ideal conditions for hesitancy. In *Finnegans Wake*, hesitancy is a celebrated word, popping up on page after page in many different spellings. It seems the letter used as proof that Parnell approved of the Phoenix Park murders was proven forged by a man named Pigott from his misspelling "hesitancy" as "hesitency." HCE even appears as "HeCitEncy!" (See **Anonymay's, erronymously,** & **hasitate**.) ("And that salubrated sickenagiaour of yaours have teaspilled all my hazeydency.")

hearseyard *FW* 621.35 *n.* Area of the graveyard in a churchyard where a form of transport for a carrying dead persons to their graves or a hearse parks to unload coffins for burial. Irish novelist Joseph Sheridan LeFanu's *The House by the Churchyard* figures prominently in *Finnegans Wake* with "In the church by the hearseyard." as one example. Joyce's father had an enthusiasm for this novel, and it is one of the few books he owned. In keeping with the *Wake's* death and resurrection theme, a character in the book is unconscious and near death but is revived by an operation. I think of going from bed to hearse, the old pun on going from bad to worse.

hearhere *FW* 147.3 *n.* The approving cry of a crowd, "Hear Hear!" combined with the importance of the location, here, of what there is to hear. Here. Hear it here! ("It's our toot-a-toot. Hearhere! Sensation!") The reverse, "herehear," is heard on *FW* 237.12 ("dearer dearest, we herehear, aboutobloss") and *FW* 584.36-585.1 ("exclusive pigtorial rights of herehear fond tiplady his weekreations").

heathvens *FW* 426.21 *n.* A special place reserved for pagans or heathens in Heaven, that place usually restricted to the blessed to live with God after death. Jesus said his Father's house had many mansions (See **dimentioned.**), just as the Greeks and Romans had different sections of Hades reserved for special groups. Dido, for example, was put with the other unrequited lovers after her self-immolation when Aeneas left her to found Rome. Heathens do believe in God(s), just not the one(s) in political favor at any given moment in a given country or culture. After Constantine converted Rome to Christianity, many well-regarded religious adherents who worshiped Jupiter et al. awoke one morning to find themselves pagans, and Joyce, being more inclusive than the writers of the New Testament, has kindly assigned them an address in the "heathvens." ("the wieds of pansiful heathvens of joepeter's gaseytotum as they are telling not but were and will be")

Hebrewer *FW* 104.12 *n*. A Jewish or Hebrew man who brews an alcoholic drink made from malted barley and hops or beer. Beer plays a prominent part in *Finnegans Wake*, beginning with "Rot a peck of pa's malt had Jhem or Shen brewed by arclight" on the first page. Jhem and Shen are not only HCE's sons Shem and Shaun but Noah's three sons, Ham, Shem, and Japhet, morphed into two, making each of them a "Hebrewer." (*"Hoebegunne the Hebrewer Hit Waterman the Brayned"*) Rather than beer, McHugh reads "water on the brain" here.

heimlocked *FW* 450.31 *v*. The Heimlich Maneuver, another Wakean anticipation, administered to one dying from the poison hemlock in the mistaken belief that the person is choking. Even if the Heimlich Maneuver had existed at the time of Socrates, its application would have done him no good. ("Lethals lurk heimlocked in logans.") McHugh tells us that *heimlich* is German for "secretly," suggesting that if a person was secretly poisoned by hemlock, unlike Socrates, the Heimlich Maneuver might reasonably be considered as a treatment, though its effect would still be negligible.

hercy *FW* 326.19 *n.* Pity or mercy for beliefs rejected by authorities or heresy. Dr. Kevorkian's hope for "hercy" for his mercy killings or euthanasia of those wishing to end their great physical suffering was dashed when he received a prison sentence for his humanitarian efforts. ("that the loyd mave hercy on your sael!") When giving a death sentence, a judge will often end with, "May the Lord have mercy on your soul." McHugh also finds the insurance giant, Lloyds of London, here.

hereditatis *FW* 131.30 *n.* Regarding this word, Richard Beckman writes: "All accounts of ultimate knowledge and seeing things as they really are, are blather. The past is recorded by 'hereditatis' (131.30); heredity; hearsay ['dit = say]; according to what it says 'here' in unreliable historians such as Herodotus." ("*hereditatis columna erecta, hagion chiton erephon*") McHugh gives the Latin reference here as "hereditatis columna erecta: the lofty column of inheritance." HCE's initials are appropriately found as he assumes the role of "everybody," a monument to the qualities all of us have inherited from him.

heroticisms *FW* 614.35 *n.* Sexually passionate and amatory acts or eroticisms that are distinguished by valor and courage, or heroic. Leander's nightly swimming of the Hellespont to visit his lover, Hero, is one of legend's "heroticisms" and the one that provided the derivation for "hero." ("so that the heroticisms, catastrophes and eccentricities transmitted by the ancient legacy of the past") You no doubt noted the initials HCE in this passage and, while HCE's alleged sexually tinged sin in Phoenix Park was catastrophic for him and considered eccentric by some, there was nothing resembling "heroticisms" about it. ALP, HCE's staunchest defender, is present through her initials as well. If any movie star at once exuded the erotic and the heroic on the silver screen, it was Errol Flynn.

herobit *FW* 498.22 *adj.* A little or a bit of brave or heroic deeds. In the middle ground between the hero and the antihero, we find the doer of "herobit" deeds. ("for to nobble or salvage their herobit of him, the poohpooher old bolssloose, with his arthurious clayroses") McHugh references "nobble or salvage" as Rosseau's "noble savage" and "nobble" as slang for "appropriate dishonestly." Modern studies have shown the noble savage to be less noble than Rosseau imagined, perhaps more of a "herobit" savage. Is it just me, or are there Hobbits hiding here, those unlikely heroes during the Third Age of Middle-earth?

hestens *FW* 135.11 *v.* Hurries or hastens on horseback. The trick here is knowing that the Danish *Hesten* means "the horse." ("he hestens towards dames troth and wedding hand like the prince of Orange and Nassau while he has trinity left behind him") McHugh adds that an equestrian statue of William III faced Dame Street and had its back to Trinity College. As a member of the Dutch House of Oranje Nassau, King Billy was also known as Prince of Orange. His statue made an inviting target for the repressed Irish who often smeared it with paint, among other less savory substances, before finally destroying it completely.

higherdimissional *FW* 395.1 *adj.* Special work, service, or mission that is above and beyond or higher in its extent and scope or dimension. With the licensed-to-kill double-O designation of 007, James Bond's assignments are "higherdimissional" than the missions given the average spy. With the Latin *dimissio* for "sending forth, the *Wake*'s "intuitions of reunited selfdom (murky whey, abstrew adim!) in the higherdimissional selfless Allself," perhaps a double 0 spy is being sent out on an above average mission.

himals *FW* 5.1 *n.* With both the Danish and German *Himmel* for "sky or heaven," Dounia Bunis Christiani finds a suggestion of the Himalayas in the spelling. Since Mount Everest is the highest mountain on our planet and it's in the Himalayas, it's the place closest to heaven on earth. ("erigenating from next to nothing and celescalating the himals and all") McHugh gives the Latin *erigo* for "I erect." Celestial, of the sky or heavens, becomes a verb with "celescalating."

himpself *FW* 313.33 *pron.* In *Wandering and Return in "Finnegans Wake,"* Kimberly J. Devlin writes that HCE's anxieties about being a "'himpself'—a chimp-self and a humped self—permeate the dreamtext, particularly in 2.3, where the visions of descent from apes or other ignominious sources combine with visions of being physically misshapen." ("that fellow fearing for his own misshapes, should he be himpself namesakely a foully fallen dissentant from the peripulator") We learn in the *Wake* that HCE has a hump on his back, as does the Norwegian captain that the tailor finds impossible to fit with a new suit, and that the middle initial "C" stands for "Chimpden." (See **furbear**.)

hir *FW* 63.14 *pron.* Her or his or him. Just as Ms unites Miss and Mrs., Joyce unites her, his, and him into one word and eliminates the awkwardness of him/her and/or his/her. ("for ann there is but one liv and hir newbridge is her old") McHugh gives the Danish *liv* for "life," adding that "New Bridge, in Leixlip, is probably the oldest bridge in Ireland," and hears in this phrase the Islamic belief, "There is but one God & Mohammed is his prophet."

histry *FW* 161.22 *n.* A record of the past or history with an emphasis on the masculine or his attempts or try to accomplish some feat or achieve some goal with an added element of the theatrical or histrionic. ("The seemsame home and histry seeks and hidepence which we used to be reading for our prepurgatory, hot, Schott?") McHugh reads "seemsame" as "selfsame" and "home and histry" as "Roman history," the last being one of those occasions when it is important to follow Joyce's advice to read *Finnegans Wake* aloud as an assist to understanding. Julius Caesar stands out as a man in Roman "histry" who was not above histrionics in promoting his agenda in conquering Gaul.

There is a touch of theatrical flourish to: "I came. I saw. I conquered." and "The die is cast." McHugh also finds "Same old six and eightpence (i.e. unchanged)," "hide and seek," and "preparatory" in this sentence. All this suggests that "histry" hasn't changed, that we all try to hide what we don't want known, that historians keep seeking for the facts, and that life on Earth is a sort of "prepurgatory" in preparation for purgatory itself, though our lives of suffering and punishment seem purgatorial enough without adding another level. The Romans cut out the middleman by placing a coin on the tongue of a corpse so that it could pay to bypass Purgatory and proceed across the River Styx straight into the underworld. I've not found any suggestions for "hot, Schott," but the first to come to my mind is "hot shot" or an extraordinarily accomplished person who is not without conceit. Julius Caesar certainly was a "hot, Schott?" without the question mark. Could the *Wake* be giving us a choice between purgatory and the hot spot better known as Hell?

hoaxites *FW* 239.12-13 *n.* This is another *Wake* word that derives its meaning by combining two or more languages. Here we have the German *Hochzeit* for "marriage" and the English *hoax* for "mischievous jest or trick." When James and Nora Joyce were formally married in London after their children were adults, Joyce claimed that they had really married secretly in Trieste years before with Nora using the name Gretta Greene, the name of a town on the Scottish border known for runaway marriages. Most Joyce scholars would file this story under "hoaxites." ("No more hoaxities! Nay more gifting in the mennage!") McHugh gives the French *ménage* for "household" and reads this as "giving in marriage."

homogenius *FW* 34.14 *n.* A man with great natural ability in a specific area or a genius who is similar or homogeneous to others. Joyce, Tolstoy, and Proust might be said to be a "homogenius" to each other. ("our good and great and no ordinary Southron Earwicker, that homogenius man, as a pious author called him")

homosodalism *FW* 352.20 *n.* A society, fellowship, or sodality for those with sexual feelings for those of the same sex or homosexuals. In the Roman Catholic Church a sodality is a lay society with religious purposes and, as a student, Joyce was elected prefect of the Sodality of the Blessed Virgin Mary. But "*homosodalism*" suggests a society within the church for homosexual purposes, something Joyce may have heard hints of in his day, or else the *Wake* anticipates the Catholic sexual scandals involving priests and boys coming to light only in our own time. ("*effaces himself in favour of the idiology alwise behounding his lumpy hump off homosodalism which means that if he has lain amain to lolly his liking-combrune!-he may pops lilly a young one to his herth – combrune –*") Given McHugh's reading of "*behounding*" as "behind" and "*combrune*" as the Spanish *cabron* for "he-goat, cuckold," combined with "*has lain amain to lolly his liking*" and "*he may pops lily a young one*," the suggestion of religious homosexual associations is certainly strengthened. (See ***idiology***.) There also exists the hint that there is "*homosodalism*" behind HCE's encounter with the "Cad with a Pipe" in Phoenix Park at midnight. (See **contrawatchwise**.) For a much more thorough analysis of "*homosodalism*," see page 106 of Finn Fordham's *Lots of Fun at Finnegans Wake: Unravelling Universals*.

horrhorrd *FW* 378.7 *v.* Listened to or heard in great fear or horror. ("oversense he horrhorrd his name in thuthunder") Joyce had a great horror of thunder and avoided cities that were known to have many thunderstorms. Vico believed that it was God's voice heard through thunder that brought the third or human age to an end and frightened humanity back into caves where the cycle of ages began anew. There are ten thunder words in *Finnegans Wake*, nine with 100 letters and the tenth with 101 letters. The first thunder word begins "bababa…" in imitation of thunder with the idea that stuttering signals God's guilt for messing up the creation business in so horrid a manner. (See **thuthunder**.)

houdingplaces *FW* 127.11 *n.* A place of concealment or hiding place used by the famed magician and escape artist Harry Houdini. Houdini was clever in concealing objects necessary for his remarkable performances, supposedly, in one instance when he got out of a jail cell in which he was locked naked, by secreting a key within his anatomy in an era when strip searches were less thorough than those of today. ("is escapemaster-in-chief from all sorts of houdingplaces") Houdini is just one of hundreds of references from popular culture that Joyce enjoyed hiding in *Finnegans Wake*.

howd *FW* 6.8 *n.* The top part of anything or the head combined with the prominent Dublin promontory known as Howth Head. Howth comes from the Danish *hoved* for "head," making the name Howth Head redundant. It is the head of Finn MacCool, the sleeping giant in *Finnegans Wake* who is stretched under the city landscape and whose feet and toes pop up "well to the west" in Phoenix Park. This headland is also the site of Howth Castle, home to the earls of Howth since arriving with Henry II's Irish invasion fleet. It is mentioned in the *Wake*'s first sentence as "Howth Castle and Environs," giving the initials HCE for Humphrey Chimpden Earwicker, one of the book's two main characters along with his wife Anna Livia Plurabelle or ALP. ("His howd feeled heavy, his hoddit did shake.") In this reference it is Tim Finnegan's head that is feeling heavy from liquor, making him shaky as he climbs a construction ladder with a hod loaded with bricks and causing him to fall and break his head.

howsoclever *FW* 426.3 *adv.* To whatever extent or degree something is intelligent or clever and in whatever way or by whatever means something intelligent or clever is done, making it howsoever clever. With a different style for each chapter, Joyce wrote *Ulysses* howsocleverly. ("I will commission to the flames any incendiarist whosoever or ahriman howsoclever who would endeavour to set ever annyma roner moother of mine on fire.")

148 | A *Finnegans Wake* Lextionary

McHugh gives as references here "annyma roner" as "Ahriman," the "Zoroastrian principle of evil" and the song "Little Annie Rooney," and "moother of mine" as the song "Mother of Mine."

howsomendeavour *FW* 624.35 *adv.* By whatever means or howsoever an earnest effort or endeavor is made. ("Howsomendeavour, you done me fine!") Here the tailor's daughter is talking about the Norwegian captain. Her father made an earnest endeavor to make a new suit for the captain, "Howsomendeavour," the hump on his back made a perfect fit impossible.

hundt *FW* 335.10 *n.* Pursuit of game or hunt and Danish and German *Hund* for "dog" or "hound." ("when the hundt called a halt on the chivvychace of the ground sloper") A hunting dog is called to halt here, though there's a good deal more going on in this lead-in for another reference to the story of how "burgherly shut the rush in general."

hussyband *FW* 226.18 *n.* A married man or husband whose taste in wives is for a woman who is shameless, saucy, too forward by far, almost if not immoral, or a hussy, a word that seems to invite the adjective "brazen" to precede it. The Confederate Railroad's lyrical line from their hit song "Trashy Women" sums up some men's taste in wives: "I like my women just a little on the trashy side." ("For though she's unmerried she'll after truss up and help that hussyband how to hop.")

hwere *FW* 311.22 & 34.28 *adv.* Contraction of here and were. ("Hwere can a ketch or hook alive a suit and sowterkins?" & "garthen gaddeth green hwere sokeman brideth griling") In the first usage, McHugh references "Hwere" with the Norwegian *hvor* for "where" and in the second usage with the Middle English *hwer(e)* for "where." I must admit that my computer spell checker gave "where" as its first suggestion, although "here" and "were" also appeared on the list. But for those with little knowledge of Norwegian or Middle English, my definition is more practical. All three can be combined for an even better effect. A statement such as "Here is where the bodies were buried." can be shortened to "'Hwere'" bodies buried."

hystry *FW* 535.18 *n*. A record of the past or history presented with unrestrained emotion or hysteria. Much of human history is certainly hysterical and apt to cause hysterics, fits of both hysterical laughing and crying. (See **cryzy**.) A history of the surgical removal of the uterus or hysterectomy may also be inferred given the Greek *hystera* for "womb." ("Lowest basemeant in hystry!") This sentence appears in the midst of references to Joyce's favorite playwright, Ibsen, such as "Ibscenest nanscence!" While this may be read as obscenest nonsense written by or about Ibsen, Joyce has garnered a greater reputation for the obscene in literature than this Norwegian author.

I

ideareal *FW* 262.R1 *adj.* A mental image or an idea that is at once ideal, real, and sidereal. An astral idea that exists perfectly in thought yet is thought to be genuine, a Black Hole for instance. ("PROBAPOSSIBLE PROLEGOMENA TO IDEAREAL HISTORY.")

idiology *FW* 352.19 *n.* The science of ideas or ideology of the Id. Freud is our best guide to the "idiology" or pleasure principle of the unconscious. ("*effaces himself in favour of the idiology alwise behounding his lumpy hump of homosodalism*") Finn Fordham writes that "'Idiology' is Joyce's simple neologism, ten years before the word 'idiolect' was first used." "A discourse peculiar to an individual because of certain elements unique to it," Fordham continues regarding idiolect, "chimes well as a description of the language of *Finnegans Wake.*" For a much greater discussion of "idiology," see all of page 107 in Fordham's *Lots of Fun at "Finnegans Wake:" Unravelling Universals*. One would have to be an idiot not to suggest that meaning here, especially since idiots see themselves as all wise. The "*lumpy hump*" suggests HCE and the Norwegian captain who each have a hump on their backs as well as Humpty Dumpty, and "*homosodalism*" hints at HCE's alleged improper actions in Phoenix Park, one of which was purported to be of a homosexual nature. The presence of "sodality" suggests a homosexual fellowship or society and brings in HCE's encounter with the Cad later that same night. (See **contrawatchwise**.) As a student, Joyce was elected prefect of the Sodality of the Blessed Virgin Mary, perhaps prefiguring the "*homosodalism*" scandals the Catholic Church was yet to face. (See ***homosodalism***.)

idself *FW* 611.21 *pron.* That part of itself made up of the Id or, in psychoanalysis, the basic part of the unconscious that wants what it wants when it wants it and that precedes the ego and the superego. As a literary work concerning the unconscious, *Finnegans Wake* "idself" is the id to be analyzed in attempting to understand what Joyce called his "book of the dark." The id often shows up in the *Wake* as Finn Fordham illustrates with one of the complications Joyce added to his continuously changing text. Referring to Shem, the word "self" was changed to "squidself." "Perhaps," comments Fordham, "in 'squid' Joyce is hearing the 'id' as well—Freud's component of the self that harbours all the repressed, deeply hidden, or screened elements and drives." This ties in nicely with the squid's ability to conceal itself by squirting black ink. *Finnegans Wake* is no slouch in hiding its elements and drives as well. Within the *Wake*'s "inside true inwardness of reality, the Ding hvad in idself id est, all objects (of panepiwor) allside showed themselves in trues coloribus resplendent" is found Kant's "Ding an sich" for "thing in itself," the Latin *id est* for "that is," and the Danish *hvad* for "what."

illas *FW* 626.34 *interj.* Alas as an exclamation of sorrow or grief, specifically for a person who is sick or ill as opposed to other types of regret. Tim Finnegan's alcoholism, "Illas," caused him to fall and crack his head but, somewhat like satisfaction for the cat, it was alcohol that brought him back. ("And can it be it's nnow fforvell? Illas!")

illformation *FW* 137.34-35 *n.* 1. Knowledge, news, or information that is bad, wrong, disagreeable, or ill. It's been said that everything you read in the newspaper is true, except for that occasional story you just happen to know something about. Which, of course, makes you realize that all the other stories are probably filled with mistakes and "illformation." It goes without saying that the majority of the stories are filled with bad or disagreeable news. 2. Information that is so upsetting as to make one sick or ill. 3. Information about those who are sick or ill. ("pours a laughsworth of his illformation over a larmsworth of salt")

imageascene *FW* 331.30 *v.* To create a mental image or imagine a place or scene through the powers of the imagination. Wordsworth related his ability to "imageascene" daffodils when he wrote:

> For oft, when on my couch I lie
> In vacant or in pensive mood,
> They flash upon that inward eye
> Which is the bliss of solitude;
> And then my heart with pleasure fills,
> And dances with the daffodils."

("in imageascene all: whimwhim whimwhim") With "imageascene" Joyce is referring to the wall of the Magazine Fort, a storehouse for war munitions in Phoenix Park that was satirized in a poem by Jonathan Swift:

> Behold a proof of Irish sense!
> Here Irish wit is seen!
> When nothing's left, that's worth defence,
> We build a magazine.

In *Finnegans Wake* Joyce parodies Swift's verse with: "Behove this sound of Irish sense. Really? Here English might be seen."

immarginable *FW* 4.19 *adj.* That which can be conceived of or that is imaginable about an extra amount beyond what is necessary, or a margin. With *Finnegans Wake*, Joyce subscribes to Oscar Wilde's comment that "Moderation is a fatal thing. Nothing succeeds like excess." It is certainly true that the *Wake* contains far more than most critics and readers have considered necessary, spreading far beyond the margins of its pages into "immarginable" territory. It's been said that no one ever wished Milton's *Paradise Lost* to be longer than it is, and the same might be said about *Finnegans Wake*. ("Bygmester Finnegan, of the Stuttering Hand, freemen's maurer, lived in the broadest way immarginable in his rushlit toofarback for messuages") McHugh gives "rushlight" as slang for "liquor" and as a "candle made from rush dipped in grease." He gives "farback" as Dublin slang for a "house with 2 back rooms" and "messuage" as "dwelling house plus adjacent land & buildings." But there's a risqué reading to be had with "Stuttering Hand," and that's an indelicate use of the hand that Buck Mulligan refers to in *Ulysses* as "A Honeymoon in the Hand" and that the *Wake* mentions as "Master Bates." Though we'll never know for sure, it's possible this could be the impropriety that HCE committed, if in fact he did commit an impropriety, that fateful night in Phoenix Park. All these details, among many more not enumerated here, demonstrate that *Finnegans Wake* was written "in the broadest way immarginable."

immartial *FW* 149.7-8 *adj.* Living or remembered forever or immortal for warlike or martial qualities. In Scandinavian mythology, warriors dying bravely in battle went to Valhalla ("waulholler"), a banqueting hall where they feasted forever with the god Odin. Muslims seem to have a better deal where virgins replace the Viking feasts as an immortal reward for martial heroism. Mars, the Roman god of war, is both immortal and "immartial." ("if the fain shiner pegged you to shave his immartial, wee skillmustered shoul") McHugh references "fain shiner" as the Irish *Sinn Féin* for "We Ourselves," which became the name of an

Irish nationalist movement, and "shinner" as slang for a member of Sinn Féin. He translates the rest of this phrase as "begged you to save his immortal . . . soul." The Roman poet Martial became immortal through his satiric epigrams rather than any martial qualities other than his name.

impalsive *FW* 386.29 *adj*. At once impulsive and impassive which is a contradiction in terms. If one feels impelled to take sudden action while indifferent and apathetic to any movement, the result is an impasse. For instance, one might feel an impulse to do some good, such as write a check for a charity, but somehow stop short of actually writing it. ("going to the tailturn horseshow, before the angler nomads flood, along with another fellow, active impalsive") McHugh gives "angler nomads" as "Anglo-Norman (invasion of Ir.)" and "active impalsive" as "active & passive."

improssable *FW* 609.6 *adj*. Something that is somewhere between can't be done or impossible and unlikely or improbable. Thus, while possible, it is even less likely to happen or be true than merely being improbable would suggest. ("like so many unprobables in their poor suit of the improssable.") This is one more instance in which Oscar Wilde's satirical comment on foxhunting is worked into the *Wake*: "The unspeakable in full pursuit of the uneatable."

indead *FW* 505.21 & 560.18 *adv*. In truth, really, or indeed inanimate or dead. One reason for wakes for the dead, aside from the wonderful, celebratory spin the Irish put on them, was to be certain that the person was "indead." Scratches later found on the inside of coffin lids are no laughing matter! ("But that steyne of law indead what stiles its naming?" & "Yesses indead it be!")

inexcessible *FW* 285.28 *adj*. Difficult to reach or attain more than enough or too much or, in Wakean terms, an inaccessible excess. As Mark Twain said, "Too much of anything is bad, but too much whiskey is just enough." ("Inexcessible as thy by god ways.") McHugh reads this as "bygone days" and as Yeats's "A Vision 143: 'as inaccessible as God or thou.'"

infester *FW* 600.11 *n.* One who puts money into such securities as stocks or bonds with the expectation of making a profit is an investor and, when the economy is in a bull market and securities are rising, a large number of people invest with such irrational exuberance that the market is infested and the investor becomes an "infester." ("the kongdomain of the Alieni, an accorsired race, infester of Libnud Ocean") McHugh gives the Latin *alieni* for "foreigners," and this fits the average "infester" since this type is foreign to the stock market and jumps in only when stocks are rising rapidly. He identifies "accorsired" with "accursed" and "corsair," a pirate, descriptions in some ways of an "infester." (See **accorsired**.)

inhebited *FW* 224.11 *v.* A combination of receive as an heir or inherited, hinder or inhibited, and live in or inhabited. In England an entailed estate inhibited an inheritor from selling the family home he was to inhabit. ("And all the freightfullness whom he inhebited after his colline born janitor.")

inher *FW* 4.30 & 546.21 *adj.* Inside or inner with the added distinction of being within a female or in her. Since one meaning of "inner" is "more intimate" or "private," readers are left to their own conjectures as to what is in what part of her or "inher." ("Wither hayre in honds tuck up your part inher." & "my otherchurch's inher light, in so and such a manner as me it so besitteth")

inkbattle *FW* 176.31 *n.* A fight or battle fought with ink from an inkbottle, that is words printed on paper. The old maxim, "The pen is mightier than the sword," comes to mind here along with a more recent saying, "Never get in a fight with someone who buys ink by the barrel," meaning newspapers and other publishers. ("kuskykorked himself up tight in his inkbatrtle house")

McHugh's reference here is: "The Inkbottle House: Church of the Seven Dolours, Botanic Avenue, D (shape said to have been suggested by Swift)." One meaning of "penisolate war" on the *Wake*'s first page is the isolated war Joyce fought with his pen as he transformed literature. He never ceased to battle despite the terrible criticisms leveled against his last work. But, in the end, it was an "inkbattle" he handily won.

innkempt *FW* 13.8 *n.* A public house offering lodging and food for travelers or an inn that is untidy or ill-kempt and unkempt. The pub run by the Porters or HCE and ALP is on the order of an inn but its tidiness or lack thereof is unclear. It was travelers' dissatisfaction with unkempt "innkempt"(s) that led to the standardization of inns such as Holiday Inns and Quality Inns. ("It reminds you of the outwashed engravure that we used to be blurring on the blotchwall of his innkempt house.")

instopressible *FW* 568.16 *adj.* At once insuppressible and unstoppable, therefore adding even greater emphasis to something or someone that cannot be quelled, crushed, subdued, or suppressed and arrested, ended, or stopped. McHugh references the newspaper term "stop press," an order only given when a story is so "hot" or important that the newspaper's production must be halted to permit the story to be included. McHugh also identifies the *Insuppressible* as an antiparnellite newspaper. With these two connections, any breaking story confirming Parnell's approval or support of the Phoenix Park murders would have instantly stopped the *Insuppressible*'s presses, presenting something of a paradox. ("It stands in *Instopressible* how Meynhir Mayour, our boorgomaister, thon staunch Thorsman") By capitalizing and italicizing *Instopressible*, Joyce strengthens the connection to the newspaper. Though Parnell survived the Phoenix Park accusations, once his adulterous affair with Kitty O'Shea was discovered, he proved not to be "*Instopressible*" after all. (See **fairescapading**.)

intelligentius *FW* 464.16-17 *adj.* Quick to understand or intelligent with a touch of great natural powers of the mind or genius. A country's intellectual geniuses or intelligentsia is implied. ("Ah, he's very thoughtful and sympatrico that way is Brother Intelligentius, when he's not absintheminded, with his Paris addresse!") A thoughtful, sympathetic, and nice (Italian *simpatico* for "nice") St. Patrick is intelligent and absentminded here.

intermisunderstanding *FW* 118.25 *n.* Between having knowledge or understanding of a subject and a mistake in meaning, a failure to understand, or misunderstanding. Many of the problems of the world result from incomplete knowledge of a subject, which causes errors in judgment and mistakes in execution as explained in the old saying, "A little knowledge is a dangerous thing." Rather than the exception, "intermisunderstanding" is most often the rule. ("the continually more and less intermisunderstanding minds of the anticollaborators")

inthrusted *FW* 356.29 *v.* Push with force or thrust upon someone what is consigned, committed, or entrusted to them. In *Finnegans Wake*, the trustworthy knight, Sir Tristram, was entrusted with delivering the Irish princess and bride-to-be, Iseult the Beautiful, to his uncle, King Mark II of Cornwall. After Tristram and Iseult mistakenly drink a love potion brewed by Iseult's mother that she meant only for her daughter and the king, the young couple spend a lustful night in the ship's cabin where, among other activities, we learn that "as quick, is greased pigskin, Amoricas Champius [Tristram was a champion from Amorica, ancient name for Brittany.], with one aragan throust, druve the massive of virilvigtoury flshpst the both lines of forwards (Eburnea's down, boys!) rightjingbangshot into the goal of her gullet." In other words, Tristram violated his uncle's trust when he "inthrusted" himself upon a more than willing Iseult. ("a reputation coextensive with its merits when inthrusted into safe and pious hands upon so edifying a mission as it, I can see, as is his")

inuendation *FW* 194.32 *n*. A flood or inundation of insinuation or innuendo. HCE certainly suffers from an "inuendation" after his midnight encounter with the Cad in Phoenix Park. Even though the resulting trials prove nothing definite, the "inuendation" still remains, and HCE continues to suffer guilt simply from accusation. ("all waived to a point and then all inuendation") (See **contrawatchwise**.)

invision *FW* 626.28 *v*. To see through imagination, dream, or vision an enemy force entering a country for conquest or an invasion. The Trojan princess Cassandra had an "invision" of the wily Greeks invading her city in a large wooden horse but, unfortunately, was not believed. ("The invision of Indelond. And, by Thorror, you looked it!") The reference here is to the Viking invasion of Ireland led by Thorir. (See **inwader** & **Thorror**.)

inwader *FW* 581.3 *n*. One who enters a country with force for conquest or an invader who walks through shallow water or wades ashore during the invasion. The most famous "inwader" of all must be General Douglas McArthur who, after being driven from the Philippines by the Japanese, retook the country after having to wade from a landing craft to the shore, proclaiming, "People of the Philippines, I have returned." ("have they not called him at many's their mock indignation meeting, vehmen's vengeance vective volleying, inwader") But then "inwader" could just be invader pronounced with a lisp.

irised sea *FW* 318.34 *n*. Infusing an arch of light containing all the colors of the spectrum or a rainbow into a large body of salt water smaller than an ocean or a sea. Iris was the rainbow goddess from Greek mythology. Rainbows and the sea feature prominently in *Finnegans Wake*, beginning with the third sentence of the first page: "Rot a peck of pa's malt had Jhem or Shen brewed by arclight and roary end to the regginbrow was to be seen ringsome on the aquaface." With Dublin as the *Wake*'s setting, "irised sea" naturally refers to the Irish Sea, the body of water into which Anna Livia Plurabelle as the River Liffey flows. ALP's daughter Issy is often accompanied by a group of friends known as the Rainbow Girls. ("But his spectrem onlymergeant crested from the irised sea in plight")

ivanmorinthorrumble *FW* 353.24 *n*. A deep, continuous sound or rumble like that caused by the thundering hammer of the Scandinavian god Thor, yet even more terrible than the infamous raging of the Russian Czar Ivan. Joyce was famously afraid of thunder. He once took his tall son Georgio with him when visiting a friend to serve, Joyce only half-jokingly said, as a lightning rod. ("*the first lord of Hurteford explodotonates through Parsuralia with an ivanmorinthorrumble*") The terrible rumble heard here is of the splitting of the atom by Lord Rutherford in 1919. (See **explodotonates** & **thonthorstrok**.)

J

jesterday *FW* 570.9 *n.* A joke or jest that occurred the day before today or yesterday. Yesterday's jest sometimes seems less funny the day after and is often a cause for regret. The lyrics of Paul McCartney's song "Yesterday," the entire melody of which he composed one night in a dream, could be rewritten to fit a new title of "jesterday." The *Wake* works this word into: "I have heard anyone tell it jesterday (master currier with brassard was't) how one should come on morrow here but it is never here that one today."

jewses *FW* 423.36 *n.* Jesus with an emphasis on his Jewishness. ("Then he caught the europicolas and went into the society of jewses.") In this context Joyce is referring to the Society of Jesus whose priests are known as Jesuits. Though Joyce rejected the Catholic Church in his teens, he owed all of his formal and extremely excellent education to the Jesuits, most of it with waived fees. Maren Linett writes of this sentence: "The pun on Society of Jesus is ironic, since the Jesuits were strict about preventing even descendents of converted Jews from taking orders (those of 'Hebrew or Saracen stock' were banned from the Society of Jesus in 1593.)" Evidently even Saints Peter and Paul would be

162 | A *Finnegans Wake* Lextionary

ineligible to be Jesuits, and Peter was the rock upon which Jesus Himself said His church would be built. (See **thuartpeatrick**.)

joyoust *FW* 414.1 *adj*. A descriptive term for a meeting of two great literary minds, James Joyce and Marcel Proust. They met only once, at a grand dinner party at the Hotel Majestic in Paris. Naturally, everyone wanted to hear what these literary lions had to say to one another but, as is usual for eyewitnesses, the reports of the great men's conversation varied. Whether they talked about truffles or their various ailments will never be known for certain, but Joyce recounted that "Proust would only talk about duchesses, while I was more concerned with their chambermaids." (Joyce's wife Nora was a chambermaid at Finn's Hotel in Dublin when they first met.) Joyce did work *Swann's Way*, the first book in Proust's seven-volume novel, *Remembrance of Things Past*, into *Finnegans Wake* with "flashing down the swansway" and "watch the swansway." ("some rhino, rhine, O joyoust rhine, was handled over spondaneously by me") McHugh gives "rhino" as slang for "money," which fits with being handed over spontaneously, something Joyce was often inclined to do. But Joyce was a great lover of white wine, and Rhine wine is white, so it might be this wine handed by Joyce to Proust, except for the fact that Proust preferred iced beer.

jungfraud's *FW* 460.20 *adj*. The dishonest trickery or fraud of psychoanalysis as practiced by Sigmund Freud and Carl Jung. Though Joyce didn't like Jung or trust his work, he did, in desperation, send his daughter Lucia to him for treatment. "To think that such a big fat materialistic Swiss man should get hold of my soul," was her response. Within *Finnegans Wake*, Jung is found hiding in "cans of Swiss condensed bilk." It's been said that psychiatry is the care of the id by the odd, but here it's the care of the id by the fraud. ("while m'm'ry's leaves are falling deeply on my Jungfraud's Messongebook") McHugh notes that *Jungfrau* is German for "virgin."

junglemen *FW* 348.13 *n*. 1. Gentlemen who are not far evolved from the jungle. While not apes or even the missing link, they certainly are seldom invited as guests to a formal dinner party. Tarzan comes to mind as one born an English gentleman, not to mention the title Lord Greystoke, but who ended up a "junglemen." 2. Men who are students or followers of the theories and treatment techniques of C. G. Jung. Joyce was not one of these "Junglemen" and he lost the financial support of a wealthy American woman by refusing her request to be psychoanalyzed by Jung. Joyce did, in desperation, send his daughter Lucia for treatment with Jung years later, though "the law of the jungerl" did not help her. ("Junglemen in agleement, I give thee our greatly swooren") (See **jungfraud's**.)

Junuary *FW* 332.25 *n*. Some date in the six months of the year from January 1st through June 30th. ("that hoppy-go-jumpy Junuary morn when he colluded with the cad out on the beg") McHugh reads this as the phrase "let the cat out of the bag." It's also a reminder of HCE's midnight collision with the Cad in Phoenix Park that begins all the accusations and trials to follow. It was HCE's stuttering, guilty-sounding, thou-doth-protest-too-much denials that made the Cad suspicious, so in a way Mr. Earwicker did seem to let, if not a cat, a cad out of the bag. After the Cad let out his suspicions to his wife, rumors about HCE were soon all over Dublin. (See **contrawatchwise**.)

L

lacessive *FW* 68.12 *adj.* Causing lust or lascivious combined with too much or excessive to give an excessive lasciviousness, how some might describe Madonna's concert tours. ("arrah of the lacessive poghue") Here are ALP's initials, the Latin *lacesso* for "I provoke" and the Irish playwright Boucicault's *Arrah-na-Pogue* or Nora of the Kiss.

landshape *FW* 474.2-3 *v.* To give a more pleasant look to the land by forming or shaping it with plants or landscaping. The task of a "landshape" architect is not only in the selection and placement of plants but also in the leveling of the land or the creation of hills and terraces. Most landscape paintings are not completely true to form but involve some landshaping by the artist in order to give an improved and more beautiful view of the landscape. ("On the mead of the hillock lay, heartsoul dormant mid shadowed landshape, brief wallet to his side, and arm loose, by his staff of citron briar")

langscape *FW* 595.4 *n.* A view or picture of a storybook land described by words or a language landscape. Books carry readers away to distant lands they may never see. In *Finnegans Wake* many languages combine to create langscapes in which *Wake* words paint a picture, however distorted, of the cyclical fall and resurrection of humanity. This picture, if painted with pigments on canvas rather than words on paper, would combine elements of the intricate elaborations of the famed Irish Book of Kells, Dali's surrealist watches wilting into the rocky landscape, Monet's impressionism's of nature, Picasso's cubism, and touches from all the abstract artists of the last century, creating a "langscape" unlike any other. And, just as painters mix different colors to create new shades, Joyce mixed many languages to create new shades of meaning. Since *lang* is German for "long" or "tall," as well as an abbreviation for language, and "scape" is an obsolete term for "escapade," "langscape" can suggest a tall tale of an escapade which, in *Finnegans Wake*, would chiefly concern H. C. Earwicker and his family. ("gives relief to the langscape as he strauches his lamusong untoupon gazelle channel and the bride of the Bryne")

langwedge *FW* 73.1 *n.* Spoken or written speech or language used to split or separate like a wedge. The "langwedge" of *Finnegans Wake* is infamous for splitting words of different languages and then reassembling them to create new or expanded meanings. ("this backblocks boor bruskly put out his langwedge and quite quit the paleologic scene")

laughtears *FW* 15.9 *n.* 1. Tears that result from making sounds of mirth or laughing as in, "He laughed so hard he cried." 2. Laughter mixed with sorrow as described in a stanza of Percy Bysshe Shelley's poem "To a Skylark:"

> We look before and after
> And pine for what is not;
> Our sincerest laughter
> With some pain is fraught;
> Our sweetest songs are those
> that tell of saddest thought.

Laughter becomes the handmaid of sorrow because humor is so often the only way to deal somewhat successfully with tragedy. ("Year! Year! And laughtears!") This sounds like a cheer, "Let's hear it for laughter!"

laysure *FW* 24.16 *n*. 1. Time free from work or responsibilities or leisure that is certain or sure such as vacation days earned through employment. 2. Leisure in which one is certain or sure to lie down, in my book, the best "laysure" of all. ("And take your laysure like a god on pension and don't be walking abroad.") This is the advice in *Finnegans Wake* that the mourners at Finnegan's wake give Tim when he awakes from being splashed with whiskey and tries to get up.

leareyed *FW* 590.2 *adj*. Organs of sight or eyes that are wary or leery and that also have elements of evil in their glance or leer. Shakespeare's King Lear, from his play of that name, comes into sight here with the suggestion of madness and/or blindness. ("his most favoured sinflute and dropped him, what remains of a heptarch, leareyed and letterish") McHugh gives the German *Sintflut* for "the Flood" and reads "leareyed and letterish" as "bleary-eyed and liverish." Both of these readings can refer to James Joyce, who suffered greatly from glaucoma and naturally became bleary-eyed from all the exacting work he put into *Finnegans Wake*. He often resorted to writing only a few words in large print on each page so that in his near-blindness he was able to read what he wrote. Certainly the critics were "leareyed" at the "letterish" experiments Joyce worked into the *Wake*. And naturally he was somewhat testy or liverish from the negative reviews they wrote. Yet, while it might be safe to assume that Joyce was liverish in the sense of having a disordered liver from his love of liquor, his autopsy gave this internal organ a clean bill of health. It was surgery for a duodenal ulcer that finally caused his death or, as the *Wake* puts it, "when the angel of death kicks the bucket of life" he "went under the grass quilt on us." I may be so far off base as to be out of the ballpark, but with "sinflute

170 | A *Finnegans Wake* Lextionary

and dropped him" I hear an echo of, or at least the meter of, the Duke of Wellington's order for the last charge at Waterloo, "Up guards and at 'em!" This command is heard throughout *Finnegans Wake* in "upright and add them" and "Nip up and nab it" along with many others. And who's to say I'm wrong?

legintimate *FW* 495.25 *adj*. Very closely acquainted or intimate in a lawful or legitimate way as opposed to an illegitimate intimacy. Marriage is a "legintimate" institution in that it legitimizes intimacy. ("to both the legintimate lady performers of display unquestionable")

lentling *FW* 607.9 *v*. Giving for a time or lending small, flat peas or lentils, particularly during the Christian season of Lent when fasting requires food to be meager and plain. The most famous "lentling" in the Bible occurred when Jacob lent his older, twin-brother Esau a bowl of lentil soup in exchange for his birthright. What the Bible terms a mess of pottage of lentils in the *Wake* becomes "messes of mottage" and "the hash of lentils." (See **Peacisely** and **Eatsoup**.) ("with Essav of Messagepostumia, lentling out his borrowed chafingdish")

lethelulled *FW* 78.4 *v*. Soothed or lulled by forgetfulness of the past by drinking the waters of the Lethe, the river in Hades that caused departed souls to forget their past lives and sink into oblivion. McHugh translates the Greek phrase in "whaling away the whole of the while (*hypnos chilia eonion!*) lethelulled between explosion and reexplosion" as "sleep for thousands of ages."

letterread *FW* 425.5 *adj*. Learned, literate, or lettered, emphasizing both being able to read well as well as being well read. Joyce was certainly "letterread," an invaluable asset in his writing of *Finnegans Wake*. James S. Atherton's classic work, *The Books at the Wake*, investigates Joyce's printed sources—the structural and literary books and, in addition, a list of literary allusions—

and gives ample evidence of just how "letterread" Joyce actually was. ("—Still in a way, not to flatter you, we fancy you that you are so strikingly brainy and well letterread in yourshelves") I love the subtle changes in words Joyce makes in the *Wake*, such as "yourshelves" that sounds like "yourselves" while reading like "your shelves," the place a "letterread" person would place and display books.

lettrechaun *FW* 419.17 *n.* 1. A leprechaun of letters. In Irish legends the leprechaun is an elf or fairy disguised as a little, old man. He harbors knowledge of hidden treasure, usually a pot of gold, which he must reveal if caught. But a leprechaun is full of tricks and always gets the best of his captors. If *Finnegans Wake* is thought of as a book filled with literary treasures, Joyce becomes the leprechaun who leads us to it while keeping its full possession from us through elaborative, labyrinthine language. 2. The French *lettre de cachet* (*lettre* meaning "letter" and *cachet* meaning "seal") or letter under seal of the king may be a farfetched finding but, as it was often used to order an exile without trial or hearing, it's reminiscent of Joyce's play, *Exiles*, as well as his actual, though voluntary, exile from Ireland. The *Wake* works this word into: "But could you, of course, decent Lettrechaun, we knew (to change your name of not your nation) while still in the barrel." For my one encounter with a leprechaun's trick when I found a pot of god at the end of the rainbow, see my previous book, *Riverrun to Livvy: Lots of Fun Reading the First Page of James Joyce's "Finnegans Wake,"* page 201.

liquorally *FW* 321.1 *adv.* Actually or literally through the influence of an alcoholic drink or liquor. HCE falls "liquorally" to the floor of his pub after draining the dregs of his customers' glasses. Alcohol often loosens the lips and a drinker is apt to say, and later regret saying, "liquorally" what would not be said when sober. ("liquorally no more powers to their elbow")

litter *FW* 93.24, 202.2, & 615.1 *n*. A real word in real life meaning scattered rubbish, "litter" in *Finnegans Wake* becomes a letter that a hen scratches out of the litter of a midden heap. (See **middenst**.) Since the majority of the letters delivered by mail these days come under the heading "junk mail," perhaps this might be a good time to switch to the *Wake*'s way by spelling "letter" as "litter." ("The letter! The Litter! And the soother the bitther," "nordsihkes and sudervers and ayes and neins to a litter," & "type by tope, letter from litter, word at ward, with sendence of sundance")

litterey *FW* 422.35 *adj*. Having to do with writing that is the opposite of the best and most beautiful writings or literary works. (See **litteringture**.) Litter or scattered rubbish best describes "litterey" works. Joyce could have written conventional novels quite easily, but he didn't consider it worth doing, considering them "litterey" rather than literary. ("I regret to announce, after laying out his litterey bed, for two days she kept squealing down for noisy priors") McHugh gives "noisy pryers" for "noisy priors." The British term "nosey parkers" for "busybodies" or "prying persons" may also be suggested

litteringture *FW* 570.18 *n*. The body of writings of a country or language that is the opposite of the best and most beautiful writings or literature. Litter or scattered rubbish categorizes the compositions of "litteringture," many of which can often to be found on each week's best-seller list. ("One would say him to hold whole a litteringture of kidlings under his aproham.")

llarge *FW* 17.32 *adj*. A little bigger than large. In clothing a "Llarge" size would be for the chubby or portly person who needs something larger than large but is not yet ready for extra-large. ("Llarge by the smal an' everynight life olso th'estrange") (See **smal**.) Giving the Danish and Dutch *smal* and the German *schmal* for "narrow," along with the Danish *large* for "generous or liberal," Christiani writes: "Besides opposing large to

litter - loveleavest | 173

small, the context does not rule out generous versus narrow in the figurative sense, although Danish *smal* means physical narrowness only."

loonely *FW* 627.34 *adj.* Crazy or loony from depression caused by being all alone, without company of any kind, or lonely. Anna Livia Plurabelle, in her final, seaward-flowing soliloquy, speaks of being "Loonely in me loneness."

loudship *FW* 53.31 & 332.23 *n.* A noisy or loud peer of the realm or lord. Due to his exalted status, his "loudship" may lord it over his inferiors in a demanding and loudt (my creation from "loud" and "lout") manner. ("the bannocks of Gort and Morya and Bri Head and Puddyrick, your Loudship" & "But before that his loudship was converted to a landshop") McHugh translates the first quote as the Irish *beannact Dé agus Muire agus Brighid agus Phádraic* for "the blessing of God & Mary & Bridget & Patrick."

loveleavest *FW* 624.22 *adj.* The most beautiful or loveliest creation from the foliage of plants and trees or leaves. ("I am so exquisitely pleased about the loveleavest dress I have.") Joyce recited Anna Livia Plurabelle's loveliest soliloquy at the close of *Finnegans Wake* from memory one evening to Jacques Mercanton who writes: "With angelic tenderness, so moving in that rebellious angel, and on a tone of confidence and wonder, Joyce evoked the last voyage of his heroine. She wears her most beautiful gown, all leafy; but, behold, little by little the fiancée's moving dress is coming apart: one leaf and then another flees toward the sea on the fugitive waters; one leaf glides on a wave that goes to mingle its foam with eternal waves. 'A leaf, just a leaf, and then leaves.'" The account of ALP, as the Liffey, leaving Dublin to return to her "cold mad feary father," the Irish Sea, is the "loveleavest" part of the *Wake*. "My leaves have drifted from me," she sighs. "All. But one clings still. I'll bear it on me. To remind me of. Lff!" Gulls call. The sea calls. But ALP reminds readers that she will be "Finn, again!" Then appears the *Wake*'s famous suspended sentence—"A way a lone a last a loved a long the"—that flows back to the book's beginning, "riverrun."

loveliletter *FW* 459.23 *n*. Beautiful or lovely love letters. Meeting Noel Olivier at a luncheon, Virginia Woolf asked why she had never married the handsome young poet Rupert Brooke. Noel gave various reasons but, as Woolf wrote in her diary, Noel replied that "when she read his love letters – beautiful beautiful love letters – real love letters, she said – she cries & cries." What could be "loveliletter" than that? ("My latest lad's loveliletter I am sore I done something with.")

lowquacity *FW* 424.34 *n*. Talkativeness or loquacity that meets one of the many definitions of "low." As examples, excessive talking can be humble or lowly, poor in quality, coarse or vulgar, soft or not loud, depressed or dejected, or several of these at once. It has been my experience that those who are loquacious are often low on the totem pole in either work or social settings. ("The lowquacity of him! With his threestar monothong! Thaw!") McHugh references "threestar" with "three-star whiskey" and "threestar monothong" with "interior monologue," the style of writing that Joyce made famous with *Ulysses* and infamous with Molly Bloom's soliloquy that closes the novel. Some critics thought Joyce took interior monologue from Freud, but Joyce maintained he borrowed it from *Les Lauriers sont coupés* by Édouard Dujardin, a French novel he picked up at a train station as he left for Tours. With "monothong," monotone is suggested and, coupled with loquacity, lowers the talker even more in the estimation of listeners.

luistening *FW* 384.19 *v*. Attempting to hear or listening in a sensual, lewd, or lustful manner. (Dutch *luisteren* for "to listen") When Tristram and Iseult, on their voyage from Ireland to Cornwall, innocently drank the love potion Iseult's mother brewed especially for her daughter and the king to share when they first meet before their marriage, the four old men who are both the four apostles known in the *Wake* as "Mamalujo" and the four barons who spy on the young couple for the king are peering "through the steamy windows, into the honeymoon cabins," "spraining their ears, luistening and listening to the oceans of kissening, with their eyes glistening, all the four, when he was kiddling and cuddling and bunnyhugging scrumptious his colleen bawn." There's lots more salacious stuff which no doubt escaped the censors from the sheer obscurity of the text. (See **amotion** & **inthrusted**.)

lyncheon *FW* 372.30 *n.* A formal midday meal or luncheon during an unlawful hanging or lynching. In less enlightened times or, if today, less enlightened places, public hangings were a source of entertainment, and it was not unusual for the spectators to make a day of it with food and drink carted in for the occasion. As a lynching is usually a more spontaneous event, "lyncheon" parties are not frequently given due to the lack of time for proper preparation. ("Are now met by Brownaboy Fuinnninuinn's former for a lyncheon partyng of his burgherbooh.") McHugh reads "burgherbooh" as "bugaboo," that ties in with this type of hanging, as the person lynched is often feared for emotional and/or imaginary reasons rather than an actual crime.

M

macroscope *FW* 275.L2 *n.* 1. While a microscope is an optical instrument for viewing very small objects that are either invisible or indistinct to the naked eye, a "*macroscope*" is an optical instrument for viewing very large objects that are clearly visible to the naked eye. This may explain the vast discrepancy in the sales figures for microscopes compared with macroscopes since the naked eye is equally effective as the use of a "macroscope." 2. A variation on the first type of "macroscope" makes very large objects look smaller by allowing them to be viewed as though from a greater distance. A "macroscope" comes in handy when one's closeness to a very large object makes it impossible to see completely, such as being so near an elephant that one sees only the trunk, the tail, or a leg. ("*Two makes a wing at the macroscope telluspeep.*") The Latin *tellus* for "earth" tells us that a "*telluspeep*" is a "*macroscope*" that allows us to get a peep at our Earth that we can not see fully otherwise. Somewhat in this neighborhood is an entry in the diary of Joyce's brother, Stanislaus: "there are scientists whose work is concerned with infinite stellar spaces and who are hailed as great, and others deemed no less great whose work is at the end of a microscope. I opined that on a far smaller scale an analogous difference existed between writers,

178 | A *Finnegans Wake* Lextionary

and that my brother would belong to the latter class." Joyce, who was in the habit of reading his younger brother's diary, thought Stanislaus might be right.

madgetcy *FW* 112.28 *n*. A royal personage or Majesty who is insane or mad. King George III of England, subject of the successful film *The Madness of King George*, comes first to an Anglophile's mind, though there are a host of others to choose from in the history of monarchies. Ivan the Terrible of Russia may or may not have been insane, but he was definitely mad when in anger he struck and killed his son and successor. ("She may be a mere Marcella, this midget madgetcy, Misthress of Arths.") McHugh references "Marcella" in this sentence to "Marcella, the midget queen" in Joyce's novel *Ulysses*.

magistrafes *FW* 443.12 *n*. A judge or magistrate who is permitted to hand down punishments, with the Danish *straf* and German *Strafe* for "punishment." ("the joyboy before a bunch of magistrafes and twelve good and gleeful men") McHugh indicates that "joyboy" is slang for "homosexual," so the one accused of such acts is to appear before a magistrate and a jury of twelve men who seem only too full of glee to sentence him to punishment. This could refer to HCE's trials regarding his alleged misdeed in Phoenix Park that many believe was of a homosexual nature or even to the trials of the Irish Oscar Wilde who was convicted on a similar charge. (See **contrawatchwise**.)

maimeries *FW* 348.7 *n*. Remembrances or memories that have been crippled or maimed. When we have been done a terrible wrong it is not unusual for the memories of that time to haunt us and maim our minds. ("I've a boodle full of maimeries in me buzzim and medears runs sloze") McHugh gives "boodle" as "lot," "buzzim" as "bosom," and "medears runs sloze" as "my tears run slow."

malestimated *FW* 125.21 *v.* Ill or badly and calculated approximately or estimated. ("still today insufficiently malestimated notesnatcher") The projected budget that an American president sends each year to Congress is invariably "malestimated." This is especially true for the cost of our wars.

malttreating *FW* 322.29 *v.* 1. Treating ill or maltreating by means of alcoholic drinks made with malt such as beer and whiskey. Malttreatment may be self-inflicted or inflicted by others when one is over-served. 2. Opposite to the first definition, alcoholic drinks made with malt are gifts that bring pleasure or are a treat. There are tee shirts available printed with "Beer is proof that God loves us and wants us to be happy." In this case, beer is gift made of malt that is given as a treat. 3. Treating malt in the proscribed manner for brewing beer. ("they had been malttreating themselves to their health's contempt") The context here fits the first definition.

mamafesta *FW* 104.4 *n.* A proclamation or manifesto made by a mother or mama. ("Her untitled mamafesta memorializing the Mosthighest has gone by many names at disjointed times.") The Wakean "mamafesta" is the letter ALP wrote or dictated to her son Shem defending her husband HCE from accusations made against him for unspecified perversities one night in Phoenix Park. The letter or "litter" is pecked out of a kitchen midden or garbage dump by a hen named Biddy Doran. Various versions of the "litter" appear throughout *Finnegans Wake* before a complete copy is finally made available. If this "mamafesta" is intended to prove HCE's innocence, he would have been better off with a Public Defender straight out of law school. Scholars have seen this letter as a miniature version of the *Wake* itself. The quoted sentence above indicates that this "mamafesta" has "gone by many names," and the three pages that follow it list these names. Some contain HCE's initials, such as "*He Can Explain,*" or HCE and ALP's with "*Amy Licks Porter While Huffy Chops Eads.*" Some are easy to understand as is "*Lapps for Finns This*

180 | A *Finnegans Wake* Lextionary

Funnycoon's Week," while others are a bit more obscure.

manorwombanborn *FW* 55.10 *n.* A man or woman who is, while still in the womb, destined to inherit an estate with a manor house, that is to be "to the manor born." There is a hint here of Shakespeare's *Macbeth* who is told by three witches that he will not be defeated by any man of woman born. Thinking that this means he is invulnerable, Macbeth is brought down by a man delivered by Cesarean section. ("a phrase which the establisher of the world by law might pretinately write across the chestfront of all manorwombanborn")

manyoumeant *FW* 318.31 *n.* A structure to commemorate a person or persons who have done something notable or a monument meant to be a memorial to many. The Tomb of the Unknown Soldier in Arlington National Cemetery is one such "manyoumeant" out of many. ("Not a knocker on his head nor a nicknumber on the manyoumeant.")

mardred *FW* 517.11 *v.* A person killed or murdered for beliefs or principles who becomes a martyr may be said to have been "mardred." ("The author, in fact, was mardred.") Joyce was, in a literary sense, "mardred" by most critics as sections of *Finnegans Wake* were published. McHugh references King Arthur's nephew Modred who murdered his royal uncle.

marmorial *FW* 9.34 *n.* A statue or other object raised in reminder of some great person or event or a memorial that is disfigured or marred. Pigeons routinely mar memorials, while others are purposely marred as attacks against the person or event commemorated. The Protestant King William III of England, known as William of Orange as he was of the Dutch House of Orange, appears on the first page of *Finnegans Wake* as "where oranges have been laid to rust upon the green." His memorial equestrian statue in Dublin was repeatedly marred by Irish Catholic Greens who smeared it with paint and other less savory substances before finally laying it to rest through complete destruction. The famous video footage of the giant statue of Iraq's Saddam Hussein being toppled in Baghdad is a more recent example of a "marmorial." ("This is the Willingdone branlish his same marmorial tallowscoop") This reference is to the Wellington Monument in Dublin's Phoenix Park, a 205-foot granite obelisk and thus somewhat difficult to mar easily. This *Wake* word is very close to the actual word "marmoreal" meaning "like marble," a substance of which so many memorials are made. With all memorials and monuments it's wise to take Stanislaw Lee's advice: "When smashing the monuments, save the pedestals—they always come in handy later."

marrage   *FW* 514.4 & 607.21   *v.* To damage or mar by wedlock or marriage with the suggestion of mirage, which the hopes for wedded bliss sometimes become. ("—In sum, some hum? And other marrage feats?" & "in somes incontigruity coumplegs of heoponhurrish marrage from whose I most sublumbunate")

marrimoney   *FW* 423.30   *n.* Monetary matrimony or, in common usage, marrying for money. The *Wake* refers to "the ricecourse of marrimoney," suggesting that there is a race on in the pursuit for wealthy spouses with rice thrown as they race down the aisle upon marriage. The truth in the old adage, those who marry for money earn it, usually kicks in shortly after the rice is thrown. Since the thrown rice is symbolic for prosperity and fertility, the money part fits well with the first of these wedding wishes. (See **ricecourse**.)

martyrolgy   *FW* 349.24   *n.* The science or branch of knowledge dealing with those who have died for a cause or belief or martyrs and, if I may create a Wakean-type word of my own, their martyrdoom. ("*the puffpuff and pompom of Powther and Pall, the great belt, band and bucklings of the Martyrology of Gorman*") McHugh references "*Martyrology*" with O'Gorman's *Martyrology* and with Herbert Gorman who served as Joyce's authorized biographer. (See **biografiend**.)

mascarete *FW* 206.14 *n*. In *How Joyce Wrote Finnegans Wake*, Patrick A. McCarthy expands on the passage in which ALP "made herself tidal to join in the mascarete." "The puns here encapsulate the main events of the last part of I.8, as Anna Livia tidies up for an innocent evening party (a masquerade) that is also a deadly revenge spree (a massacre). She is of course 'going out' in another sense as well: reaching the end of her course as a river, flowing out to sea, merging into the tide. This aspect of the story is suggested both by 'tidal' and by the pun on French mascaret, 'tidal wave in estuary' (McHugh)."

massacreedoed *FW* 515.25 *v*. A statement of faith, belief, or a creed that has been slaughtered, torpedoed, or massacred. Catholics have "massacreedoed" Protestants and vice versa in Christianity for centuries just as Sunnis and Shiites are doing in Islam, all over minor points of their creeds, at least minor to those who don't believe in those particular creeds. ("massacreedoed as the holiname rally round took place")

mathness *FW* 182.7 *n*. Either insanity or great anger but definitely madness about the science of numbers or mathematics. Something often experienced by anyone trying to balance a checkbook. ("his fear in saddishness, to ensign the colours by the beerlitz in his mathness") McHugh suggests that there may be "a method in his madness." Joyce taught English at the Berlitz School in Trieste. (See **beerlitz**.)

maudelenian *FW* 153.36 *adj*. A silly sentimentally concerning Magdalen College at Oxford, England. Many alumni are apt to become maudlin when reflecting fondly on the institutions of higher learning where they spent their student years. Alumni associations find "maudelenian" graduates great targets for fundraising drives. ("a wherry shaggy maudelenian woice and the jackasses all within bawl laughed and brayed")

mayour *FW* 568.16 *n.* "Your" and/or "our" head of city government or mayor. ("It stands in *Instopressisble* how Meynhir Mayour, our boorgomaister, thon staunch Thorsman") McHugh offers "stop press" here as well as the Antiparnellite newspaper *Insuppressible*. He gives the Dutch *mijnheer* for "sir." (See *Instopressible*.)

meandertale *FW* 18.22 *n.* A story or tale that wanders or meanders. *Finnegans Wake* is a model "meandertale" with its meandering tales like the Norwegian Captain and the Tailor, the "Pranksome" "prankquean," or how Buckley shot the Russian General, among many, that come and go within the circular structure of the *Wake*. ("The meandertale, aloss and again, of our old Heidenburgh in the days when Head-in-Clouds walked the earth.") McHugh finds "Neanderthal Man," "Heidelberg Man," "Edinburgh," and the German *Heiden* for "heathen" in "Heidenburgh." You may have spotted HCE in "when Head-in-Clouds walked the earth," but McHugh also notes that "after enlightenment Buddha walked the world."

meanderthalltale *FW* 19.25 *n.* 1. A story or tale, perhaps a tall tale, of the aimless wandering or meandering of the prehistoric cave people named Neanderthal. 2. Since Neanderthal is also a term for a political reactionary and, since at one time George W. Bush was the head of the reactionary wing of the Republican Party, his tall tales of the the great success of his aimlessly meandering policies in the Middle East can quite easily be called a "meanderthalltale." ("What a meanderthalltale to unfurl and with what an end in view of squattor and anntisquattor and postproneauntisquattor!")

megalogue *FW* 467.8 *n.* Large or mega (Greek *megas* for great) part of a play for an actor speaking alone or monologue. The final chapter of *Ulysses* is composed entirely of Molly Bloom's almost unpunctuated, stream of consciousness "megalogue." ("Did you note that worrid expressionism on his megalogue?")

mehind *FW* 350.15   *n.* Mental ability or mind and buttocks or behind, giving thoughts centered on a person's posterior. This is a special *Wake* word that must be read in its context: "*Mr. Lhugewhite Cadderpollard with sunflawered beautonhole pulled up point blanck by mailbag mundaynism at Oldbally Court . . . the whyfe of his bothem was the very lad's thing to elter his mehind.*" I recommend you fasten your seat belt for this one so, with help from McHugh, here goes—The large, huge, white caterpillar is the Irish playwright Oscar Wilde, as described by Lady Campbell. He was often characterized carrying a sunflower and always wore a flower in his buttonhole. Blackmailed for some love or, as Wilde maintained, lovely letters he wrote his young friend Lord Alfred Douglas, Wilde later saw them used in evidence against him at his trial for gross indecency at the Old Bailey Court. With "whyfe of his bothem" as "wife of his bosom" or "wipe of his bottom," "lad's" as slang for "penis," and "elter his mehind" as "alter his mind" or "enter his behind" and, if your mind is in the wrong place and you make the right selections, you'll see how Wilde's dalliances with young lads got him two years hard labor. I can't resist throwing in the pun, since the *Wake* is a punny book, of the butcher who, while his mind was distracted, backed into the meat grinder and got a little behind in his work. (See **beauhind**.)

mememormee *FW* 628.14   *v.* To recall or remember combined with the capacity to recall or memory with the implication of remembrance after death or of something that is gone and won't return. In the Roman Catholic Mass, "Memento" is the first word of two prayers, one for the living and one for the dead. There is the suggestion of the Latin "memento mori" meaning "remember that you must die." Medieval scholars once kept a human skull on their desks as a memento mori. Today we often keep souvenirs as mementos of a special time or place that is long past or build memorials for the dead and gone. In *Finnegans Wake*, Anna Livia Plurabelle as the river Liffey is asking her family to remember her as she prepares to flow into death in the Irish Sea, returning to her "cold mad feary father." ("Far calls. Coming, far! End here. Us then. Finn, again! Bussoftlhee, mememormee!") Being a fan of Byron, as was the young Joyce, "mememormee" makes me remember the poem his lordship wrote in response to the words "Remember me!" that Lady Caroline Lamb wrote on the first page of *Vathek*, a book she found on the table when she once visited Byron's London apartment in his absence:

> Remember thee! Remember thee!
> Till Lethe quench life's burning stream
> Remorse and Shame shall cling to thee,
> And haunt thee like a feverish dream!
>
> Remember thee! Aye, doubt it not.
> Thy husband too shall think of thee:
> By neither shalt thou be forgot,
> Thou *false* to him, thou *fiend* to me!

Christopher Nolan's captivatingly complex film *Memento*, in which the scenes are screened in reverse sequence so that time travels backwards, is an excellent exercise of one's ability to "mememormee" and the perfect mental preparation for tackling *Finnegans Wake*.

metandmorefussed *FW* 513.31 *v.* Physically transformed in trifling ways or metamorphosed through excessive worry over small matters or fussing. Women are often accused (unfairly of course) of no sooner having met a man than they attempt to change some little habit of his, resorting to fussing if necessary. ("in an amenessy metting, metandmorefussed to decide where-againwhen to meet themselves, flopsome and jerksome, lubber and deliric") McHugh finds in this word "met & more fussed" and gives "amenessy" as "amnesty" and "amnesia" and "flopsome and jerksome" as a quote from *Ulysses*: "flotsam, jetsam, lagan and derelict."

metween *FW* 570.24 *prep.* In the space or time that separates me from two or more people or things, such as "metween" the devil and the deep blue sea. ("he has his mic son and his two fine mac sons and a superfine mick want they mack metween them") McHugh gives the Irish *mac* for "son."

middayevil *FW* 423.28 *adj.* 1. Something wicked or evil that occurs at noon or midday. The shootout in the film *High Noon* effectively took care of an evil at midday. 2. Evil during the Middle Ages or the Medieval Period. Though evil is always relative, medieval times are considered a particularly evil time in which to live, at least when compared with the civilizations of the earlier Greeks and Romans and our own "enlightened" times. ("He's weird, I tell you, and middayevil down to his vegetable soul.")

middenst *FW* 350.2 *adj.* In the center or middle of a refuse heap or midden. A story central to *Finnegans Wake* is the finding of a letter or, in Wakese, a "litter" in a kitchen midden. The discovery is made by a hen, Biddy Doran, an embodiment of ALP. There are multiple versions of the "litter" and, like the *Wake*, they are difficult to interpret. As are many artifacts found by archeologists in refuse heaps, the "litter" raises more questions than it answers, though some scholars have seen the final and complete "litter" as a *Reader's Digest* condensed version of *Finnegans Wake* itself. (See **mamafesta**.) ("*he touched upon this tree of livings in the middenst of the gareden*") McHugh matches this with *Genesis* 2:9: "the tree of life also in the midst of the garden."

millentury *FW* 32.32 *n.* A thousand periods of 100 years or a millennium of centuries which equal 100,000 years. ("the homedromed and enliventh performance of the problem passion play of the millentury, running strong since creation, *A Royal Divorce*") McHugh references "homedromed and enliventh" with "hundred & eleventh" and ALP's "111 children." *A Royal Divorce* is a play by W. W. Wills about Napoleon's divorce from Josephine.

minnowaurs *FW* 272.10 *n.* A warship or man-of-war that, in relation to other ships, is comparatively small, as a minnow is to larger fish, yet as ferocious and deadly as was the monstrous Minotaur of ancient Crete (See **Allmaziful** & **dazecrazemazed**.) and particularly effective in small or mini-wars. ("Stop, if you are a sally of the allies, hot off Minnowaurs and naval actiums, picked engagements and banks of rowers") McHugh identifies the song "Sally in Our Alley" and finds "maneuvers" in "Minnowaurs," which describes navel actions in which the ships were partly powered by "banks of rowers," such as the Battle of Actium where Octavius outmaneuvered Mark Antony and Cleopatra.

mirage *FW* 340.28 *n.* Mirror, marriage, and mirage combined to give the illusory reflection of a marriage. ("*his pollex prized going forth on his visitations of mirrage or Miss Horizon, justso allour fannacies daintied her*") "Fantasies" as "fannacies" fits well with a mirage and with many brides' illusionary visions of marriage. Oscar Wilde may have seen marriage as a "mirrage" when he wrote: "Men marry because they are tired, women because they are curious. They are both disappointed."

mirrorminded *FW* 576.24 *adj.* 1. Mental ability or mind that reflects images in reverse to reality such as objects seen in a mirror. Alice found a "mirrorminded" land when she went through the looking glass. 2. McHugh suggests "myriadminded," which might be a mind that can deal with countless or innumerable thoughts or objects. 3. When the two meanings above are combined, there is found a mind that handles a huge number of thoughts or objects which it reflects on in a reversed fashion. Mirrormindedness is an excellent quality to possess when reading *Finnegans Wake*. ("mirrorminded curiositease and would-to-the-large which bring hills to molehunter") Curiosities that tease fit well with "curiositease. McHugh gives "making a mountain out of a molehill" and "mountains to Mohammed" for "brings hills to molehunter."

mischievmiss *FW* 20.31 *n*. A naughty or mischievous unmarried young woman or Miss. In *Finnegans Wake* it refers to the two girls in Phoenix Park who are either spied upon by HCE or who observe him in some unseemly act or, perhaps, encourage him in such an act as hinted at with "what the mischievmiss made a man do." McHugh gives the following reference to this word, though I must admit it's over my head: "medieval chansons de mal mariée relate wife's escape from jealous husband."

miseffectual *FW* 118.28 *adj*. Producing a bad result or effect. While ineffectual means without effect or useless, "miseffectual" is stronger in its negative effect, being not only useless but bad. ("it is not a miseffectual whyacinjthinous riot of blots and blurs and bars and balls hoops and wriggles")

missaunderstaid *FW* 363.36 *v*. Wrongly understood or misunderstood to be fixed, unchanging, or staid. I'll go even farther out on a limb than I normally do by suggesting that "Miss" as an "unmarried woman" and "aund" as close to the Scottish *auld* for "old," provides an old maid who, though thought to be staid in her marital status, would abandon her spinsterhood in a New York minute for a gentleman's marriage proposal. Perhaps the most "missaunderstaid" theory in physics was Einstein's fierce defense of a static universe, despite his general theory of relativity that showed the universe was either contracting or expanding ("an extense must impull, an elapse must elopes"). Since a static universe was the accepted notion at that time, he fixed his numbers to make the universe stand still. Einstein said this was his biggest blooper. ("It was merely my barely till their oh offs. Missaunderstaid. Meggy Guggy's giggag.") McHugh translates "barely" as Irish *Béarla* for "Eng. Language" and "bare lie." He references "Meggy Guggy's giggag" with "*Ulysses* 550 (emended): The NANNYGOAT (bleats) Megeggaggegg!"

Missisliffi *FW* 159.12-13 *n*. A combination of the Mississippi and Liffey rivers, both important and prominent in *Finnegans*

Wake. The Liffey is the lifeblood of Dublin and the primal form of Anna Livia Plurabelle who begins and ends the book and embodies the historical circularity of humanity as proposed by Vico. The Mississippi brings in the *Wake*'s new-world theme while also introducing Mark Twain, Tom Sawyer, and, especially, Huckleberry Finn, an American incarnation of the Irish giant Finn MacCool. ("her muddied name was Missisliffi") The Mississippi is popularly known as "The Big Muddy."

mistery *FW* 270.22 *n.* Something hidden or a mystery and hazy or misty. Many mystery stories take place in mist-shrouded settings, casting a mysterious, hidden aspect on the story. Sir Arthur Conan Doyle's Sherlock Holmes novel, *The Hound of the Baskervilles*, with its mist-shrouded moors, is an example of a near-perfect "mistery." ("Liddell lokker through the leafery, ours is a mistery of pain.") McHugh identifies Alice Liddell as the basis for Lewis Carroll's Alice in *Through the Looking Glass*. He also sees in "Liddel lokker" the Dutch *lokker* for "tempter" and "little looker," both of which fit the photographs Carroll took of the nude, real-life Alice.

mistomist *FW* 340.5 *n.* This is one of those Wakeisms composed entirely of foreign words used to make an English connection. It's difficult to even venture a guess as to how many words of this type there are, and Joyce himself predicted that within a few years following the publication of *Finnegans Wake* even he wouldn't be able to identify everything he put in it. So, with that caveat, here goes. McHugh gives the Ukrainian *misto* for "town," *mist* for "bridge," and *mistomist* as "town of towns." He also adds in the Italian *misto* for "mixed." While Joyce's feelings for his home town were definitely mixed, he did consider it the "town of towns." Now bring in Petr Škrabánek's suggestion of "the town of bridges," that fits Dublin accurately, and his addition of the German *Mist* for "dung," and there is Lady Morgan's comment on Ireland's capital, "Dear Dirty Dublin." This description is woven into the fabric of the *Wake* with "Dear

Dirty Dumpling" and "dire dreary darkness" as two out of many. For Joyce, Dublin was "distinctly dirty but rather a dear." ("*after his tongues in his cheeks, with pinkpoker pointing out in rutene to impassible abjects beyond the mistomist towards Lissnaluhy*") Joyce plants a clue here with "*rutene*" as a reference to Ruthenian, the name for Ukrainian but, even so, "*mistomist*" only goes to prove that it takes more than a Ruthenian village to read *Finnegans Wake*, it takes the world.

mistributed *FW* 371.12 -13 *v.* Divided, separated, or distributed wrongly, badly, or mistakenly. While communism's goal was the redistribution of the world's wealth that had been "mistributed," it seems much of it was "mistributed" to the party leaders. Under Leonid Brezhnev's leadership of the Soviet Union, a joke quietly circulated about his attempts to impress his mother by showing her his spacious apartment, chauffeured limousine, private plane, country dacha, and other party perks. When his mother made no response, he asked, "Well, mother, what do you think of all these beautiful things?" "This is all very well, Leonid," his mother replied, "but what will you do if the communists get back into power?" ("That he had mistributed in port, pub, park, pantry and poultryhouse")

misunderstruck *FW* 126.7 *v.* 1. Hit or struck through a mistake in meaning or misunderstanding. People are often "misunderstrurk" by those following the shoot now, ask questions later philosophy of conflict resolution. 2. To strike out and miss the target from striking somewhere below or under it, as batters sometimes do in baseball. ("He misunderstruck and aim for am ollo of number three of them")

mmmmany *FW* 171.19 *adj.* The simple word many means numerous or consisting of a great number, so "mmmmany" implies quadruple a numerous or great number. It receives greater emphasis in the *Wake* by being paired with "mmmmuch" to give "mmmmuch too mmmmany." This visual representation of the superfluous is prefigured at *FW* 122.36 with "toomuchness, the fartoomanyness." (See **mmmmuch**.)

mmmmuch *FW* 171.19 *adj.* The simple word much means great in amount, degree, or number, so "mmmmuch" implies quadruple a great amount, degree, or number. It receives greater emphasis in the *Wake* by being paired with "mmmmany" to give "mmmmuch too mmmmany." This visual representation of the superfluous is prefigured at *FW* 122.36 with "toomuchness, the fartoomanyness." (See **mmmmany**.)

moananoaning *FW* 628.3 *n.* A lovely onomatopoeic word based on the Maori *moana* for "sea" to describe the monotonous moaning of the Irish Sea that ALP hears on the *Wake*'s last page as she rushes into the arms of her "cold mad feary father." ("till the near sight of the mere size of him, the moyles and moyles of it, moananoaning, makes me seasilt saltsick") McHugh identifies Moyle as the sea between Ireland and Scotland as well as suggesting miles and miles.

moaning pipers *FW* 23.31 *n.* Persons complaining or moaning with a loud, shrill voice by transmission through radio or television frequencies or piping. Rush Limbaugh is presently the king of American "moaning pipers." ("the moaning pipers could tell him to his faceback, the louthly one whose loab we are devourers of") No doubt "morning papers" is the reference here and, with their concentration on bad news, accidents, and catastrophes, the morning papers certainly pipe out plenty of moans.

Mockerloo *FW* 73.5 *n.* A humorous reference to the battle of Waterloo in which the British and their allies ridiculed or made a mockery of Napoleon's attempt at an imperial comeback. ("to cocoa come outside to Mockerloo out of that for the honour of Crumlin")

moighty *FW* 623.5 *n.* A half, part, or moiety of the powerful or mighty. While the "moighty" falls short of a majority, its might and power alone is usually great enough to carry a cause to victory. ("Like the score and a moighty went before him.")

moisturologist *FW* 608.2 *n.* A scientist studying atmospheric conditions related to weather or a meteorologist with a specialty in various forms of moisture such as rain, snow, hail, fog, and mist. ("as accorded to by moisturologist of the Brehons Assorceration for the advauncement of scayence") McHugh references the "British Association for the Advancement of Science" and "Brehon Law: ancient Ir. legal system." Sorcerers and séances are worked in as well. McHugh writes that this highlights the hostility that 19th Century scientific bodies had toward spiritualists.

monofractured *FW* 310.10-11 *n.* Having one thing that is broken or fractured while being manufactured. ("monofractured by Piaras UaRhuamhaighaudhlug, tympan founder") McHugh gives the Irish *Piaras Ua Raghallaigh* for "Piers O'Reilly" that brings in the spurious song, "The Ballad of Persse O'Reilly," Hosty composed to spread the rumors about HCE's alleged misdeeds in Phoenix Park.

morphomelosophopancreates *FW* 88.9 *n.* A wise (Greek *sophos*), overpowering (Greek *pan krates*) dream (Greek god of dreams *Morpheus*) that has a musical or melodious (Greek *melos*) shape or structure. This Wakism is self-referent since *Finnegans Wake* is filled with the wisdom of all ages and cultures as well as predictive of what is yet to come. The novel is certainly overpowering, as testified by those who have come to it cold all the way to Wakean scholars. It certainly is a dream world, as Joyce himself called it such, and melodiously musical, since Joyce was always more concerned with sound than sense, as he aptly demonstrated with a recorded reading from the Anna Livia Plurabelle chapter of the *Wake*. ("That he was only too cognitively conatively cogitbabundantly sure of it because, living, loving, breathing and sleeping morphomelosophopancreates, as he most significantly did, whenever he thought he heard he saw he felt he made a bell clipperclipperclipperclipper.") No other sentence describes so perfectly Joyce's creation of *Finnegans Wake*.

mother-in-lieu *FW* 220.22-23 *n*. One who stands in place of or in lieu of the mother of one's husband or wife or mother-in-law. A substitute "mother-in-lieu," giving a husband or wife a choice of adopting their own would, in many cases, be preferred to the genuine article. ("their poor little old mother-in-lieu, who is woman of the house")

mousterious *FW* 15.33 *adj*. Secret, hidden, or mysterious as a mouse. Mice are "mousterious," covert creatures who prefer to secrete themselves into hidden places. ("He hath locktoes, this shortshins, and, Obeold that's pectoral, his mammamuscles most mousterious.") McHugh references "Mousterian man = Neanderthal man." Agatha Christie's long-running play, *The Mousetrap*, is a "mousterious" work for the stage.

movely *FW* 318.1 *adj*. Put in motion or move in a beautiful or lovely way. Instead of "She walks in beauty as the night," Lord Byron might more concisely have written "She movely as the night," though it would have messed up his meter. ("and that proud grace to her, in gait a movely water, of smile a coolsome cup") The "gait" of this "movely water" could be ALP as she moves from the mountains to the sea as the lovely Liffey.

muchrooms *FW* 625.19 *n*. A great number or much fast-growing, umbrella-shaped fungi or mushrooms. ("Why, them's the muchrooms, come up during the night.") McHugh references *Ulysses* with "Kerwan's mushroom houses."

muddlecrass *FW* 152.8 *adj*. People between the poor and the wealthy or in the middle-class but who are both in a mess or muddle and coarse, gross, or crass. People of the "muddlecrass" might be described as tasteless trash with a moderate amount of money. ("I shall revert to a expletive method which I frequently use when I have to sermo with muddlecrass pupils.")

muftilife *FW* 261.19 *n.* That part of a life lived in ordinary clothes or mufti by one who has the right to wear a uniform. Career service personnel begin a "muftilife" on their retirement. ("tumulous under his chthonic exterior but plain Mr Tumulty in muftilife, in his antisipiences as in his recognisances") HCE is hiding here and, with McHugh giving "chthonic" as "dwelling underground," he is in his aspect as Finn MacCool interred in the Dublin landscape.

murkblankered *FW* 612.22 *adj.* Appearing empty or blank from a covering or blanket of darkness, gloom, or murk. London was once famous for its enveloping fogs that gave the city a "murkblankered" appearance. ("beingtime monkblinkers timeblinged completamentarily murkblankered in their neutrolysis") McHugh translates "beingtime" as "for the time being," "monkblinkers" as "blinkered," "completamentarily" as the Italian *completamente* for "completely," "murkblandered" as "blankminded," and "neutrolysis" as "electrolysis" and "neutrality."

murmoirs *FW* 387.34 *n.* A record of a person's life experiences or memoir that contains complaints or murmurs inserted as though spoken under the breath or indistinctly. Autobiographical memoirs allow persons to grumble about others after the fact, something that they were unable to do at the time. ("And his widdy the giddy is wreathing her murmoirs as her gracest triput to the Grocery Trader's Manthly.") When "wreathing her murmoirs" is read as "writing her memoirs" and "gracest triput" as "greatest tribute," there is the suggestion of memoirs which twist and bend events to make the author appear wreathed in accolades or awarded wreaths as an honor. Most memoirs show their writers to the best advantage while overlooking certain faults.

muftilife - mythametical | 195

murmurrandoms *FW* 358.3 *n.* Informal notes or memorandums based on random grumbles or murmurs. The Latin *murmurandum* refers to "something to be murmured." Such memorandums are the bane of the business world, an indirect method of addressing a complaint or problem that is best dealt with openly and directly. ("I am cadging hapsnots as at murmurrandoms of distend relations from ficsimilar phases") McHugh translates "cadging hapsnots" as "catching snapshots," "murmurrandoms of distend relations" as "memoranda of distant relations," and "ficsimilar phases" as "familiar faces." He provides the Latin *murmurandum* as "(something) to be murmured."

museyroom *FW* 8.9, 8.10, & 10.22 *n.* A building containing a collection of objects or a museum that compels deep thought, mediation, or musing. In *Finnegans Wake*, readers are taken on a tour of the Wellington Museum with its collection of artifacts from Wellington's defeat of Napoleon at Waterloo. The tour is conducted by the Earwicker's cleaning lady, Kate, who gives these directions: "This the way to the museyroom. Mind your hats goan in," "Now yiz are in the Willingdone Museyroom," & "This way the museyroom. Mind your boots goan out." Joyce took his family on a tour of the Waterloo battlefield, traveling on the same bus with the later-to-be-famous American writer Thomas Wolfe. Wolfe certainly recognized Joyce but was too shy to speak to him.

myselx *FW* 444.18 *pron.* Specifically the sexual side of "myself" and, possibly, a reference to one's male or female sexual characteristics. This is one of those Wakean words in which the meaning is completely clear when read in context. ("I'll be all over you myselx horizontally") Here Shaun as Juan is voicing incestuous thoughts of his sister Issy. (See **encestor**.)

mythametical *FW* 286.23 *adj.* A combination of myths and mathematics or that which is exact or accurate regarding what is legendary or imaginary. Joyce may also be suggesting that numbers are not real but an invention much like ancient myths. Like Joyce, I prefer letters to numbers and agree with humorist Fran Lebowitz who, when asked what should be taught in schools, replied, "The Three R's, give or take arithmetic." ("On the name of the tizzer and off the tongs and off the mythametical tripods.") McHugh identifies this as the Christian blessing, "In the name of the Father, & of the Son, & of the Holy Ghost." In the final book of the New Testament, The *Revelation to John*, the number 666 has attained and retained "mythametical" status as the number of the beast who will bring about an apocalyptic end time. With the Hebrew letters for Nero Caesar (Neron Kesar) adding up to 666 and, given his brutal persecution of Christians, many scholars believe John identified this infamous emperor as the beast. But this has not prevented later ages from finding new names to link with 666, Napoleon and Hitler being two of the more recent ones.

mythelated *FW* 266.9-10 *adj.* A mentholated myth. To add the cooling and pleasing effect of menthol from oil of peppermint to make what is legendary or imaginary or a myth more easily swallowed, just as mentholated cigarettes mask the harsh effect of fire on a smoker's throat. The promise of eternal life in paradise is one of the more common mentholated benefits for following rules decreed by God(s). ("Which assoars us from the murk of the mythelated in the barrabelowther") McHugh suggests connections with the Greek *methysos* for "drunk" and "methylated spirit in lamps" and gives both "assails" and "answers" for "assoars."

mythified *FW* 393.33 *v.* To puzzle, bewilder, or make mysterious through the creation or recounting of a story not based on fact or reality or mystified by a myth. ("all puddled and mythified") McHugh gives "puddled" as slang for "insane, very eccentric." It is generally found that the beliefs of all the world's religions since the dawn of time have mythified almost everyone, the exceptions being those specific beliefs adhered to by the members of a particular faith. A cannibal who has no problem appeasing the gods through the sacrificial slaughter and consumption of a missionary may refuse to swallow the Roman Catholic doctrine of transubstantiation.

N

nabsack *FW* 11.19 *n.* A canvas sack or knapsack for carrying on the back items that have been caught, suddenly seized, or nabbed. ("all spoiled goods go into her nabsack") When Snuffy Smith of the Sunday comics goes after his neighbors' chickens under cover of night, he's always seen carrying a "nabsack."

naughtingels *FW* 359.32 *n.* Zero or naught European thrushes with a sweet song or nightingales. If "naughtingels" sang in Berkeley Square, then we would not have one of our sweetest songs. With "We are now diffusing among our lovers of this sequence (to you! to you!) the dewfolded song of the naughtingels (Alys! Alysaloe!) form their sheltered positions," it's difficult to understand how no song of nightingales could be heard, unless it's the song of "naughty girls" that McHugh hears, along with the "to-whit, to-whoo" of an owl in "to you! to you!"

nayophight *FW* 425.31 *n.* A novice or neophyte at saying no or the archaic nay. Two year olds are new to human speech, but they quickly master the art of saying "NO!" ("as a papst and an immature and a nayophight") With the German *Papst* for Pope, the definition of neophyte as a recent religious convert comes into play.

nekropolitan *FW* 80.1 *adj.* Being part of a large city or metropolitan in nature, but a large city, not of the living, but of the dead. A person buried in a large cemetery may be considered a "nekropolitan" and, one hopes and trusts, dead before burial. ("there being no macadamized sidetracks on those old nekropolitan nights") McHugh gives the German *nekropolis* for "cemetery" and sees "Neapolitan" in "nekropolitan."

nethermore *FW* 57.26 *adv.* Never again or nevermore because of a sentence to that lower or nether place, the netherworld of Hell. It's good that Edgar Allan Poe's "stately raven," "bird or devil" from "the Night's Plutonian shore" said "Nevermore" rather than the *Wake*'s "nethermore," which might have implied that "the lost Lenore" was indeed lost in the darkness of the netherworld forevermore. ("watching bland sol slithe dodgsomely into the nethermore") McHugh reads "the pleasant sun" for "bland sol" and Lewis Carroll's invented word "slithy" from *Jabberwocky* for "slithe." (See the Introduction to this Lextionary. Carroll's real name, C. L. Dodgson, is referred to with "dodgsomely."

neuthing *FW* 455.22 *n.* With the German *neu* for "new," there is a combination of nothing and a new thing. Beckman comments on the context of this word in the *Wake* with: "We are left, epistemologically, 'dead certain however of neuthing whatever.' With one more head-turning twist: being certain of 'neuthing' or nothing may open the door, the only door there is, to a neuthing in the sense of a new thing." ("you sprout all your abel and woof your wings dead certain however of neuthing whatever to aye forever")

nevar *FW* 203.36 *adv.* Not ever or never the Neva, the Russian river that flows through St. Petersburg, the capital Peter the Great created as a window on the West. After their successful revolution, the communists moved the capital back to

Moscow, saying "nevar" to the Neva River and yes once more to the Moskva River. After the communist government of the USSR fell, St. Petersburg once more became the capital of Russia. ("as he warned her niver to, niver to, nevar") This word appears in Book I, Chapter 8 of *Finnegans Wake*, the ALP chapter that is generally regarded as the most beautiful chapter of the book. Joyce wove hundreds and hundreds of river names into this chapter saying, "I think it flows." (See **nevay**.)

nevay *FW* 322.4 *n.* The navy on the Neva. (See **nevar**.) Peter the Great not only created St. Petersburg on the Neva River but also created Russia's navy that was based at this Baltic seaport. ("he's like more look a novicer on the nevay") McHugh reads this as "looks more like an officer in the navy." It can also be read as "looks more like a novice officer in the navy." (See **novicer**.)

newseryreel *FW* 489.35 *n.* A tale in rhymed verse for children or nursery rhyme in the form of a reel of motion pictures portraying current events or a newsreel. You must be of a certain age and remember well back into the last century to have seen a newsreel at a movie theater before the feature film began. Could Joyce be implying here that the news we are fed, whether in the form of newsreels or television, amounts to nothing more than nursery rhymes? ("—This nonday diary, this allnights newseryreel.") *Finnegans Wake* in many ways is a nighttime diary and an all night newsreel, though the reported stories are confused and complex as stories usually are in a dream.

nicknumber *FW* 318.30-31 *n.* A number given to a person in place of his or her legal name or a numerical nickname. A boy who is the third of that name in a family is sometimes nicknumbered "Trey." The "nicknumber" of the man who services my water softener is "Quarter," as his last name is followed by IV. The ancient Romans skipped numerical nicknames and used numbers as actual names, such as Sextus for the sixth child. ("Not a knocker on his head nor a nicknumber on the manyoumeant.")

nightinesses *FW* 51.5 *n*. Improper or naughty things that happen between evening and morning or the night. The field is wide open here but, as far as *Finnegans Wake* is concerned, HCE's alleged "nightinesses" in Phoenix Park commands the forefront. Also suggested is nightie, an informal term for nightgown or nightshirt. Since Joyce's hero, the Irish Party leader Charles Stewart Parnell, was mistakenly reported to have climbed down the fire escape in his nightshirt to avoid being discovered in his married mistress's bedroom, his naughtiness in a nightie ("fairescapading in his natsirt" with the Danish *nat* for night) comes to mind. ("since in this scherzarade of one's thousand one nightinesses that sword of certainty which would indentifide the body never falls") Scheherazade with her thousand nights and a night's store of stories from *The Arabian Nights* (also a reference to the 1,001 letters in the *Wake*'s ten thunder words) as well as the Sword of Damocles are in play here.

nightmaze *FW* 411.8 *n*. A state of confusion or a maze that must be navigated in the dark of night during sleep, better known as a nightmare. Nightmares often impart the fearful feeling of being in a maze or labyrinth from which one never finds the exit. In *Ulysses*, Stephen Dedalus says that "History is a nightmare from which I am trying to awake" and, as if *Ulysses* was not enough of a labyrinthine maze, the nighttime, dreamlike setting of *Finnegans Wake* provides a literary "nightmaze" unlike any other. ("Go thou this island, one housesleep there, then go thou other island, two housesleep there, then catch one nightmaze, then home to dearies.") McHugh references this with "Edward Clodd: *The Story of the Alphabet* 64 deciphers an Alaskan pictogram: 'I there go that island, one sleep there; then I go another island, there 2 sleeps; I catch 1 sealion, then return mine.'"

nightynovel *FW* 54.21 *n*. A somewhat improper or naughty long, fictitious story or a novel, the action and plot of which takes place during the dark of night. *Finnegans Wake* immediately comes to mind with its dream/sleep structure and its abundance of sexual scenes and naughty innuendos. Unlike its predecessor, *Ulysses*, the *Wake* escaped the censors' wrath only through the obscurity of its multilingual language. As Joyce said to a friend, "It's natural things should not be so clear at night, isn't it now?" And his wife, Nora, said, "I guess the man's a genius, but what a dirty mind he has, hasn't he?" If you are 18 or over and want to check this out for yourself, I recommend reading Book II, Chapter 4 beginning on page 383. ("Maggis, nick your nightynovel!")

noarchic *FW* 80.25 *adj*. Extremely archaic; antiquated to the point of going back to Noah's ark and the rainbow's arch as a sign of the first covenant. ("the obluvial waters of our noarchic memory withdrew") McHugh gives the Greek *nauarchos* for "admiral," a fitting title for Noah as the highest ranking man in the entire world's navy at that time.

noer *FW* 286.28 *n*. One who is sure of or knows when to refuse or to say no, à la Nancy Reagan's "Just say no." ("Can you nei do her, numb? Asks Dolph, suspecting the answer know. Oikkont, ken you, ninny? asks Kev, expecting the answer guess. Nor was the noer long disappointed for easiest of kisshams, he was made vicewise.") McHugh gives the Norwegian *nei* for "no" and translates "suspecting the answer know" as "expecting negative response" and "Oikkont, ken you" as "I can't, can you?" He reads "easiest of kisshams" as the phrase "easy as kissing hands." Naturally, you are free to read these in any way you want.

nollcromforemost *FW* 362.5 *n*. One who does not accept the conduct or worship of an established social group or church or a nonconformist in the manner of Oliver Cromwell. With "Old Nol" as one nickname of the English reformer Oliver Cromwell, we have a Nonconformist with a capital "N," that is a Protestant who is not a member of the Church of England. The civil war that this foremost Nonconformist Cromwell fought as the leading general cost Charles I his head and England and Ireland many deaths and much damage to priceless religious buildings and art objects. Cromwell's actions against Irish Catholics were "Prepatrickulary" harsh and have been characterized as near if not genocidal. ("till his repepulation, upon old nollcromforemost ironsides, as camnabel chieftain") "Old Ironsides" was another of Cromwell's nicknames. McHugh points out Cain and Abel in "camnabel," as well as a cannibal.

nomomorphemy *FW* 599.18-19 *n*. ("Nomomorphemy for me!") A morpheme is the smallest unit of language that still retains meaning. Finn Fordham writes that "Joyce has been turning these units—affixes, prefixes, suffixes, and infixes—and morphing them into new words, displaying a 'nomomorphology'—a concern with laws ('nomo') of the units of language." Fordham compares Joyce's language game to an addiction such as morphine, reading this sentence as "No more morphemy for me!" Conversely, and still in keeping with an addiction, he also reads it as "No! More, more for me, for me!" "The game and the addiction—the addictive game of addition—continue," Fordham believes, "in the etymological unravelling that readers engage in." The Wakean language known as Wakese becomes an addiction from which the *Wake*'s addicts seek no cure.

nonsolance *FW* 562.32 *n*. A combination of insolence, nonchalance, and nonsense or a boldly rude indifference to foolishness. In *Finnegans Wake* it is applied to Jonathan Swift, Dean of St. Patrick's Cathedral in Dublin, referring to him as "That keen dean with his veen nonsolance!"

nonthings *FW* 598.1 *n*. A nonentity that is even more not a thing than a nothing. The use of the prefix "non" heightens the nothingness. On the other hand, this may be a double negative with non nothings being something. ("Every those personal place objects ifnonthings where soevers and they just done been doing being in a dromo of todos withouten a bound to be your trowers.") There is the old schoolroom definition of a noun as "a person, place, or thing" here and McHugh gives the Greek *dromos* for "race" and reads "dromo of todos" as "drama of today."

nopussy   *FW* 28.10   *n.* Censored but self-explanatory. ("It's an allavalonche that blows nopussy food.") McHugh translates this as the phrase "It's an ill wind that blows nobody good." Of course we know better—wink wink, nudge nudge.

Norewheezian   *FW* 67.13   *n.* A Norwegian who breathes hard with a whistling noise or a wheeze. Asthmatic-like breathing may result from the intense cold of a Norwegian winter. ("swore like a Norewheezian tailliur on the stand before the proper functionary") McHugh gives the Irish *ta'illiu'r* for "tailor." The context here is to the story of the Captain and the Norwegian tailor that Joyce heard from his father and worked into the *Wake* in various, multiple ways. (See **ashaped**.)

noughttime   *FW* 349.6   *n.* None, zero, or nought time when it is dark or at night time. In the world of the subconsciousness of sleep, time no longer exists or, in dreams, becomes an extremely flexible commodity where different historical people and events can occur together, effectively making time disappear or, as the *Wake* puts it, "Yet is no body present here which was not there before. Only is order othered. Nought is nulled." Events and people from all places and periods of the world's history merge in the dream world of *Finnegans Wake*, one of several reasons it is so difficult to read and assimilate. ("*In the heliotropical noughttime following a fade of transformed Tuff and pending its viseversion, a metenergic reglow of beaming Batt*")

noughty   *FW* 261.24, 284.11, & 597.15   *adj.* Not disobedient or having nothing or nought in the way of bad or naughty behavior. While the implication is that a person's conduct is not bad or naughty, it does not follow that it is necessarily good, either, more on the borderline between good and bad with a little leaning toward the naughty side. ("Ainsoph, this upright one, with that noughty besiged him zeroine," "may be involted into the zeroic couplet, palls pell inhis heventh glike noughty times ∞," & "it is the alcovan and the rosegarden, boony noughty, all puraputhry") McHugh reads "palls pell inhis heventh glike" as "God's in his heaven, All's right...," and gives the Italian *buona notte* for "goodnight" as a reference for "boony noughty."

novembrance *FW* 226.32-33 *n*. 1. Recollection or remembrance of the month following October or November. For the English, Guy Fawkes' ("Gaoy Fecks") thwarted attempt to blow up Parliament on November 5, 1605 is a strong "novembrance" and is best remembered with a popular rhyme:

> Remember, remember the fifth of November,
> The gunpowder, treason and plot,
> I know of no reason
> Why gunpowder treason
> Should ever be forgot.

There's a "novembrance" of the plot on *FW* 87.4 with "remember the filth of November" and on *FW* 205.28 Guy Fawkes is mocked with "cammocking his guy." (See **funpowtherplother**.) 2. McHugh gives: "*Hamlet* IV.5.174: 'rosemary, that's for remembrance' (purple flower, in bloom in November)." This reference is obviously most in line with the *Wake*'s "waters the fleurettes of novembrance," but the connection with Guy Fawkes Day is my personal remembrance preference.

novicer *FW* 322.4 *n*. A beginner or novice commander or officer. ("his top gallant shouldier so was, lao yiu shao, he's like more look a novicer on the nevay") (See **nevay**.) McHugh identifies "top gallant" as "top-gallant flag on mizzen mast" and, in Chinese, *lao* for "old" or "senior," *yü* for "compared with, together with," and *shao* for "junior." So this may now read as a brave or gallant senior soldier who, compared with a junior, looks more like a beginning officer in the navy. This is a prime example of why it's crazy to try and do a literal translation of *Finnegans Wake*. It must be read in relation to the context of each passage and its referents throughout the book as well as to the personal associations it engenders.

nubtials *FW* 324.36 – 325.1 *n.* With McHugh's reference of "nub" as slang for "copulation," a wedding ceremony or nuptials with sexual intercourse. The sex may follow the couple's ritual kiss or replace it entirely. Nuptials would suddenly become rather tame and boring in comparison. Joyce and Nora skipped the nuptials when they "eloped" to Italy in 1904, but the birth there of their son and daughter is tangible proof that they didn't skip the sex. ("Birdflights confirm abbroaching nubtials.") McHugh also notes that "Birdflights" relates to "divination by flight of birds."

nuder *FW* 268.18 & 493.19 *adj.* Neither masculine nor feminine but neuter when without clothes or nude. Only clothes give a male or female appearance to someone who, when nude, is clearly seen to be neither one nor the other but neuter. The exact opposite of one who is "nuder" is a hermaphrodite who also requires nudity to reveal this special feature of the physique. ("From gramma's grammar she has it that if there is a third person, mascarine, phelinine or nuder, being spoken abad it moods prosodes from a person speaking to her second" & "And there is nihil nuder under the clothing moon.") *Nihil* is Latin for "nothing," and McHugh reads this as both the Bible's "there is no new thing under the sun" and Shakespeare's *Antony and Cleopatra*'s "there is nothing left remarkable Beneath the visiting moon."

O

occidentally *FW* 589.22 *adv.* Unexpectedly or accidentally happening to be Western or Occidental. Columbus sailed west in confident expectation of reaching the East but "occidentally" ended up in the Americas. The *Wake* takes a turn west with: "Then ('twas in fenland) occidentally of a sudden, six junelooking flamefaces straggled wild out of their turns." If "fenland" is Finland, then it is certainly Occidental.

odable *FW* 53.4 *adj.* Able to be both heard or audible and smelled or odorous. ("this mimage of the seventyseventh kusin of kristansen is odable to os across the wineless Ere no oedor nor mere eerie nor liss potent of suggestion than in the tales of the tingmount") Homer's oft-repeated "wine dark sea" is worked into "wineless," while its companion, the "rosy-fingered dawn" that is always over the sea, fails to make an appearance here. Perhaps I failed to spot it somewhere else.

oddmitted *FW* 222.15 *v.* 1. Left out or omitted from being strange, unusual, or odd. The saying "odd man out" comes to mind. adj. 2. By general consent or admittedly strange, unusual, or odd. *Finnegans Wake* has certainly suffered being "oddmitted" from lists of great books because of its "oddmitted" difficulties, obscurities, and oddities. ("the portions understood to be oddmitted as the results of the respective titulars neglecting to produce themselves")

o'gong *FW* 26.27 *n.* Of or by a piece of metal shaped like a saucer that makes a bell-like noise when struck or a gong used to tell the hour, such as six "o'gong" is six o'clock. Just as both hands of a clock pointing straight up signal twelve o'clock, twelve strikes of a gong signals the same. In English country homes, the butler would signal the time to dress for dinner with the use of a gong. ("The horn for breakfast, one o'gong for lunch and dinnerchime.") As this indicates, a chime can be used in place of a gong to announce dinnertime.

onanymous *FW* 435.31 *adj.* By or from someone who remains nameless or anonymous concerning uncompleted sexual intercourse, masturbation, or onanism. In the Wakean context of "onanymous letters," it is understandable, given the subject matter, that the letters are left unsigned. ("Secret satieties and onanymous letters make the great unwatched as bad as their betters.") The suggestion of sexual satiety within these secret societies provides another cause to keep the letters anonymous. The suggestion is that the "great unwatched" or the great unwashed of the proletariat may be just as promiscuous or bad, sexually speaking, as their betters in the upper classes.

optimominous *FW* 613.28-29 *adj.* Hoping for the best or optimistic about what is unfavorable, threatening, or ominous. A wonderful word to describe the typical human outlook on life. ("The folgor of the frightfools is olympically optimominous") McHugh gives the Italian *folgore* for "thunderbolt" and reads "frightfools" as "frightful." Joyce was famously among the "frightfools" when it came to thunder and was far from seeing it in an optimistic light. (See **ivanmorinthorrumble** & **thonthorstrok**.)

ouraganisations *FW* 86.21 *n.* A group united for some purpose or an organization of large anthropoid apes or orangutans. Some human organizations somewhat resemble "ouraganisations," especially at this writing the American Republican Party. ("The gathering, convened by the Irish Angricultural and Prepostoral Ouraganisations to help the Irish muck to look his brother dane in the face") McHugh references "The Irish Agricultural Organisation Society founded by Sir Horace Plunkett" to deal with Denmark's competition with the Irish bacon industry. (See **angricultural** & **prepostoral**.) The fact that that political cartoons in American newpapers once portrayed Irish immigrants as monkeys, illustrating the severe discrimination to which they were subjected, may play a part here. Our papers only did what the English had been doing for years. In *Stephen Hero*, Joyce's abandoned precursor to *A Portrait of the Artist as a Young Man*, Stephen's friend Madden says, "You are simply giving vent to old stale libels—the drunken Irishman, the baboon-faced Irishman that we see in *Punch*."

outhue *FW* 182.8 *v.* Surpass or outdo regarding the varieties of a color or its hue. Ireland's forty shades of green undoubtedly "outhue" the colors of any other country. ("to ensign the colours by the beerlitz in his mathness and his educandees to outhue to themselves in the cries of girlglee: gember! inkware! chonchambre! cinsero! zinnzabar!") McHugh identifies these last five words as Dutch, German, Latin, French, and Italian for "ginger." Redheads are sometimes nicknamed "Ginger" for the reddish hue of their hair. Did you hear the "hue and cry" here?

outlex *FW* 169.3 *n.* Away, forth, or out from the law (Latin *lex* for law) and/or from the word (Greek *lexis* for word). *Finnegans Wake* employs an outlaw language that breaks the accepted rules of writing and vocabulary, creating a unique work outside the known literary boundaries. It's the "outlex" aspect of the *Wake* that makes it at once so difficult and delightful. ("he was an outlex between the lines") To really read it requires not only looking between the lines but often between the words and even the letters. When one of Joyce's friends remarked that *Finnegans Wake* was outside literature, Joyce agreed, "Yes, but it's future is inside literature." Joyce was too modest to say so, but the truth is that all literature is inside *Finnegans Wake*.

outlusts *FW* 444.25 *v.* 1. To outlast or last longer than excessive sexual desire or lust, which is quite a long time, as lust, it seems, lasts a lifetime. 2. To outdo or to lust to a greater degree. Whether Warren Beatty has outlusted Errol Flynn is open to conjecture, but we all have lusts in our hearts that we don't care to let out like Jimmy Carter did for a *Playboy* interview. ("The pleasures of love lasts but a fleeting but the pledges of life outlusts a lifetime.")

outragedy *FW* 425.24 *n.* Great offense or outrage combined with a sad or terrible happening or tragedy. Most critics found *Finnegans Wake* an outrageous work and considered it a terrible tragedy that Joyce wasted his genius during the 17 years of its composition. ("Outragedy of poetscalds! Acomedy of letters!") It's important to recall that Joyce referred to the *Wake* as "my nocturnal comedy" and always insisted, "It's meant to make you laugh." Joyce is calling his book not only a comedy of letters but, with a reference to Shakespeare's play, *The Comedy of Errors*, may also be acknowledging the critics' view that his last book was an error.

overgoat *FW* 35.13 *n.* An outer coat worn over regular clothes in cold weather or an overcoat that is made of the skin of a horned, bearded mammal related to sheep or a goat. The most infamous "overgoat" of all was the crude one Jacob wore to deceive his father, Isaac, into believing that he, Jacob, was actually his older twin, Esau, who was a hairy man. The deception succeeded and Isaac gave his blessing and entire inheritance to the wrong boy. In all fairness to Jacob, Esau shortly before had stupidly traded his birthright to Jacob for a pot of pea soup. (See **Eatsoup**,

lentling, & peacisely.) ("carryin his overgoat under his schulder, sheepside out, so as to look more like a coumfry gentleman") The person wearing the "overgoat" in his instance is "the cad with a pipe" who accosts HCE in Phoenix Park one fateful evening asking for the time. With the German *Schuld* for "guilt," there is the hint of a scapegoat here. If the "cad with a pipe" is the real guilty party (See **contrawatchwise** & **saddenly**.), then HCE is the scapegoat and ALP's "litter" defending him is valid. (See **mamafesta**.)

overlasting *FW* 499.2 *adj*. Everlasting with a special emphasis on its lasting much too long, that is, lasting over the time that something should, such as Sunday sermons. Too much of a good thing, Mae West to the contrary, is not always wonderful, as Dorian Gray found that life everlasting was really "overlasting" and required desperate measures to terminate it. ("as it turned up, after his life overlasting, at thus being reduced to nothing") Christians repeat the Apostles' Creed, affirming they believe in life everlasting, without wondering if it might turn out to be "overlasting."

overstand *FW* 444.30 *v*. To get the meaning of or understand over and above the normal understanding from a position of higher knowledge, experience, or insight. A medical specialist will no doubt "overstand" the intricacies of a disease merely "understood" by a general practitioner. This word may also refer to "topsawyer's" on the *Wake*'s first page, a reference not only to Mark Twain's Tom Sawyer but to the practice of using a pit to saw logs, in which the top sawyer is the favored position because the sawyer in the pit gets covered in sawdust. Joyce's father, John Joyce, the main model for HCE, is described in *Finnegans Wake* as "always bottom sawyer," the way his son Stanislaus once described him. In this sense, "overstand" can mean a position of power or privilege over others. ("I overstand you, you understand.")

owlwise *FW* 78.30 *adv*. At all times or always as learned or wise as an owl. Other than our "owlwise" politicians, most of us admit to an erudite error every now and then. As Rabbit remarked about Winnie-the-Pooh's scholarly friend Owl, "you can't help respecting anybody who can spell TUESDAY, even if he doesn't spell it right; but spelling isn't everything." (For a view contrary to Rabbit's, see **erronymously**.) Since even Microsoft Word's spellchecker throws up its figurative hands over some of my desperate grasps for the correct letters in their correct order, I freely admit to being anything other than an "owlwise" speller. ("on the purely doffensive since the eternals were owlwise on their side every time")

P

pacnincstricken *FW* 599.28 *adj*. A sudden, unreasoning fear or panic-stricken during an outdoor meal or while on a picnic. Vladimir Nabokov's line from *Lolita* is the most concise example that comes to mind: "My very photogenic mother died in a freak accident (picnic, lightning) when I was three." ("eminently adapted for the requirements of pacnincstricken humanity.") In his novel *Larva*, that is filled with Joycean wordplay, Julián Ríos creates the wonderful word "pignic" that suggests "pigging out" or stuffing yourself at a picnic.

painapple *FW* 167.15 & 246.29 *n*. 1. An apple that causes suffering or pain. The most famous example is the one *Finnegans Wake* references as the "forebitten" apple "eaden" by Eve and Adam in the Garden of Eatin'. This so-called original sin resulted not only in pain for the first couple (childbirth, work, death, etc.) but for all of humanity for centuries afterwards. 2. Pineapple is also suggested here in two ways—the fruit that's sharp spikes can certainly cause pain if not carefully handled and as slang for a bomb. ("blesphorous idiot who kennot tail a bomb from a painapple when he steals one" & "Adam Leftus and the devil took our hindmost, gegifting her with his painapple") The first

216 | A *Finnegans Wake* Lextionary

quote basically reads as a blasphemous idiot who cannot tell a bomb from a pineapple (bomb) when he sees one. McHugh explains that "Adam Leftus" in the second quote refers to Adam Loftus who "suggested the establishment of Trinity College, Dublin." Then there's the phrase "devil take the hindmost." in "the devil took our hindmost" and the German *vergiften* for "to poison" suggested by "gegifting." McHugh finds in "painapple" "Adam's apple," and "cain-apple: fruit of strawberry-tree" and mentions that according to Kabbalists, Cain was the offspring of Satan and Eve.

paraidiotically *FW* 615.5-6 *adv.* 1. With "para" meaning "that which protects from," as in parasol, here the protection is from those extremely deficient in intelligence or idiots. If only Congress could be so protected. 2. With "para" meaning "parallel with" or "related to," the relationship is to an idiot, something we have all experienced within a family, in the work place, or at one time or another. ("anastomosically assimilated and preteridentified paraidiotically") For the other words in this phrase, McHugh gives "anastomosis: connection of 2 vessels, esp. blood vessels, by a cross branch," the Latin *praeter* for "previously," and the Greek (artif.) *paraidiôtikos* for "almost privately."

patrified *FW* 87.11 *v.* Paralyzed with fear or petrified of Saint Patrick. A prime example is Mileac, Patrick's owner during his years as a slave in Ireland. Patrick had, with God's blessing, escaped his slavery, studied for the priesthood, and returned to convert the Irish to Christianity. The first thing he wanted to do was meet his old master and repay him in gold for what he had lost when his slave ran away. Hearing that Patrick was approaching his home and, fearing the worst, the "patrified" Mileac barricaded himself in his great hall with his most valuable possessions and put it all to the torch, himself included. According to legend, the snakes of Ireland were so "patrified" they all slithered into the sea, though the truth is Ireland had not had snakes since the last Ice Age. ("the striking thing about it was that he was patrified to see, hear, taste and smell, as his time of night") (See **thuartpeatrick**.)

peacisely *FW* 89.4 *adv*. Exactly or precisely small or the size of a pea. ("And both as like as a duel of lentils? Peacisely.") This reference is to the Biblical story in which Esau sells his birthright to his younger twin brother Jacob for a pottage of lentils or a pot of pea soup. The first of the *Wake*'s many references to Jacob and Esau is found on the first page with: "venissoon after, had a kidscad buttended a bland old Isaac." After buying his brother's birthright for the very small sum of some peas, Jacob then had to pretend to be Esau by wrapping himself in some hairy skins and taking his father, blind old Isaac, some cooked venison or meat from a kid or young goat, thereby butting his brother out of the rightful line of inheritance. You no doubt heard the old phrase "like two peas in a pod," though Jacob and Esau, like Shem and Shaun, were as different as night and day.

peatrick's *FW* 361.3-4 *n*. (See **prepatrickularly**.)

peeptomine *FW* 361.1 *n*. A play in which gestures replace words or a pantomime that one gets only a furtive look or peep at, perhaps through a small hole or peephole. Someone without the price of admission might find a secret way to get a peep at the performance. Pantomimes were popular in Dublin's theaters and as a child Joyce saw a number of them. The "Mime of Mick, Nick, and the Maggies" is only one way in which pantomimes appear in *Finnegans Wake*. In her book *Joyce's Anatomy of Culture*, Cheryl Herr mentions "the playfully reflexive use of outrageous puns" used to describe pantomime characters ("two characters from the Gaiety's *Ali Baba and the Forty Thieves* [26 December 1890] are described on the programme as 'Two young Gentlemen from across the seas—Who seize everything they sees.'") and believes that these "verbal devices no doubt appealed to Joyce and influenced the verbal comedy of *Ulysses* and *Finnegans Wake*." ("let harleqwind play peeptomine up all our colombbinations") Here we also find the popular pantomime characters Halequin and his sweetheart Columbine.

peequuliar *FW* 606.30 *n.* Strange, unusual, or peculiar urine or pee. Definitely a sign to visit a urologist. Critics of *Finnegans Wake* might have used "peequuliar" to describe this most peculiar of books, if they had ever read far enough to find this particular word. A micturition motif flows through the *Wake*, the stream having started with Molly Bloom on her chamber pot in her closing soliloquy of *Ulysses*. ("Panniquanne starts showing of her peequuliar talonts") McHugh gives as a reference here the P/Q split—"a type of consonant split in Celtic languages."

peerfectly *FW* 527.26 *adv.* A man belonging to the British nobility or a peer (See **peersons**.) who is absolutely faultless or perfect. As a boy, Joyce was a great admirer of Lord Byron's poetry and was even beaten by some of his school chums for claiming that Byron was the greatest poet. Joyce's schoolmates were more concerned with his lordship's moral character than his verses. But Byron's last mistress, Countess Guiccioli, sets the record straight in her memoir, *My Recollections of Lord Byron; and Those of Eye-Witnesses of His Life*, in which she describes her lover as "the perfect peer." Lady Byron chose not to put her views in print, except second hand through her manipulative influence on Harriet Beecher Stowe's *Lady Byron Vindicated*, in which Byron was portrayed impeerfectly. ("Of course it was downright verry wickred of him, reely meeting me disguised, Bortolo mio, peerfectly appealling") The reference here is to a disguised Tristram's clandestine rendezvous in the castle garden with his lover, Iseult, who is technically his aunt as she is the wife of his uncle King Mark II of Cornwall. McHugh identifies Bartolo as the old man in *The Barber Of Seville* and the song as "O Sole Mio." As an example of just how far one's thoughts can wander with the *Wake*'s words, I wonder if Joyce's spelling of *really* as "reely" is meant to suggest the reel, a lively dance, given his description of the young couple's lively and erotic dance of love on the ship bringing Iseult from Ireland to Cornwall.

peersons *FW* 60.25 *n.* 1. A human being or person who looks closely at something or peers. Readers attempting to understand *Finnegans Wake* must by necessity become "peersons," as the complexity of the work requires close scrutiny and study. Many characters in the *Wake* spend some time peering, in the sense of peeping, into the private details of others lives. The four old men are "peersons" who with "their pair of green eyes and peering in" "through the steamy windows, into the honeymoon cabins" watch Tristram and Iseult's lovemaking (I coined the word "voyeugers" to describe them.) as Tristram "with one aragan throust, druve the massive of virilvigtoury flshpst the both lines forwards (Eburnea's down, boys!) rightjingbangshot into the goal of her gullet." There are also a number of "peersons" involved in HCE's evening activities in Phoenix Park, and this is the context here, but who and what is peered at is less clear than the straightforward sex of the couple above. There is no question, though, that *Finnegans Wake* is something of a peeping tome. 2. Noblemen, especially British, bearing the title of duke, marquis, earl, viscount, or baron, or persons of the peerage, peers of the realm. 3. Someone equal to another. In our judicial system, defendants in court are to be tried by a jury of their peers or "peersons." ("concerning the coincident of interfizzing with grenadines and other respectable and disgusted peersons using the park")

pelagiarist *FW* 182.3 & 525.7 *n.* One who represents as his/her own the writing of another or a plagiarist, with a reference to Pelagian, an ascetic Christian monk of the late Roman Empire who was also a heretic and possibly Irish. He denied original sin and was condemned by the church. While Joyce does not deny original sin in *Finnegans Wake*, he does ascribe it to God for having created the world. ("piously forged palimpsests shipped in the first place by this morbid process from his pelagiarist pen" & "Tallhell and Barbados wi ye and your Errian coprulation!

220 | A *Finnegans Wake* Lextionary

Palegiarist!") In the first quote, "piously" relates to Pelagian as a religious man and, in the second quote, McHugh mentions that Cromwell deported many Irish to Barbados.

penisills *FW* 566.9 *n.* Male organs of copulation or penises and graphite enclosed in wood used for writing or pencils combined, having similar shapes and both being possible instruments of creation. The old saying "that will put lead in your pencil" comes to mind along with the Wakean connections of the Wellington Monument in Phoenix Park. Known to Dubliners as the "overgrown milestone," it appears in *Finnegans Wake* as the "overgrown leadpencil." There's also a humorous comment about "burstall boys with their underhand leadpencils climbing to her crotch for the origin of spices." ("all balaaming in their selladoutes and sharping up their penisills") If "sellaboutes" refers to celibate, it could also suggest the selling of celibacy." (See **celibrate**.)

penproduct *FW* 108.31 *n.* That which is produced through the use of a writing instrument or pen. The famous "penproduct" in *Finnegans Wake* is the "litter" from Boston that the hen pecks out of the dump. (See **anomorous** & **middenst**.) The "penproduct" produced by Pigott that attempts to implicate Parnell in the Phoenix Park murders but fails from the misspelling of hesitancy is another example. (See **Anoymay's** & **hazeydency**.) In the secret language of the revolutionary Irish Fenians, "pen" meant "revolver," so a "penproduct" might also be an injured or dead body. And one of the readings of the first page's "penisolate" is the isolated war fought with a pen, that is Joyce's struggle to produce *Finnegans Wake* despite all the critics calling for him to quit. (See **inkbattle**.) Pen refers not only to what is written but how it's written, making the *Wake*, through its subject and style, the most original of "penproducts." ("its page cannot ever have been a penproduct of a man or woman of that period or those parts")

penultimatum *FW* 424.26 *n.* The next to the last or the penultimate final terms or ultimatum. ("Peax! Peax! Shaun replied in vealar penultimatum.") I hear the Latin *pax* for "peace" here combined with "peat" that is so prominent in Ireland, though how they fit together is a puzzle, unless it's connected to St. Patrick's Irish mission. (See **Prepatrickulary**.)

perhelps *FW* 238.19 *adv.* Maybe or perhaps willing to assist or help. ("You don't want to peach but bejimboed if ye do! Perhelps. We ernst too may.") Playing off the song lyrics, "We Don't Want to Fight, but, by Jingo, If We Do," we find the advice Stephen's father gave him when he went off to school in *Portrait* at the age of half past six: don't peach or tell on other students. Joyce's father had given him the same advice and here the exclamation "By jingo!" becomes "bejimboed," containing Jim Joyce's name along with the militaristic policy of jingoism. McHugh notes that the "Buddha did not wish to preach the law but was persuaded by Brahma" and gives the German *wie ernst* for "how seriously."

perlection *FW* 94.10 *n.* Faultlessness or perfection combined with the Latin *perlectio* for "a reading through" to give the reading of a text to complete perfection. Joyce's recorded reading from the *Wake*'s Anna Livia Plurabelle chapter is an example of "perlection." That Joyce did not read it word for word but improved his writing through improvisation only adds to a performance of "perlection." ("The old hunks on the hill read it to perlection.")

persins *FW* 48.16 *n.* Human beings or persons who have broken the law of God or sinned. Since this includes everyone since the original sin of Eve and Adam, "persins" should probably replace "persons" so as not to be "confused" before entering the "confusional." McHugh gives the Italian *persi* for "lost," which could imply that "persins" are lost in sin without confession and repentance. "Of the persins sin this Eyrawyggla saga (which, thorough readable to int from and, is from tubb to buttom all falsetissues" suggests that the supposed sin of the person HCE in Phoenix Park is, from top to bottom, a false issue. For "Eyrawyggla saga," McHugh references "*Eyrbyggia saga*: one of the great Icelandic sagas." It's also an Earwicker saga.

phaked *FW* 264.19 *adj.* An uncovered or naked penis or phallus. ("phaked of philim pholk, bowed and sould for a four of hundreds of manhood") McHugh sees "faked," "film folk," and "bought & sold" here. Mainstream movies are moving more and more to full-frontal male nudity, though the sex scenes are still simulated or faked, and a faked phallus is sometimes used to augment a male actor's natural endowment.

phall *FW* 4.15 *v.* A special term for the quick descent from an erect position or the fall of the penis or phallus. As science teaches us, everything that goes up must come down, even if the descent is delayed by Viagra. ("Phall if you but will, rise you must") McHugh references "Macpherson: *Fingal* II.52: 'If fall I must, my tomb shall rise.'" and sees "will . . . must" as "indeterminism (free will) v. determinism (necessity)."

pharahead *FW* 292.19 *adv.* 1. Seen before or far ahead by means of a strong and powerful light. *Pharos* is Greek for "lighthouse," something ships can see at a great distance. *adj.* 2. Blond, light, or fair-haired and thus in an advantageous position for advancement as the fair-haired boy. ("search lighting, beached, bashed and beaushelled *à la Mer* pharahead into faturity") McHugh translates these last three words as "far ahead into futurity." (See **faturity**.)

pigstickularly *FW* 87.9 *adv.* Unusually or particularly in the manner of a pig stuck by a sharp stick. Anything that is characterized by loud squeals, such as a group of teenage girls attending a concert given by the latest rock heartthrob. ("one thing which would pigstickularly strike a person of such sorely tried observational powers") The young boys in William Golding's *Lord of* *the Flies* can be said to have particularly or "pigstickularly" sharp skills at sticking pigs with sticks.

pigtorial   *FW* 584.36   *adj.* Pigs illustrated in pictures or a pig pictorial. The children's story of *The Three Little Pigs* is usually presented in a combined print and pictorial format. ("begging your honour's pardon for, well, exclusive pigtorial rights of herehear fond tiplady his weekreations, appearing in next eon's issue") With books like *The Three Little Pigs* or *Charlotte's Web*, film studios can be said to have acquired the "pigtorial rights" to them. *Porky's* and its sequels are "pigtorial" films of a different nature and are aimed at a more "mature" audience.

pillgrimace   *FW* 423.8   *n.* A journey to a holy place as a religious act or pilgrimage, such as that made by the pilgrims in Chaucer's *The Canterbury Tales*, but made under compulsion or duress, thus causing a twisting of the face in a grimace. ("making his pillgrimace of Childe Horrid") Lord Byron's *Childe Harold's Pilgrimage*, the first canto of which caused him to remark—"I awoke one morning to find myself famous."—comes into play here. There may also be the suggestion that the pilgrimage through life is a bitter pill that causes a grimace when swallowed.

platoonic   *FW* 348.8   *adj.* An ideal, spiritual, nonsexual or platonic love for a small military unit led by a lieutenant or a platoon. Battles are often won or lost based on the degree of camaraderie and "platoonic" feelings soldiers have for their comrades in their platoon. ("I now with platoonic leave recoil in (how the thickens they come back to one to rust!)") You no doubt noticed that "recoil" serves for both "recall" and the "recoil" of a rifle, which fits the platoon motif, and that "leave" can be both "love" and a military "leave of absence." McHugh reads "the thickens they come back to one to rust!" as "chickens that come home to roost."

popetithes   *FW* 326.6   *v.* Baptize—a Christian sacrament in which a person is dipped into or sprinkled with water as a sign of washing away the sins of the world and being born again. Joyce combined pope, the title of the head of the Roman Catholic Church, and tithes, the giving of one tenth of one's income for the support of the church. In the *Wake* it is used in "I popethithes thee" meaning I baptize thee. The use of tithes suggests a monetary cost for baptism and, since Joyce mounted a production of Oscar Wile's play, *The Importance of Being Earnest*, in Zurich during the First World War, he may have been thinking of the scene in which Jack Worthing asks Lady Bracknell if he had been christened as a baby (given a name during baptism). She replies, "Every luxury that money could buy, including christening, had been lavished on you by your fond and doting parents.' Other Waken terms for baptism include "dipdip" and "tauftauf" with the German *taufen* meaning "baptize." (See **thuartpeatrick** for "tauftauf.")

poseproem *FW* 528.16 *n.* 1. With "proem" meaning an introductory invitation or preface, a "poseproem" is a preface to a work written in ordinary language or prose that has a poetic touch, giving it an extra, artistic quality or a prose-poem. *v.* 2. Pretending or posing as a preface or proem. Due to its poetical/musical qualities, the opening of Part I, Chapter 8 is an excellent example of a "poseproem," the one part Joyce chose to read for a recording. An essay by Victor Llona in the Joyce-encouraged *Our Exagmination Round His Factification for Incamination of Work in Progress* is titled "I Don't Know What To Call It, But Its Mighty Unlike Prose." ("Hear we here her first poseproem of suora unto suora?")

pranksome *FW* 508.28 *adj.* Causing tricks or pranks. ("Peequeen ourselves, the prettiest pickles of unmatchemable mute antes I ever bopeeped at, seesaw shallshee, since the town go went gonning on Pranksome Quaine.") (See **whyre** for the story of the "Pranksome" Prankquean.) There are two nursery rhymes playing pranks here, "Little Bo Peep" and "She sells seashells by the seashore."

praverbs *FW* 242.12 *n.* With the Latin *prava* for "depraved" or "crooked," "praverbs," unlike wise maxims or proverbs such as are found in the Biblical book of *Proverbs*, are wicked or perverted proverbs meant to mislead rather than to enlighten readers. Oscar Wilde's *Phrases and Philosophies for the Use of the Young* contains many wonderful "praverbs"—"Wickedness is a myth invented by good people to account for the curious attractiveness of others;" "Religions die when they are proved to be true. Science is the record of dead religions;" and "Dullness is the coming of age of seriousness" are but three examples." ("crime ministers preaching him mornings and makes a power of spoon vittles out of his praverbs") Joyce makes a sharp, political point by referring to prime ministers as "crime ministers," although we all know that politicians are just here to serve us citizens. At least that's what they keep telling us.

preadaminant *FW* 617.23-24 *adj.* Superior or predominant by predating Adam. There is a word, preadamite, found in everyday dictionaries that names a believer in the existence of a race that predated Adam. In *The Devil's Dictionary*, Ambrose Bierce writes of preadamite: "Little is known of them beyond the fact that they supplied Cain with a wife and theologians with a controversy." ("Femelles will be preadaminant as from twentyeight to twelve.") If females did appear before Adam, this may explain why Joyce placed Eve in the "preadaminant" position on the first page of *Finnegans Wake*— "riverrun, past Eve and Adam's."

preausteric *FW* 266.R1 *adj.* Before conditions were severe or austere, which can only apply to the Garden of Eden, but before recorded history or prehistoric is also suggested. If Adam and Eve were indeed the first humans, and since their story is recorded in the book of Genesis, there can properly have been no prehistoric time. And since life in the Garden of Eden was far from austere, "preausteric" must apply to the period of time before the first couple were expelled to the east of Eden. ("PREAUSTERIC MAN AND HIS PURSUIT OF PANHYSTERIC

WOMAN.") McHugh gives the Greek *panhysterikos* for "all-womb-suffering," childbirth pain being one of the consequences of eating that damn apple in "preausteric" times.

precondamned *FW* 418.30 *v.* To at once denounce or condemn and curse or damn in advance or beforehand. The addition of swearing with condemnation makes for a stronger statement of disapproval. ("*We are Wastenot with Want, precondamned, two and true*") In *Finnegans Wake*, the original sin is God's creation of the world, but in the Bible it's Adam and Eve's eating of the fruit from the Tree of the Knowledge of Good and Evil, an act against God's strict instruction that "precondamned" all of humanity from that time forward. I suppose it could be said that God damned us and, since he supposedly knows everything that is going to happen, he "precondamned" us knowing in advance what would result from the temptation he placed before Eve and Adam. As Oscar Wilde so epigrammatically put it, "I can resist everything except temptation." The proverb "Waste not, want not" also appears here.

prediseased *FW* 423.27 *v.* To die before or predecease as a result of an illness or a disease. George, Joyce's younger brother, "prediseased" him when he died of typhoid fever at the age of 14. ("He was down with the whooping laugh at the age of the loss of reason the whopping first time he prediseased me.") McHugh references "The Age of Reason: time of Pope, C18" and "age of the use of reason: for Catholics, the age at which a child is capable of committing sin."

prepatrickularly *FW* 316.5 *adv.* Especially or particularly to a great degree like Patrick. As a *Wake* word, this refers "prepatrickulary" to St. Patrick, patron saint of Ireland, who is all over *Finnegans Wake*, beginning on the first page in the pun "thuartpeatrick." (Jesus said to Saint Peter, "Thou art Peter, and upon this rock I will build my Church.") "Peter" came from the Greek *Petros* meaning "rock," thus Jesus' pun and evidence that he had a sense of humor. (See **thuartpeatrick**.) Since Ireland is composed to a large extent of peat, which, when cut into bricks and dried on ricks, is used for fuel ("peatrefired"), Patrick's or "peatrick's" church is particularly built on peat rather than rock. "Prepatrickulary," or particularly before Patrick, the Irish were of the druidic persuasion. ("Prepatrickularly all, they summed. Kish met. Bound to.") McHugh gives the Norwegian *summe* for "collect oneself." For "Kish" he references "kismet (= bound to happen)" and "Kish lightship off Dublin."

prepostoral *FW* 86.21 *adj.* A senseless or preposterous view of the natural beauty of country life or the pastoral. Marie Antoinette's mock village adjacent to her small, personal palace, Petit Trinon, where she and her ladies-in-waiting dressed as shepherdesses, while undoubtedly eating cake, comes immediately to mind as a "prepostoral" playground. ("The gathering, convened by the Irish Angricultural and Prepostoral Ouraganisations, to help the Irish muck to look his brother dane in the face") McHugh references the "competition from Denmark as obstacle to Ir. Bacon industry." He also relates "muck," moist farmyard manure, to the Irish *muc* for "pig." (See **angricultural**.)

pressantly *FW* 295.29 *adv.* At this time or presently pleasing or pleasant, giving pleasantly present. The temperature of the Earth is "pressantly" for humans, but the greenhouse effect could make the future unpleasant for them as well as many other creatures. ("Now, as will pressantly be felt, there's tew tricklesome poinds") The French *pressant* for "urgent" adds a note of warning about the Earth's warming.

pridejealice *FW* 344.32-33 *n.* A bias or prejudice stemming from both conceit or pride and enviousness or jealousy. I believe "pridejealice" would make a perfect title for a sequel to Jane Austen's novel *Pride and Prejudice*. ("I confess withould pridejealice")

228 | A *Finnegans Wake* Lextionary

probapossible *FW* 262.R1 *adj*. Likely to happen or be true or probably and what can be done or be true or possible, that is what is probably possible or possibly probable. A qualification or, in other words, hedging your bet or giving no guarantee. ("PROBAPOSSIBLE PROLEGOMENA TO IDEAREAL HISTORY.") In *FW* 110.11-12 is found "where the possible was the improbable and the improbable was the inevitable," that McHugh identifies with Aristotle's *De Poetica* 24: "Accordingly, the poet should prefer probable impossibilities to improbable possibilities." As Sherlock Holmes more than once reminded Dr. Watson, "When you have eliminated all that is impossible, whatever remains must be the truth, no matter how improbable."

promisus *FW* 238.15 *adj*. Pledge or promise us not to be casual or promiscuous in one's sexual relationships. The abstinence-only sex education promoted by the W. Bush administration and the rings worn to symbolize sex only after marriage as worn most prominently by the Jonas Brothers among others are examples of "promisus." ("Now promisus as at our requisted you will remain ignorant of all what you hear and, though if whilst disrobing to the edge of risk") Shaun is hearing his sister Issy and her rainbow girls' confession and asking them to promise not to be promiscuous, though all the while he has incestuous designs on Issy.

propendiculous *FW* 493.10 *adj*. An upright, erect, or perpendicular position that is laughable or ridiculous. With one meaning of "pro" being "forward" as in project, McHugh's reference to the Latin *propendulus* meaning "hanging down in front," and given the multitude of phallic references in *Finnegans Wake*, the meaning in its Wakean context is quite clear. ("whom I dipped my hand in, he simply showed me his propendiculous loadpoker") McHugh further gives us "poker" as slang for "penis."

prophitable *FW* 240.32 *adj*. Gaining a financial benefit, useful information, or profitable advice from either a person who can foretell the future, one to whom some divine truth has been revealed, or a prophet. Joyce's self-proclaimed prophetic abilities are evident throughout *Finnegans Wake*, beginning on the first page with the great Wall Street ("wallstrait") financial fall of 1929, though he failed to profit from his own prophecy. ("to look most prophitable out of smily skibluh eye")

prosplodes *FW* 249.15 *v.* Ordinary language or prose that blows up or explodes. The publication of *Finnegans Wake* violently burst all the bounds of ordinary language and writing. It still "prosplodes" to this day. ("It vibroverberates upon the tegmen and prosplodes from pomoeria.") For "tegmen" McHugh gives "hardened wing cover of some insects. Those of some Orthoptera resonate to the song." (See **poseproem**.)

pseudoselves *FW* 576.33 *n.* Fake, sham, or pseudo persons or selves. In place of using a false name or pseudonym while remaining the same person, people may create false selves by changing their physical and mental characteristics. In time we can become so confused about which self is our self that, as the *Wake* has it, we "don't know whose hue." ("guide them through the labyrinth of their samilikes and the alteregoases of their pseudoselves, hedge them bothways from all roamers whose names are ligious, from loss of bearings deliver them")

pseudostylic *FW* 181.36 *adj.* Fake, sham, or pseudo way of writing or stylistic. Many critics considered *Finnegans Wake* "pseudostylic." In *Ulysses*, Joyce writes of Bloom's flirtation from a distance with Gerty MacDowell on Sandymount Strand in a "pseudostylic" prose form reminiscent of romance novels. ("Who can say how many pseudostylic shamiana") McHugh identifies "shamiana" as a cloth canopy in India. It is certainly a reference to HCE's twin son Shem who is often considered a sham.

psocoldlogical *FW* 396.14 *adj.* Science or study of the mind or psychological processes that are based on pure, cold logic rather than fanciful thinking. McHugh's suggestion here of "so-called logical" fits perfectly with Joyce's distrust of psychology. (See **junglemen** and **jungfraud**.) ("Could you blame her, we're saying, for one psocoldlogical moment?")

pubably *FW* 608.23 *adv.* Likely to be true of or probably related to the front of the pelvis or pubic area. ("A kind of thinglike all traylogged then pubably it resymbles a pelvic or some kvind then props an acutebacked quadrangle with aslant off ohalnthenth a wenchyoumaycuddler") The pubic area probably resembles the triangular genital region of a woman (McHugh gives the Danish *kvinde* for "woman.") at times referred to as the delta of Venus. ALP's siglum in *Finnegans Wake* is an equilateral triangle representing the female pubis (See **puerity**.) and the delta of the Liffey. In fact the Anna Livia Plurabelle chapter begins in triangular fashion:

O
tell me all about
Anna Livia! I want to hear all

The gossip the two washerwomen trade about ALP in what follows this opening is just as salacious as that making the rounds about her husband HCE. With McHugh's take on "wenchyoumaycuddler" as "whatyoumaycallher," I find another reading that's fit for today's tabloids, "you may call her a wench that you may cuddle."

puerity *FW* 237.25 *n.* Innocence or purity that comes from childishness or puerility. Shaun is the one with "puerity" in *Finnegans Wake* and is taught about sex by his twin brother Shem who explains the genital geometry of ALP's siglum, an equilateral triangle that, when inverted, becomes the female pubis. ("You are pure. You are pure. You are in your puerity.") McHugh references the Latin *pueritia* for "innocence, boyhood" and a quote from *The Egyptian Book of the Dead* CXXV: "I am pure. I am pure. My purity is the purity of that great *Bennu*."

puffumed *FW* 236.2 *adj*. Having a sweet smell or perfumed through the use of an atomizer, an apparatus that produces a whiff or puff of perfume when its bellows-like ball is squeezed. In Joyce's play *Exiles*, Robert Hand is described puffuming a room: "Then he rises and, pulling out a pump from behind the piano, walks here and there in the room ejecting from it into the air sprays of perfume." ("Charmeuses chloes, glycering juwells, lydialight fans and puffumed cynarettes.") McHugh offers a bonanza here with the French "charmeuse," "clothes," "U.416: 'Glycera or Chloe' (girls in Horace's *Odes*," "glittering jewels," "glycerin," "ladylike," "fanlights," "Lydia & Cynara: girls in Horace's *Odes*," and "perfumed cigarettes." The "puff" in "puffumed" is appropriate for smoking a cigarette that is given a pejorative touch with the suggestion of sin in "cynarettes."

pulpititions *FW* 276.F1 *n*. Rapid heart beats or palpitations caused by a sermon preached from a church platform or pulpit. The "pulpititions" could be experienced by the preacher and/or members of the congregation. The two hellfire sermons in *A Portrait of the Artist as a Young Man* cause "pulpititions" in the young Catholic student Stephen Dedalus that send him straight for the confessional. ("¹He gives me pulpititions with his Castlecowards never in these twowsers and ever in those twawsers and then babeteasing us out of our hoydenname." For "Castlecowards" McHugh gives the slang "coward's castle" for "pulpit." With my love for Evelyn Waugh's wonderful novel *Brideshead Revisited*, I hear Castle Howard, the actual stately home that Waugh used as a model for his fictional Brideshead Castle. The PBS television series based on the novel was shot at Castle Howard. The fact that *Finnegans Wake* was published five years before *Brideshead Revisited* is insignificant in the everything-exists-at-once world of the *Wake*.

puncheon *FW* 69.33, 373.20, & 455.2 *n*. A light noonday meal or luncheon served with a drink of mixed beverages or punch. Puncheon in regular language is a large cask that holds in the neighborhood of 100 gallons of liquor. ("digging in number 32 at the Rum and Puncheon," "You would think him Alddaublin staking his lordsure like a gourd on puncheon," & "no cupahurling nor apuckalips nor no puncheon jodelling nor no nothing") For the second quote McHugh gives "old Dublin taking his leisure" and a line from *Finnegans Wake*, "take your laysure like a god on pension." For the third quote he reads "cupahurling" as "hurling cups" and "coupling," "apuckalips" as both "Apocalypse" and "kissing," and "puncheon jodelling" as "Punch & Judy."

pungataries *FW* 352.36 *n.* Funny or comical through the use of words that can have different meanings or puns and a place of purification from sin by punishment or purgatory. Considered the lowest form of humor, those, such as Joyce, who constantly pun may be sentenced to some level of "pungataries." In a *New Yorker* cartoon by P. Byrnes, a demon in Hell says to two of his accomplices while escorting a couple of new arrivals, "Put the punster in with the mime." ("*has been sulphuring to himsalves all the pungataries of sin praktice in failing to furrow theogonies of the doomed*") Into this fragment is packed suffering, Hell's smell of sulfur, salvation, purgatory, and the theological agonies of the doomed.

punical *FW* 32.6 *adj.* 1. Funny or comical through the use of words that can have different meanings or puns. This is a perfect adjective to describe *Finnegans Wake*. If some readers of the *Wake* connect the first three letters of "punical" with punishment, I wouldn't hold that against them. As Joyce himself said of his "punical" creation, "Such a book, all in puns!" 2. With "punic" meaning "treacherous" or "deceiving," there are in "punical" puns used for some evil intent hidden in the humor. That the *Wake*'s puns can operate on many levels, often all at once, is demonstrated in Joyce's response to the question, "Aren't some of your puns trivial?" "Yes," he replied, "and many are quadrivial."

("Heave we aside the fallacy, as punical as finikin") With "finikin" suggesting Tim Finnegan whose wake gave Joyce the title of his last book, there is a hint of what lies ahead. Finnegan can be read as the French *fin* for "end" and "egan" sounds similar to "again," giving end and again or the cyclical structure of *Finnegans Wake* that ends with the first part of a sentence that is completed at the book's beginning. It also suggests that Finnegan will be fine again. That, added to the reading of "wake" as both a ceremony for the dead and a waking or rising from sleep or death, illustrates how Joyce played with words in a "punical" way. (See **apun** & **thuartpeatrick**.)

punman *FW* 93.13 & 517.18 *n.* A penman, that is a writer such as James Joyce, whose style, as in *Finnegans Wake*, is greatly infused with the comic use of words that can have different meanings or puns. In the *Wake* this also refers to "Shem the Penman," Shaun's twin brother and Jim the Penman who was a famous forger, both of whom are associated with Joyce himself. ("Shun the Punman!" & "No but Cox did to shin the punman.") With "Shun the Punman" Joyce recognizes that punsters are often shunned since the pun is considered the lowest form of humor. (See **apun, punical,** & **thuartpeatrick**.)

punplays *FW* 233.19 *n.* Comical wordplays based on words that can have different meanings or puns as well as plays composed of puns. ("letting punplays pass to ernest") This is a play on Oscar Wilde's play, *The Importance of Being Earnest*, a comedy that Joyce produced in Zurich during his stay there in World War I. Wilde "punplays" with Earnest as a man's name and its meaning of being serious or strong of purpose. (See **apun** & **thuartpeatrick**.)

punsil *FW* 98.30 *n.* A writing instrument of a rod of graphite enclosed in wood or a pencil used for the comic writing of words that can have different meanings or puns. Joyce did use a broad pencil while writing parts of *Finnegans Wake*. ("Batty believes a baton while Hogan hears a hod yet Heer prefers a punsil shapner and Cope and Bull go cup and ball.") In "punsil shapner" is found both a pencil sharpener and Joyce as a shaper of puns.

puntomine *FW* 587.8 *n.* A play of gestures without words or a pantomime that is comical through the use of words that can have different meanings or puns. Take for example the following pun from the book *Punishment: The Art of Punning or How to Lose Friends and Agonize People* by Harvey C. Gordon—"Last Saturday night we had a great idea. We went to see the play *Dracula* and then went out for a bite." You can picture to yourself how a mime troupe might present such a pun. ("pepped from our Theoatre Regal's drolleries puntomine") McHugh references "Theatre Royal, Hawkins St, noted for pantomimes" and gives the Italian *punto* for "point, passage in story or play." A variation is "punnermine" on *FW* 519.3—"And this pattern pootsch punnermine of concoon and proprey went on."

puraduxed *FW* 611.19-20 *n.* A contradictory statement or a paradox combined with a curtain, screen, or veil to seclude women from the sight of men or a purdah. This is the perfect portmanteau word for what the language of *Finnegans Wake* has done to readers through its veils of paradoxes. ("whereas for numpa one puraduxed seer in seventh degree of wisdom") McHugh writes that Seven Degrees of Wisdom is "twelve-year program incumbent upon ollaves in ancient Ireland." He also gives the Latin *dux* for "leader," which is a humorous twist in the middle of "puraduxed" since leaders and politicians are so often full of contradictory statements and paradoxes to veil their actions.

purefusion *FW* 222.2 *n.* A great abundance or profusion of unadulterated or pure melting together or fusing. An effusion of tremendous energy results from the "purefusion" of two atomic nuclei in the nuclear fusion of a hydrogen bomb. ("Melodiotiosities in purefusion by the score.") Effusion can mean unrestrained expression in writing, which describes *Finnegans Wake* well, and its effusion through the pure fusion of words from a multitude of languages produced a literary explosion unlike any the literate world had or has witnessed.

purscent *FW* 181.23 *n.* A chase or pursuit of a pleasing smell or scent. Judging by the astounding number of individual perfumes and colognes bearing the names of celebrities, each highly priced and from which the famous derive a percent of the proceeds, there is also the "purscent" of the smell of money as well. ("not even the Turk, ungreekable in purscent of the armenable, dared whiff the polecat at close range") This is one of the many reworkings of Oscar Wilde's well-known comment on fox hunting: "The unspeakable in full pursuit of the uneatable." McHugh also references Greece and Armenia that were occupied by the Turks. A "polecat" is another name for a skunk.

Q

quarks *FW* 383.1 *n.* While *Finnegans Wake* is without doubt the least read masterpiece of literature, it has contributed one quite well-known word—"quarks." The Nobel Prize winning physicist Murray Gell-Mann tells the story in *The Quark and the Jaguar: Adventures in the Simple and the Complex*: "In 1963, when I assigned the name 'quark' to the fundamental constituents of the nucleon, I had the sound first, without the spelling, which could have been 'kwork.' Then, in one of my occasional perusals of *Finnegans Wake*, by James Joyce, I came across the word '*quark*' in the phrase '— *Three quarks for Muster Mark!*'" I interrupt his account to insert that the sentence he quoted is the first line of Book II, Chapter 4 and tells the tale of the love triangle of Tristram, Iseult, and King Mark II of Cornwall. Gell-Mann realizes that the generally accepted meaning of "*quarks*" is the screeching cry of seagulls mocking the cuckolded king and is meant to rhyme with "*Mark*." So, he writes, "I had to find an excuse to pronounce it as 'kwork.'" He reasons that the *Wake*'s portmanteau words represent several sources at once and, with HCE as a publican, "phrases occur in the book that are partially determined by calls for drinks at the bar. I argued, therefore, that perhaps one of the multiple sources of the cry

'*Three quarks for Muster Mark*' might be 'Three quarts for Mister Mark,' in which case the pronunciation 'kwork' would not be totally unjustified. In any case, the number three fitted perfectly the way quarks occur in nature." Joyce would have been gratified by this as he was quite interested in the latest scientific discoveries ("the whoo-whoo and where's hairs theorics of Winestain"), and Eugene Jolas writes that Joyce "once began to speculate on the new physics, and the theory of the expanding universe," that appears in the *Wake* as the "expending umniverse." And so Joyce's "*Three quarks*" became as famous as Gertrude Stein's three roses. McHugh weighs in with "quark" as archaic for "to croak" and *Muster* as German for "paragon." He also relates that "Sir Dynaden, in Malory's *Tristram*, composes a song against Mark, which is sung before him." I believe that *quark* in German may also mean "jabberwocky," which would bring us full circle back to Lewis Carroll and his portmanteau words.

quiztune *FW* 110.14 *n*. A question in a test or quiz concerning music or a tune. There was an American radio program called *Quiztunes* and later a popular television game show, *Name That Tune*, in which contestants identified a song from its opening notes. Those correctly naming the song after listening to the fewest number of notes were the winners. ("Zot is the Quiztune") McHugh gives the following associations for *Zot*: Hebrew for "this, that;" Dutch for "fool;" German for "obscenity;" and the Albanian *Zoti* for "God." If Shakespeare's *Hamlet* was made into a Broadway musical, I can imagine that insane Dane singing his famous To-be-or-not-to- be soliloquy, asking Joyce's question, "Zot is the Quiztune." Gertrude Stein's last words before being wheeled into the operating room where she died were reported to have been, "What is the question?" Receiving no reply, she said, "If there is no question, there can be no answer." As Stein was descended from German stock and, as "Zot is the Quiztune" has a Germanic inflection to it, Joyce may have anticipated these words from his former rival who lived in his Paris neighborhood. This has a personal connection for me because it was from reading about Stein's jealously of Joyce that led me first to read *Ulysses* and then to become a fan of *Finnegans Wake*.

R

refrects *FW* 612.16 *v.* To throw back or reflect but in a bent or refracted form. A Fun House mirror "refrects" and distorts your image in hilarious ways. ("Bigseer, refrects the petty padre, whackling it out, a tumble to take") McHugh gives the German *wacklig* for "tottering." Tim Finnegan no doubt did some drunken tottering before finally taking a tumble from the ladder.

remembored *FW* 384.35 & 388.18 *v.* Recalled or remembered though wearied by someone or something dull or boring and, perhaps because of boredom with the subject or event, not remembering it exactly or accurately. Memory is tricky enough without adding the element of boredom to its mix. ("they all four remembored who made the world and how they used to be at that time in the vulgar ear cuddling and kiddling her, after an oyster supper in Cullen's barn" & "Lapoleon, the equestrian, on his whuite house of Hunover, rising Clunkthurf over Cabinhogan and all they remembored") In the first quote the "four" are the four evangelists known in *Finnegans Wake* as "Mamalujo" who are spying on Tristram and Iseult's love making in the ship's cabin during their voyage to Cornwall where Iseult is to marry Tristram's uncle, King Mark II. (See **amotion** &

242 | A *Finnegans Wake* Lextionary

avunculusts.) McHugh finds in "who made the world" the first question of the Catechism and reads "the vulgar ear" as "the Vulgar era: The Christian era." The second quote contains Napoleon, Wellington's horse Copenhagen, and the emblem of the House of Hanover, a white horse, associated with William III. There was an equestrian statue of William III in Dublin that was often desecrated until it was finally destroyed. This statue is vaguely "remembored" by the Irish. McHugh gives "hun" as the pejorative of "German," a putdown on the House of Hanover.

remembrandts *FW* 403.10 *n.* A recollecting or remembrance in the manner or style of a Rembrandt painting. Beckman writes: "Memory in *Finnegans Wake* is if anything the opposite of Proust's luminous remembrance of times that are lost . . . The elusiveness of memory justifies the pun 'remembrandts;' since the objects of memory in the *Wake* are only just glimpsed in accidental light, and emerge for a moment from darkness like the dramatic scene (It's *The Abduction of Proserpina*!) in a Rembrandt painting. Retrospection in Joyce is essential yet imperfect and obscure." ("whose fixtures are mobiling so wobiling befear my remembrandts")

reprodictive *FW* 298.17 *adj.* Prophetic or predictive of that which will be created anew or reproductive. Joyce described *The New Science* of Giambattista Vico as the "trellis" upon which he built *Finnegans Wake*, just as *The Odyssey* provided structure to *Ulysses*. Vico theorized history as moving in a circle of three ages, the divine, heroic, and human, followed by a ricorso in which all is destroyed to begin the cycle again. As the *Wake* puts it, the world "moves in vicous circles yet remews the same." Thus it can be predicted what will be reproduced in this best of all "reprodictive" worlds. ("those fickers which are returnally reprodictive of themselves") McHugh gives the German *ficken* for "fuck," so you can deduce exactly who those "fickers" are who eternally reproduce themselves.

requisted *FW* 238.15 *v.* Something that is strongly asked for or requested yet not quite required or requisite. Something may be "requisted" under false authority to conceal the fact that the power to requisition is lacking. ("Now promisus at our requisted you will remain ignorant of all what you hear") McHugh gives the Provencal *requist* for "precious," which makes the requested thing that is not required also something valuable or precious. It is so often the luxuries of life that we request, though these items are not actually required to live a good life.

respunchable *FW* 29.35 *adj.* Deserving credit or blame or responsible for a blow with the fist or a punch. Mike Tyson's fist was "respunchable" for many a heavyweight fighter's downfall. ("he who will be ultimendly respunchable for the hubbub caused in Edenborough") McHugh gives the Latin *timendum* for "to be feared," the Hebrew *hibbub* for "love," and references "Edenborough" with "Eden & Burgh Quays, D, face one another" and "Edinburgh."

resymbles *FW* 608.23 *v.* Being similar to or resembling representations of ideas and/or abstractions or symbols. In *Finnegans Wake*, HCE "resymbles" all men as ALP "resymbles" all women. In fact, within the *Wake* it is difficult to find anything that doesn't resymble something else. At the most fundamental level, the letter the hen scratches out of the dump "resymbles" *Finnegans Wake* itself. ("A kind of a thinglike all traylogged then pubably it resymbles a pelvic or some kvind ") McHugh reads "pubably it resymbles" as "probably it resembles" and finds a hint of "pubic" in "pubably," which goes with the Danish *kvinde* he gives for "woman."

retrophoebia *FW* 415.10 *n.* 1. An irrational fear or phobia of moving back or retrocession, a phobia or a fear of what is behind or backward. Whoever wrote the song lyrics, "I was looking back to see if you were looking back to see if I was looking back to see if you were looking back at me," did not suffer from "retrophoebia." 2. With Phoebe as the moon in Greek myths, Richard Beckman writes of the characters in *Finnegans Wake*: "They brood over the past . . . and are afflicted with bitter memories; they think backwards, like the motion of one of the moons of Saturn ('retrophoebia'), burdened by their own rear view of things, 'rerembrandtsers' trying to 'reassemble' their lives from the scattered pieces of their past, whatever can be 'reromembered.'" ("soturning around his eggshell rockcoach their dance McCaper in retrophoebia")

returnally *FW* 298.17 *adv.* Forever or eternally coming back or returning. With *Finnegans Wake* ending with a sentence fragment that connects with the sentence fragment that begins it, the *Wake* is written "returnally." (See **rolywholyover**.) The same is true of so many of the book's characters, themes, and motifs, each of which "resymbles" "returnally." ("those fickers which are returnally reprodictive of themselves") McHugh reads "fickers" as "figures" and, more interestingly, as the German *ficken* for "fuck."

rheumaniscences *FW* 319.17 *n.* Recollections or reminiscences about inflammation of the joints or rheumatism. ("Ampsterdampster that had rheumaniscences in his netherlumbs.") The damp climate of Amsterdam in the Netherlands could very well cause "rheumaniscences" in the lower legs or nether limbs. At the top of my "rheumaniscences" is the "rheumatiz" medicine that Granny on *The Beverly Hillbillies* concocted in her moonshine still.

rhomes *FW* 286.F1 *n.* 1. Family dwelling places or homes in Italy's eternal city, Rome, as easily seen in Wakean context: "As Rhombulus Rebus went building rhomes one day." Romulus and Remus were the legendary founders of Rome. 2. Homes that wander or roam provide another slant, from covered wagons that gave settlers a home crossing the plains where the buffalo roamed up to our luxurious motor homes and RV's of today.

Neither "rhomes" nor Rome was built in a day.

ricecourse *FW* 423.30 *n*. A racetrack or racecourse covered with a starchy grain or rice. In its Wakean context, "the ricecourse of marrimoney," this racecourse would be, in most cases, the distance from the door of a church to the door of a car, a course covered with rice thrown by wedding guests at the bride and groom. (See **marrimoney**.)

ridy *FW* 43.11 *adj*. Prepared or ready to be carried by or to ride. Since Diana was the Roman goddess of the hunt, the *Wake*'s "deuce of dianas ridy for the hunt" presents an image of foxhunters ready to ride after the hounds or, as Oscar Wilde described it, "the unspeakable in full pursuit of the uneatable." (See **purscent** & **unfallable**.)

roade *FW* 197.35 *v*. Moved on or rode on a way made to travel on or a road. A much more accurate title for Jack Kerouac's famous novel *On the Road* would be *On the Roade* since he was not just on the road but rode on the road. ("till with his runagate bowmpriss he roade and borst her bar") This passage appears in the ALP chapter into which Joyce wove the names of hundreds of rivers, and here McHugh finds the rivers Runa, Bow, and Riss.

roaratorios *FW* 41.28 *n*. Musical compositions on a religious theme for voices and orchestra or oratorios that are loud in sound or roared. Composer and author John Cage, in the category of "roaratorios," created *Roaratorio: An Irish Circus on "Finnegans Wake"* in which he read his "Writing for the Second Time Through *Finnegans Wake*" to the accompaniment of Celtic music and over a thousand sounds recorded in locations mentioned in the *Wake*. Commenting on Cage's composition, Scott W. Klein writes: "The title is both secular and religious—an 'oratorio,' or sacred work for accompanied voice, plus the 'roar' of the crowed world—and Roaratorio says 'Here Comes Everybody' not only to environmental sounds but to the history and universal experience of music." You can listen to a sample of this music on Amazon.com and, if its roaring sounds suit you, you can purchase the CD. ("with their priggish mouths all open for the larger appraisiation of this longawaited Messiagh of roaratorios")

rolywholyover *FW* 597.3 *adj.* 1. A turning or rolling over of the entire or whole thing, that is moving a full 180 degrees. 2. Completely over or finished. ("It is just, it is just about to, it is just about to rolywholyover.") This is the big question about the oxymoronic, rolling-stop ending of *Finnegans Wake*—does " . . . a long the" on page 628 roll over to continue again at "riverrun past Eve and Adam's . . ." on page 3, or is the book really wholly over? Since scholars disagree, your conjecture is as good as any. (See **backwords** & **circumconversioning**.)

roturn *FW* 18.5 *v.* To come back or return through revolving or rotating. ("This ourth of years is not save brickdust and being humus the same roturns.") With the Latin *humus* for earth (from which the first human, Adam, was reportedly made), on this earth of ours there is a suggestion of the ubiquitous funereal quotation, "Dust thou art, to dust returnest."

rouseruction *FW* 499.1 *n.* Rising from the dead or resurrection with an added element of waking up or rousing. The revival from sleep, death, or otherwise through excitement or a stirring up. A more vigorous or brisk form of resurrection, like being awakened in the morning from shouts of "GET UP YOU LAZY BAG OF BONES" rather than the soft music from a clock radio. ("healed cured and embalsemate, pending a rouseruction of his bogey, most highly astounded, as it turned up, after his life overlasting, at thus being reduced to nothing.") For "rouseruction," McHugh gives the Latin *eructo* for "belch" and reads this as "resurrection of the body." He identifies *bog* in "bogey" as the Pan-Slavonic for "God" and "life overlasting" as the "life everlasting" from the Christian creed. I can read Rosicrucian here, but since it's a secret society with special knowledge of nature and religion, I'm unable to say what its adherents may believe concerning resurrection. (See **overlasting**.)

ruinboon *FW* 612.20 *n.* something that is at once a great destruction or ruin and a blessing or boon. In its Wakean context of "Iro's Irismans ruinboon pot," it is the rainbow, God's promise that the Earth will never be destroyed again by floodwaters, at once a ruin and a boon. It is also the Leprechaun's pot of gold at the end of a rainbow that seems like a wonderful boon until one's hopes are ruined by one of the Little People's tricks. McHugh gives the Japanese *iro* for "color" and "Iris" as the "rainbow goddess."

S

saddenly *FW* 363.13 *adv.* Quickly, unexpectedly, or suddenly unhappy or sad. After his encounter in Phoenix Park with the Cad, HCE "saddenly" found his life turned upside down and himself on trial. Even the lack of any concrete evidence against him gave HCE little comfort but his enemies some "sadisfaction." ("Is their bann bothstiesed? Saddenly now. Has they bane reneemed?")

sadisfaction *FW* 445.8 *n.* Pleased, contented, or satisfied through the love of cruelty or sadism. We can thank the Marquis de Sade for giving us a word to describe those who find "sadisfaction" in sadism. ("So skelp your budd and kiss the hurt! I'll have plenary sadisfaction") For a full catalog of activities that brought de Sade some "sadisfaction," try reading his monumental work written while he was imprisoned in the Bastille, *The 120 Days of Sodom*.

sailsmanship *FW* 325.17 *n.* Ability to exchange payment or sell cloth designed to catch the wind and move a ship or a sail, giving salesmanship. ("in sailsmanship, szed the head marines talebearer") McHugh identifies the phrase "tell that to the marines."

salvocean *FW* 623.29 *n.* A saving or salvation from the sea or ocean. This salvation may be simply from drowning, perhaps from flooding, as when the little Dutch boy was the "salvocean" of Holland when he put his finger in the hole of the dike, or even from sin and eternal punishment through Christian baptism in the ocean. ALP as a river finds "salvocean" of sorts at the end of *Finnegans Wake* when she flows into the waiting arms of her father ("Far calls. Coming, far!" [*far* is Danish for 'father']) knowing full well she will soon be resurrected through the evaporative power of the sun to fall as rain that replenishes Dublin's life-giving Liffey. ("At the site of salvocean.")

sangnifying *FW* 515.8 *v.* 1. To make known by words or signs or to signify hopeful, confident, or sanguine feelings. *adj.* 2. To be signified with bloodshed or to be sanguinary. *The Red Badge of Courage* by Stephen Crane is a "sangnifying" novel. ("—Sangnifying nothing. Mock!") This references a nihilistic line about life from Shakespeare's *Macbeth*: "a tale / Told by an idiot, full of sound and fury, / Signifying nothing."

scandalisang *FW* 188.21-22 *v.* Vocal music or singing about a shameful action or a scandal. ("I too nerve myself to pray for the loss of selfrespect to equip me for the horrible necessity of scandalisang") Once the lyrics to "The Ballad of Persse O'Reilly" with their scandalous accusations against HCE's alleged misdeeds in Phoenix Park were released, all Dublin was "scandalisang."

scandiknavery *FW* 47.21 *n.* Behavior of a tricky rascal or knave from Norway, Sweden, Denmark, or Finland or the region of Europe known as Scandinavia. HCE is of Scandinavian descent.

> ("Then we'll have a free trade Gaels' band and mass meeting
> For to sod the brave son of Scandiknavery.
> And we'll bury him down in Oxmanstown
> Along with the devil and Danes,

[Chorus] With the deaf and dumb Danes,
And all their remains.")

This is from "The Ballad of Persse O'Reilly," the song written and sung by Hosty that indicts HCE for his alleged crimes in Phoenix Park and spreads the rumor about them throughout Dublin. HCE's fall from grace is compared with the fall of Humpty Dumpty, a crackup that can't be corrected. "Scandiknavery" may also refer to the tale threaded throughout *Finnegans Wake* of the tailor and the Norwegian Captain, a favorite story told by Joyce's father about a hunchbacked (as was HCE) ship's captain who orders a suit from a Dublin tailor. When the suit doesn't fit, the captain refuses to pay the tailor and accuses him of being unable to sew, while the tailor accuses the captain of being impossible to fit. (See **ashaped**.) No doubt the story was more humorous as told by John Joyce, a well known Dublin raconteur.

scholard *FW* 215.26 *n.* A person who is half learned as a scholar and half stupid as a dullard. With the compartmentalization and specialization of knowledge in today's complex world, a scholar in one area may be a dullard in many others. In fact, it has become nearly impossible to become a renaissance wo/man as new knowledge grows greater than our ability to keep up with it, making even the smartest among us a "diller a dollar a ten-o'clock 'scholard.'" ("Latin me that, my trinity scholard, out of eure sanscreed into oure eryan!")

scribicide *FW* 14.21 *n.* The purposeful killing of oneself or suicide by a writer or scribe. ("A scribicide then and there is led off under old's code with some fine covered by six marks or ninepins") In one sense, Joyce could be considered a "scribicide" from the 17 years he devoted to writing *Finnegans Wake*, since so many critics thought of the book as a literary suicide. Pigott was an actual "scribicide" because, after his misspelling of hesitancy in the letter he forged to incriminate Parnell was disclosed in court, he did not hesitate to put a bullet through his head.

scutterer *FW* 340.1 *n.* In *Wandering and Return in Finnegans Wake*, Kimberly J. Devlin writes: "The dream's patriarch is branded a 'scuterer of guld'—a stuttering utterer of guilt and a scattering utterer of gold (in a monetary context, an 'utterer' is a passer of counterfeit currency.)" ("Scutterer of guld, he is retourious on every roudery!") McHugh gives the Danish *guld* for "gold" and gives the meaning of "scutter" as "to squitter, have diarrhea." Whether scattering fake gold or utterances resembling watery movements of the bowels, a "scutterer" seems, metaphorically, much like many American politicians. This may also be read as a stutter heard in the sound of thunder indicating guilt, another reference to Joyce's belief that the Original Sin was God's from his creation of a flawed world. (See **unpeppeppediment**.)

scygthe *FW* 341.10 *n.* In *Joyce's Rare View*, Richard Beckman suggests a double meaning for "scygthe" as a sickle or scythe which "the oppressed, the revolutionary, or the merely hostile can use as weapons" and "the Scythians, a warring people of ancient Russia thought of as barbarous." (Edmund Spenser uses the phrase "uncivil and Scythian-like" to describe the Irish over whom he tyrannized.") (*"with sickle of a scygthe but the humour of a hummer"*) McHugh finds the Communist hammer and sickle here and the German *Hummer* for "lobster."

seatuition *FW* 385.30 *n.* 1. A site, place, or situation located at or on the ocean or sea. 2. A case, condition, or situation occurring at or on the sea. 3. Teaching or instruction about the sea or occurring at or on the sea. ("the plaint effect being in point of fact there being in the whole, a seatuition so shocking and scandalous") The shocking and scandalous "seatuition" referred to in this passage is the highly sexual situation taking place in the ship's cabin between Tristram and Iseult while being observed and commented upon by the four old men (Matthew, Mark, Luke, and John) who are known throughout *Finnegans Wake* as "Mamalujo." Tristram, Iseult's "Amoricas Champius" or champion of love, undoubtedly teaches her something when "he was kiddling and cuddling and bunnyhugging scrumptious his colleen bawn." To reinforce this nautical situation, just five lines down from "seatuition" is "Rolando's deepen darblun Ossian roll," a reference to Lord Byron's famous line from *Childe Harold's Pilgrimage*—"Roll on, thou deep and dark blue ocean, roll!"

seemaultaneously *FW* 161.12-13 *adv*. To appear or to seem to exist or happen at the same time or simultaneously. Joyce said that the events and characters of *Finnegans Wake* exist in the "eternal now," that is they appear together "seemaultaneously" though in fact they may have been historically separated by hundreds of years. ("unless Burrus and Caseous have not or not have seemaultaneously sysentangled themselves, selldear to soldthere, once in the dairy days of buy and buy") McHugh points out "Brutus & Cassius" and the song "Love's Old Sweet Song: 'Once in the dear dead days beyond recall.'" (In *Ulysses*, this song is one of Molly Bloom's most requested numbers.) In "sysentangled" he gives the Greek *sys* for "together," that gives an understanding of being entangled together.

selfabyss *FW* 40.23 *n*. The lowest depth or the abyss of masturbation or self-abuse. ("suspicioning as how he was setting on a twoodstool on the verge of selfabyss") In Ulysses, Buck Mulligan speaks of "A Honeymoon in the Hand," and the *Wake*, taking the name of Gulliver's teacher from *Gulliver's Travels*, mentions "Master Bates." "Masturbation!" exclaimed Joyce, "The amazing availability of it!"

selfridgeousness *FW* 137.34 *adj*. Thinking that one's self is more firm, severely exact, or ridged than others. Combined with the suggested self-righteousness, one has the belief that one is better than others when it comes to rigidity. ("peddles in passivism and is a gorgon of selfridgeousness") McHugh references "Gordon Selfridge: 1920's director of Selfridges, London chain store."

selfthought *FW* 147.9 *n*. Instructed by one's self or self-taught through one's own study, thinking, or thought. Einstein discovered his groundbreaking theories of relativity through thought experiments he conducted in his mind while working in a patent office. The style of *Finnegans Wake* was certainly "selfthought" by Joyce. ("And you'll see if I'm selfthought.") The *Wake*'s "selfthought" is another word for "autodidact'"or "self-taught" that appears in *FW* 50.36: "It is nebuless an autodidact fact of the commonest that the shape of the average human cloudyphiz ..."

semisized *FW* 170.19 *v.* Incomplete or semi of amount or size of the foreskin cut off when circumcised. The "semisized" needs to contact a malpractice attorney as quickly as possible. ("amother when he is just only after having been semisized")

semitary *FW* 85.9 & 594.8 *n.* Graveyard or cemetery for a school for training students for a religious vocation or a seminary. ("alongst one of our unphrohibited semitary thrufahrts" & "amid the semitary of Somnionia") For the first quote McHugh provides the Latin *semita* for "path" and the German *Durchfahrt* for "passage," giving a path for passage, perhaps to the afterlife. For the second quote he again gives the Latin *semita* for "path" and the Latin *somnium* for a "dream," giving a path to a dream. *Finnegans Wake* is certainly a path and a passage through a deep, dark dream.

seomen *FW* 331.29-30 *n.* Seminal fluid of male reproductive organs or semen of a sailor or seaman. The slang of "salt" for a seaman and the salty nature of semen combine in the suggestive "seomen." ("was it the twylyd or the mounth of the yare or the feint of her smell made the seomen assault of her") (See **assault**.) McHugh reads "mounth of the yare" as "month of the year" and "mouth of the river Yare." With mouth, semen, and assault coming together in this phrase, oral sex is certainly a strong suggestion.

sensed *FW* 268.F6 *v.* To feel or sense that one has done wrong or sinned. This is another of those Wakeisms that uses a real word in an entirely new sense, as is evident from its usage. ("Leap me, Locklaun, for you have sensed!") The beginning of Catholic confession begins, "Bless me, father, for I have sinned." With "sensed" preceded by, "So that's why you ran away to sea, Mrs Lappy," in this sentence ALP is asking for forgiveness for the sin of leaving her husband and children to return to her father, the Irish Sea, though her doing so may demonstrate very good sense.

sexfutter *FW* 384.28 *n.* In his essay "A Chapter in Composition: Chapter II.4" found in *How Joyce Wrote "Finnegans Wake": A Chapter-by-Chapter Genetic Guide*, Jed Deppman explores an array of possible meanings/associations/allusions for "sexfutter." "Sexfutter" actually started out as "sixfooter." Deppman writes: "In 1924 'sixfooter' *described* Tristan, and it meant, first, that he was rather tall and fit Isolde's childish, preconceived ideas of attractiveness and, second, that Joyce was punning on poetic 'hexameter': Tristan the six-foot-tall specialist of 'six-footer' poetry came up a little short with his decasyllabic, Byronic verse to Isolde." This type of pun is relatively simple Deppman tells us but, when Joyce turns Tristan into a "sexfutter," things quickly get complicated as Deppman continues: "This linguistic bit, vocable, phoneme, or nonword 'sexfutter' brings to mind 'sixfooter,' no doubt, but also 'sexfooter,' 'sexe- fouteur,' 'six fuck her,' 'sex fuck her,' 'sexfucker,' 'sex-father,' 'sex-fooder,' and 'sex- fodder,' among other things." As if that wasn't enough, Deppman opens the spigot all the way and sees that "the first syllable, 'sex,' invites such readings as socks, six, sacks, sax, shacks, shocks, soaks, sucks, Saxe, such, sicks, sics, checks, shucks, chicks, Czechs, seeks, chokes, sheiks, shakes ... in English alone." By the time Joyce finally finished *Finnegans Wake*, he had, Deppman posits, "not only destabilized words by changing or removing a few letters, he had radicalized enough of the text on enough of its readable levels to splash suspicion upon every textual order." If this is too little for you, there's much more in Deppman's essay. ("the brueburnt sexfutter, handson and huntsem, that was palpably wrong and bulbubly improper") This word appears in one of the raciest, sexiest sections of the *Wake* and, even though it's written in Wakese, if your mind is in the wrong place, you'll find your prurient interests stirred, if not shaken. To cap this off, McHugh provides "futter" as slang for "fuck."

sexophonologistic *FW* 123.18 *n.* The study of the sexy sounds of language or phonology that can be created by the saxophone. Recordings of jazz-great Coleman Hawkins is a good place to start such a study. ("v. *Some Forestallings over that Studium of Sexophonologistic Schizophrenesis*, vol. xxiv, pp. 2-555")

shouldier *FW* 322.3 *n.* The body part to which the arm is attached or the shoulder of a person who serves in the army or a soldier. The military command to "shoulder arms" is suggested. ("dangieling his old Conan over his top gallant shouldier") McHugh references the Irish independence leader Daniel O'Connell "dangling his overcoat over his shoulder." He also provides "one of the Fianna" for "Conan" and "top-gallant flag on mizzen mast."

shoutmost *FW* 6.18-19 adj. The greatest or utmost in crying out loudly or shouting. Many "shoutmost" fans at football games go home hoarse after shouting their utmost in support of their teams. ("And the all gained in with the shoutmost shoviality.") This is a sentence from the description of Tim Finnegan's wake where all the mourners joined in with the utmost joviality that soon dissolved into shoving, throwing, and hitting. As the *Wake* asks, "E'erawhere in this whorl would ye hear sich a din again?" See the lyrics to the ballad "Finnegan's Wake" for a full account of the activities at Tim's wake. As the song so vividly shows, it took more than the utmost shouting to wake Tim from the dead, it took whiskey or *uisge breatha*, Irish for "water of life," that in Irish folklore is reputed to have power to wake the dead. (See **funferall** & **splabashing**.)

shoviality *FW* 6.19 *n.* Quality of being merry or jovial while pushing or shoving. This behavior is observed in *Finnegans Wake* at Tim Finnegan's wake, while a more modern example might be a mosh pit at a nightclub concert. ("And the all gained in with the shoutmost shoviality.") McHugh gives a reference to the song "Phil the Fluter's Ball" with the lyrics that include "Then all joined in wid the utmost joviality.")

showting *FW* 116.6 *v.* Display or show while crying out loudly or shouting. Carnival barkers make their living though "showting," as invariably do used-car salesmen in television commercials. ("what we have perused from the pages of *I Was A Gemral*, that Showting up of Bulsklivism") If you have read the story of how Buckley shot the Russian general (See **gianerant**.), then you will realize that in this instance "showting" means "shooting" which, in a way, is a way to forcibly show something accompanied by a loud noise. McHugh references George Bernard Shaw's *Shewing-Up of Blanco Posnet* and Bolshevism.

shrubrubs *FW* 420.8 *n.* Areas of bushes or shrubs in a residential section on the outskirts of a city or a suburb. Suburbs naturally have more shrubs than the center of a city as the buildings are usually not as dense, giving "shrubrubs" a more pleasing, pastoral aspect. In *Finnegans Wake* HCE's Chapelizod pub is in the "shrubrubs" of Dublin and adjoins Phoenix Park, site of HCE's supposed sin observed by three soldiers from the shrubbery. ("And why there were treefellers in the shrubrubs.") In keeping with the shrubs and trees of a park, the three fellows become "treefellers."

sibster *FW* 465.17 *n.* A brother/sister or sibling and a daughter of the same parents or a sister. ("or like boyrun to sibster, me and you") This passage provides a link to Lord Byron's relationship with his half sister Augusta, rumored to be incestuous and the cause of Byron's self exile from England. (See **peerfectly**.) For a refutation of Harriet Beecher Stowe's defamatory attack on

Byron, read John Murray's *Lord Byron and His Detractors*. Joyce's middle name, Augustine, was incorrectly recorded as Augusta at his birth.

sin beau *FW* 233.5 *n*. A Wakean way to reference a rainbow with its origination from the sins of humans that caused God to destroy the world by a great flood. There is also the thought that sin may be beautiful despite its future consequences or that God's rainbow as a sign that he will not destroy the world by flood again is a beautiful promise. ("Angelinas, hide from light those hues that your sin beau may bring to light!")

sinduced *FW* 4.9 *v*. To influence or induce to an immoral act or sin. ("What bidimetoloves sinduced by what tegotetabsolvers!") Eve and Adam, the first "sinduced" by the serpent and the second "sinduced" by Eve, appear on the *Wake*'s first page. This "sinduced" couple appear repeatedly throughout the book.

sinflowed *FW* 481.9 *n*. With the German *Sintflut* and the Danish *Sinflowed* for "the Flood" and the concept of ran like water or flowed, all the sin and sinners of the world flowed away during the forty days and forty nights that Noah's Ark floated along. ("Sinflowed, O sinflowed! Fia! Fia!") McHugh gives the Italian *fia* for "be it done."

singulfied *FW* 306.6 *v*. 1. two or more made into one, a single one and no more than one thing that has importance or that is signified. In *Finnegans Wake* HCE is the single, significant male character who represents all men, and ALP is the single, significant female character who represents all women in the entire world, past, present, and future. HCE and ALP begin as "our forced payrents," Adam and Eve, and expand from there. HCE's initials are most famously found in "Here Comes Everybody," leading Adaline Glasheen to ask, "Who is who when everybody is somebody else?" When everyone has been "singulfied," we "don't know whose hue." *Macbeth* maintains that life is "signifying nothing," but the *Wake* certainly "singulfied" something by combining the world's languages, arts, sciences, religions, histories, etc. into one remarkable work. The critic Stuart Gilbert wrote of *Finnegans Wake*, "The unusual word formation ... was called for by its subject and is thereby justified, but it will in all probability remain a unique creation—once and only once by one only." ("With this laudable purpose in loud ability let us be singulfied.")

sinscript   *FW* 421.18   *n.* Immoral or sinful writing in the ancient language of the Hindus or Sanskrit. The *Kama Sutra*'s instructions in sexual positions could be considered an example of "sinscript" by those of a puritanical persuasion. The *Wake*'s description of the ship's-cabin coupling of Tristram and Iseult is written in a Wakean form of "sinscript." (See **amotion** & **inthrusted**.) ("slanguage ten times as words as the penmarks used out in sinscript with such hesitancy by your cerebrated brother") The forged letter meant to implicate Parnell in the Phoenix Park murders would be a form of "sinscript" if reprinted in an Indian newspaper. This infamous letter is brought to mind here with the word "hesitancy" that Pigott misspelled as "hesitency." (See **anonymay's** & **hazedency**.)

sinse   *FW* 83.12, 239.2, & 338.2   *adv.* & *n.* Once more, as I did with "corpse," I'll turn things over to Philippe Sollers: "Joyce writes SINSE, reading *since*, *sense*, and *sin*. The 'syllogistic' development of this condensation is as follows: ever since sense, there is sin; ever since sin, there is sense; ever since since (time), there is sin and sense. All in a flash in SINSE. In one word, as in a thousand, you have a thesis on language and man's fall from paradise; and, simultaneously, it is funny." ("nat language at any sinse of the world," "so pleasekindly communicake with the original sinse as we are only yearning," & "We've heard it sinse sung thousandtimes.") The first quote can be read as "not language as well as night language (Danish *nat* for "night")in any sense of the word," and the second communicates "Original

260 | A *Finnegans Wake* Lextionary

Sin." For the third quote McHugh references the song "Ireland Boys, Hurrah: 'We've heard her faults a Hundred times.'" In this instance "sinse" stands in for "since" and "faults," which may also be "sins."

sinsitives *FW* 527.27 *n.* Susceptible or sensitive to immoral acts or sin. ("Their sinsitives shrinked. Even Netta and Linda, our seeyu tities and they've sin sumtim, thankus!") Coming on a page with many references to Tristram and Iseult, it could be that the two lovebirds sensitivity to sin is shrinking as they continue their assignations in King Mark's garden and that something of their sin has been seen. I leave it to you to decipher "seeyu tities."

skyerscape *FW* 4.36 *v.* To find a way out or to escape from the upper air or sky. A parachute would be a normal way to "skyerscape" but, this being *Finnegans Wake*, there is a complicating factor. Charles Stewart Parnell, leader of the effort to free Ireland from English rule, was an important figure in James Joyce's life. His first published work, a poem printed at the expense of his father, concerned Parnell's betrayal and downfall. Parnell precipitated this through his affair with the wife of one of his lieutenants. One of the rumors at that time had Parnell escaping from Kitty O'Shea's bedroom in his nightshirt by a fire escape ("fairescaping in his natshirt" with the Danish *nat* for "night") to avoid detection by her husband. ("a waalworth of a skyerscape of the most eyeful hoyth entowerly") Here we have the Woolworth Building, a skyscraper in New York, and the entire Hill of Howth in Dublin.

slanguage *FW* 421.17 *n.* Written or spoken speech or language that is primarily composed of slang. Slang has several meanings, such as the jargon of a particular group or class of society or vivid and colorful words that are not part of proper English. Slang may also be forced and fantastic, exhibiting eccentric humor or fancy, qualities common in the "slanguage" of *Finnegans Wake*. ("millions of moods used up slanguage tun times as words as the Penmarks used out in sinscript with such hesitancy by your celebrated brother")

slumbwhere *FW* 580.15 *n.* Some place or somewhere to sleep or slumber. After draining the dregs of his customers' glasses, HCE's "slumbwhere" is, briefly, the floor of his pub. ("light in hand, helm on high, to peekaboo durk the thicket of slumbwhere, till their hour with their scene be struck for ever and the book of the dates he close") For "durk," as well as referring to "dark," McHugh gives the German *durch* for "through." He also points out that *The Egyptian Book of the Dead* is closed.

smal *FW* 17.32 *adj.* Not only little or not large but slightly less large than small, somewhere between tiny and small. ("Llarge by the smal an' everynight life olso th'estrange") McHugh gives the Danish *smal* for "narrow." (See **Llarge**.)

smatterafact *FW* 183.7 *n.* As a matter of fact, "smatterafact" is a slight, superficial, or smattering of knowledge of things known to be true or facts. Political speeches are often filled with one "Smatterafact" after another while scattering a few facts here and there to cover up the lack of any depth of knowledge. ("Smatterafact, Angles aftanon browsing there thought not Edam reeked more rare.") McHugh, as a matter of fact, finds here the song "Killarney: 'Angels often pausing there Doubt if Eden were more fair.'"

sobsconcious *FW* 377.28 *n.* Crying or sobs that exist in the mind when it is not fully conscious, that is coming from the subconscious. Since *Finnegans Wake* occurs at night and has been perceived as a dream, this subconscious state explains much of it's legendary difficulties. ("all he bares sobsconcious inklings shadowed on soulskin")

sojestiveness *FW* 222.32-33 *n.* Brought to mind or suggestiveness that suggests an idea or feeling of something indecent or improper in a humorous or jesting manner. An ideal example of "sojestiveness" in *Finnegans Wake* is the description of Tristram and Iseult's love making on the ship taking Iseult to Cornwall where she was to marry Tristram's uncle, King Mark II: "Shuck her! Let him! What he's good for. Shuck her more! Let him again! All she wants!" In the final analysis, everything in the *Wake* suggests a suggestion of something else, many much more allusive than the example given here and most often in a humorous fashion. ("Aminxt that nombre of evelings, but how pierceful in their sojestiveness where those first girly stirs") The *Dubliners* story "Eveline" is suggested by "evelings," though there is no trace of a jest in that sad tale.

sorgy *FW* 392.16 *adj.* Sympathetic or sorry that one is soaked or soggy. ("They were all so sorgy for poorboir Matt in his saltwater hat") McHugh gives the German *Sorge* for "worry," which adds another element to the concern over a "sorgy" state. As he was no doubt a little drunk at the time, I doubt John Joyce was "sorgy" when he held his eldest son James by the feet and dunked him in the Liffey.

sorowbrate *FW* 518.22 *v.* To observe an event with proper ceremonies or celebrate, though with sadness or sorrow. On Memorial Day we "sorowbrate" the sacrifices of our armed forces. Irish wakes are also somewhat sorrowful celebrations, sorrow for the loss of loved ones but a celebration of their passing from this vale of tears to a happier home in Heaven. ("as betwinst Picturshirts and Scutticules, like their caractacurs in an Irish Ruman to sorowbrate the expeltsion of the Danos?") McHugh mentions the "expulsion of the Danes after the battle of Clontarf, 1014," an occasion for a happy rather than a sorrowful celebration for the Irish. (See **celibrate**.)

soupirs *FW* 453.12 *n.* McHugh translates "turning breakfarts into lost soupirs" as turning "breakfasts into Last Suppers." No doubt the main course of "lost soupirs" would be soup. Leopold

Bloom carefully breaking a fart on the street in *Ulysses* comes to mind with "breakfarts." (See **farternoiser**.)

sourface *FW* 50.10 *n*. 1. The top layer or surface of the Earth, either land or water, that has an acid or sour taste or aspect. Acid rain produced in many places by pollution has changed the surface of our planet to the "sourface" of our planet. 2. A disagreeable or bad-tempered expression or face. *Genesis* 1:2 reports that in the beginning "the Spirit of God was moving over the surface of the waters," and "God saw all that He had made, and behold it was very good." Looking at what man has made of God's creation, His look might have changed his facial aspect from one of benevolence to a "sourface." ("from the sourface of this earth, that austral plain he had transmaried himself to") Astral plane, the heavens, or God's abode is indicated with "austral plain."

sowarmly *FW* 430.20 *adv*. A great number or swarm of bees that is easily excited or warm. A swarm of bees, like other stinging insects, sends out a warm warning when a perceived danger approaches its hive, and the stings it inflicts are warm in the sense of generating some heat mixed with pain. ("on their best beehiviour who all they were girls all rushing sowarmly for the post as buzzy as sie could bie") McHugh gives the Norwegian *bie* for "bee" and reads this phrase as "busy as she could be." (See **beehiviour** & **buzzy**.)

spatialist *FW* 149.19 *n*. An expert or specialist on spatial matters, that is those pertaining to space. In the spatiotemporal story of The "Ondt and the Gracehoper" within *Finnegans Wake*, the Ondt is the "spatialist" while the Gracehoper represents issues of time. Joyce and Shem are on the Gracehoper's side while Joyce's brother Stanislaus and Shaun side with the Ondt. ("the same dime-cash problem elsewhere naturalistically of course, from the blinkpoint of so eminent a spatialist") McHugh gives the French *cache-cache* for "hide & seek" and quotes from Wyndham Lewis' *Time and Western Man*: "Bergson had said that the intellect 'spatialized' things. It was that 'spatialization' that the doctrinaire of motion and mental 'time' attacked." (See **dhrone**.)

spittyful *FW* 240.5 *adj.* Deserving contempt, scorn, or pity while also deserving to have salvia spit from the mouth upon. HCE becomes a pitiful, "spittyful" character in *Finnegans Wake* once the rumors of his "crime" in Phoenix Park are broadcast throughout Dublin. ("But low, boys low, he rises, shrivering, with his spittyful eyes and his whoozebecome voice.") McHugh references the sea shanty "What Shall We Do with the Drunken Sailor?" with its line, "Low, boys and up she rises.' This of course suggests Tim Finnegan rising from the dead after his drunken fall from a ladder. "Woebegone" can be read for "whoozebecome," but I also read it as the voice of someone who's become woozy from drinking booze. The blind man whose sight was restored by Jesus spitting on some clay and placing it over his eyes might be said to have been a "spittyful" sight.

splabashing *FW* 431.16 *v.* To smash or bash by striking or splashing with water or another liquid. In *Finnegans Wake* there was a good bit of "splabashing" of porter and whiskey in the free-for-all among the mourners that resulted in the revival of Tim Finnegan when some of the whiskey splabashed on him. ("he knowed his love by her waves of splabashing and she showed him proof by her way of blabushing") McHugh identifies the song "I Know My Love by His Way of Walking."

spotch *FW* 600.16 *n.* Spot and splotch combined to give a botched blotch or spot. ("that his harpened before Gage's Fane for it has to be over this booty spotch") Within this Wakean context, McHugh translates "booty spotch" as "beauty spot" and references "beauty spot" as slang for "cunt." Beauty spot also occurs as "Miss Butys Pott" (*FW* 220.7) and "Just one big booty's pot" (*FW* 291.F70). With "booty" as slang for "buttocks," the pot becomes a chamber pot.

SPQueaRking *FW* 455.28 *n.* The act of talking or speaking about ancient Rome. In any film about Rome, such as HBO's recent series *Rome*, the initials SPQR for Senatus Populusque Romanus or the Senate and People of Rome appear quite frequently. An entirely different twist is given by Edmund Epstein who writes that "Woolworth, a major ruin of the small trader, invented the slogan that appears elsewhere in the *Wake*, SPQR—Small Profits, Quick Returns." ("lets regally fire of his mio colpo for the chrisman's pandemon to give over and the Harlequinade to begin properly SPQueaRking") McHugh reads "mio colpo" as the Latin *mea culpa* for "my fault" and the Italian *mio colpo* for "my shot." The Harlequin appears here, perhaps as a performer in the "chrisman's pandemon" or the "Christmas pantomime" and "pandemonium."

spreach *FW* 378.32 *n. & v.* Speech or speak, preach, and possibly screech all rolled into one. Examples are available any Sunday morning on radio or television. ("Spreach! Wear anartful of outer nocense!" McHugh gives the German *sprich* for "speak" and the Latin *nocentia* for "guilt," all while reading this as "utter nonsense."

spunish *FW* 548.8 *n.* Spanish plays on words or puns that cause pain or punish. ("I chained her chastemate to grippe fuming snugglers, her chambrett I bestank so to spunish furiosos") There's some naughty stuff going on here with McHugh giving *casemate* as French slang for "cunt," *chambrette* as French for "little room," and *furioso* as Spanish for "violent." *Finnegans Wake* is famous, if not infamous, for its multilingual puns. A friend who speaks Spanish shared this pun with me: "Que' un pescado hace? Nada." This translates as: "What does a fish do? Nothing." The joke is that "nada" means "swim" in third person singular and also means "nothing." As puns go, and many wish they would, this one is pretty puny so, if you have something better, please send it along and I'll be moocow grasses.

stablecert *FW* 610.17 *n.* Steady and firm or stable while sure and without doubt or certain, giving stability with certitude. Tim Finnegan's footing on his ladder was far from "stablecert" the morning of his fall, perhaps even less so than Humpty Dumpty on his wall. (*Muta*: Haven money on stablecert?") Richard Beckman sees "stablecert" as "a horse race with the winner known in advance."

stolentelling *FW* 424.35 *n.* The reciting or telling of a story or storytelling that is taken dishonestly or stolen, another word for plagiarizing. When the painter James Whistler made a witty remark one day, Oscar Wilde said, "I wish I'd said that." Whistler replied, "You will, Oscar, you will." ("The last word in stolentelling!") Because of its utter uniqueness and its appropriations from a wide array of languages, books, and various sources, *Finnegans Wake* can be considered, in a certain sense, the "last word in stolentelling."

storyaboot *FW* 336.17 *n.* A volume of tales or a storybook with a story about a boot, possibly a shoe, pictures of which resemble a boot, lived in by the old lady who was beside herself from a surfeit of children or possibly Puss in Boots and/or Buster Brown and his dog Tiege. This word anticipates Nancy Sinatra's story in song about her boots that were made for walking. ("We are once amore as babes awondering in a wold made fresh where with the hen in the storyaboot we start from scratch.") McHugh references the song "The Babes in the Wood" that was also a pantomime and *John* 1:14: "The Word was made flesh." The *Wake*'s ubiquitous story about the hen, Biddy Doran, who scratches out a letter ("litter") from a kitchen midden is hard at work in this sentence.

strangerous *FW* 625.5 *adj.* What is at once odd, unusual, or strange and unsafe, risky, or dangerous. For HCE, the "strangerous" "Cad" in Phoenix Park indeed proves to be a dangerous stranger. ("I will tell you all sorts of makeup things, strangerous.")

strife *FW* 38.9 *n.* Another of the *Wake*'s clever uses of an existing word to do double duty, in this case as a married woman or wife who causes household quarrelling, fighting, or strife. "Our cad's bit of strife (knee Bareniece Maxwelton) with a quick ear for spittoons (as the aftertale hath it) glaned up as usual with dumbestic husbandry" is the Cad's wife who pried out of him the details of his encounter with HCE at midnight in Phoenix Park and, despite her husband's admonition not to mention it to anyone, she blabs to her priest who can't keep a confidence and, before the day is out, the story is all over Dublin and the subject of a scurrilous song, a lot of strife caused by a wife. McHugh writes that "bit of strife" is rhyming slang for "wife," that "Bareniece Maxwelton" refers to the song "Annie Laurie: Maxwelton braes are bonny," and that the French *glaner* for "glean" indicates that the wife cleaned up after the meal with efficient domestic husbandry.

sullibrated *FW* 379.7 *adj.* Tarnished, defiled, or sullied though distinguished, renowned, or celebrated. In the sense of infamous or notorious, Joyce became a "sullibrated" writer for many critics with the publication of *Finnegans Wake*. ("And be the seem talking wharabahts hosetanzies, dat sure is sullibrated word!") This is one of Joyce's many takeoffs from Mark Twain's *Huckleberry Finn*. It's said that Joyce never actually read Twain's celebrated and later "sullibrated" book but asked his step-grandson in America to read it for him and to underline passages he thought interesting. Joyce's interest in *Huckleberry Finn* was primarily concerned with the name Finn and its American setting that he could connect to Finn MacCool and his Irish setting.

summour *FW* 371.15 *n.* 1. A secret love affair or *amour*, French for "love," during summer, the season between spring and autumn. If a young man's fancies lightly turn to love in spring, in summer they find fruition. 2. A love affair or amour with summer, a love shared by all those who enjoy hot weather and its sports. ("most emulously concerned to cupturing the last dropes

268 | A *Finnegans Wake* Lextionary

of summour") One in love with summer would be concerned to capture its last drops before it dies into autumn. McHugh makes a connection with Thomas Moore's well known song, "'Tis the Last Rose of Summer."

suppraise *FW* 356.19 *v.* "I have just (let us suppraise) been reading in a (suppressed) book" Starting with its use in *Finnegans Wake*, "suppraise" might be read: let us suppose; let us appraise; let us surprise or, as suggested by McHugh, "let us pray." All of these can, in some way, be associated with the reading of a banned or suppressed book, whether the cause of its suppression be political, scatological, or religious. With the publication of *Ulysses* in 1922, Joyce experienced suppression first hand, though I "suppraise" (suppose) the lack of praise some critics had for his banned book did not come as a total suppraise" (surprise).

surview *FW* 285.26 *v.* To measure size, shape, or boundaries or survey what is within one's range of vision or view or to survey only what can be seen. McHugh suggests "purview," "preview," and "serve you" as well. ("For a surview over all the factionables see Iris in the Evenine's World.") "Evenine's World" suggests Joyce's short story in *Dubliners*, "Eveline." Her world was quite restricted, limited as it was to caring for her widowed father and her two young siblings while clerking in a Dublin store. Given a chance to start a new life in Buenos Ayres with a sailor and widen her purview, Eveline froze at the last moment and refused to board the ship, preferring to remain in what she could "surview." The old phrase, "I am lord of all I that I survey," can now be updated to "I am lord of all that I 'surview.'"

sweetmoztheart *FW* 360.12 *n.* A lover or sweetheart as sweet as the heart of Mozart's music, especially the sweet, dreamy nocturnes as seen in the context here. ("our nocturnefield, night's sweetmoztheart, their Carmen Sylvae, my quest, my queen") McHugh references Mozart's "Queen of the Night" in *The Magic Flute*.

sybarate *FW* 451.32 *v.* To divide or separate lovers of luxury or sybarites into categories such as those who love the pleasures of the finest and rarest foods from those who love the richest and costliest clothing. Those who love the most luxurious and voluptuous in every category of life can be sybarated into a special class all their own. ("the most uxuriously furnished compartments, with sybarate chambers, just as I'd run my shoestring into near a million or so of them as a firstclass dealer") This description sounds like a compartment on the Orient Express where first-class and the best of everything is standard. McHugh adds that "run my shoestring" is American slang for "make easy money."

synnbildising *FW* 332.28 *v.* With the German *Sinnbild* and the Danish *sindbillede* for "symbol" along with the Danish *syn* for "sight" and *synd* for "sin," there is the sighting of something symbolizing sin. For some, Playboy's iconic image of a bunny symbolizes pleasure, while for others it symbolizes sin. ("synnbildising graters and things, eke ysendt?") McHugh gives the French *ikke sandt* for "isn't that true?"

T

teargarten *FW* 75.1 *n.* A drop of salty liquid flowing from the eyeball or a tear and the German *Garten* for "garden," giving a garden of tears or a graveyard or cemetery. The German *Tiergarten* means "zoo," and that fits nicely within the Wakean context: "As the lion in our teargarten remembers the nenuphars of his Nile." Combining these two seemingly unrelated places, Joyce was buried in a cemetery near Zurich's zoological garden that he had compared to the one in Phoenix Park, Dublin. Nora remarked that Joyce had always loved the lions and said she was comforted by the thought of him being able to listen to them roar. This lionized writer had come home in a way, for one of the houses he lived in as a child was called "Leoville" because of a stone lion over the porch.

teartoretoring *FW* 256.17 *adj.* In *Joyce's Rare View*, Richard Beckman gives his definition as "teary, torn, but returning." This is the perfect word to describe ALP in the *Wake*'s final, haunting pages. She is teary ("saltsick") and torn about leaving her husband, HCE, and children, Shem, Shaun, and Isabel ("I'll slip away before they're up."), but still returning as she must to her father, the Irish Sea ("it's sad and old it's sad and weary I go

272 | A *Finnegans Wake* Lextionary

back to you, my cold father, my cold mad father, my cold mad feary father"). She asks us to "mememormee!" as she knows, through her tears and torn feelings, that she will return again as rain that refreshes the river that "returnally" seeks the sea. ("For they are now tearing, that is, teartoretorning.")

teasily *FW* 68.1 *adv*. Not hard to do or easily able to pester or tease. Shem is treated "teasily" in the *Wake* by Issy and her rainbow girls. ("she stripped teasily for binocular man and that her jambs were jimpjoyed to see each other") A strip tease is easily suggested here, and it seems Jim Joyce jumped for joy to see her legs since the Old French *jamb* meant "leg."

teaspoonspill *FW* 534.9 *n*. A fall or spill of a teaspoonful amount of some solid or liquid, thus a small spill. ("I protest there is luttrelly not one teaspoonspill of evidence at bottomlie to my babad, as you shall see, as this is.") This is HCE's protest against those accusing him of some sin or misdeed in Phoenix Park. One of the accusations is that he masturbated ("abusing the apparatus") while watching two girls urinate in the bushes ("Trickpissers vill be pairsecluded"). If so, the "teaspoonspill" could have been his semen. For "luttrelly" McHugh references "John Luttrel, sheriff of Dublin, 1567-8." But of course you already knew that. It can also be read as "literally." Another instance of HCE's stuttering, indicating guilt, appears with "babad," a reference going back to the first thunder word of 100 letters on the *Wake*'s first page—"bababad . . ."

tellavicious *FW* 349.28 *n*. Television that is evil, wicked, and vicious. Naturally, most television programming meets this description, as the main objective is to attract as many viewers as possible. I know I finally gave up watching reruns of *The Lawrence Welk Show* because there was just too much sax and violins. ("*He blanks his ogles because he confesses to all his tellavicious nieces.*") It should be noted that *Finnegans Wake* may be the first novel to mention television ("television" 150.33 & 254.22 and

"Television" 52.18), a medium that was not well known when the *Wake* was published in 1939.

theogamyjig *FW* 332.24 *n.* A supreme being or God, the name of whom is either forgotten or not cared to be mentioned, in other words a thingamajig, but a thingamajig the name of which incorporates a reference to the Greek *theos* for "god." McHugh gives the Greek *theogamia* for "marriage of gods." ("there was a little theogamyjig incidence that hoppy-go-jumpy Junuary morn") It seems the incidence involving a god happened on a happy-go-lucky morning during "Junuary." (See **Junuary**.)

theosophagusted *FW* 610.1 *v.* Sickened with dislike or disgusted, which is felt in the gullet or esophagus, by a philosophical or religious system that derives knowledge of God through mystical insight. Joyce may have in mind here the Theosophical Society founded in America in 1875 that combined the teachings of a wide variety of religions, but he is particularly mocking George Russell, editor of the *Irish Homestead*, who published three of Joyce's short stories but then refused to accept any others since he did not consider them appropriate for his paper. Russell was an avid member of the Dublin Lodge of the Theosophical Society. Theosophy combines the Greek *theos* for "god" and *sophos* for "wise." ("*Juva:* Bulkily: and he is fundamentially theosophagusted over the whorse proceedings.") McHugh adds that the philosopher Berkeley denied the existence of matter. (See **whorse**.)

thinkyou *FW* 232.17 *v.* To at once express gratitude or thank someone for their opinion while asking if that is what s/he really thinks. It expresses doubt, yet politely. ("He's your change, thinkyou methim.")

thonthorstrok *FW* 18.16. *adj.* Suddenly overcome or astonished as if struck by a stroke of lightening or thunderstruck. Thor, the Scandinavian god of thunder, is the clue in the word's center.

In Vico's circular theory of human history, the third and final age ends with the sound of thunder that instills the fear of God and drives man back to the shelter of the caves and to renewed religion. The reference in *Finnegans Wake* is to a conversation between the twins Shem and Shaun as the cavemen Mutt and Jute: "Mutt.—Ore you astoneaged, jute you?" "Jute.—Oye am thonthorstrok, thing mud." (See **astoneaged**.)

thorpeto *FW* 77.7 *n.* An explosive underwater missile or torpedo combined with the speed and destructive power of a thunderbolt thrown by the Scandinavian god Thor. Launched with the speed of light and the full force of a lightning strike, a "thorpeto," unlike a conventional torpedo, makes defensive maneuvers impossible. ("to sternbooard out of his aerial thorpeto, Auton Dynamon, contacted with the expectant minefield") A torpedo can be launched by submarine, torpedo boat, or a low-flying airplane, but this "thorpeto," like Thor's thunderbolts, is launched from the air, to the starboard side. McHugh gives the Greek *auto dynamikon* for "self powerful."

thorror *FW* 626.28 *n.* 1. Great fear, dread, or terror and horror caused by the Viking commander Thorir when he invaded and terrorized Ireland. ("The invision of Indelond. And, by Thorror, you looked it!") (See **invision**.) 2. Great fear or horror at the sound of thunder produced by Thor's lightning bolt. (See **thonthorostrok**.) Joyce had a through "thorror" of thunder by the second definition.

thothfolly *FW* 415.28 *adv.* Thoughtfully or acting in a thoughtful or considerate manner with the underlying dichotomy of Thoth, the Egyptian god of wisdom, with particular emphasis on reading and writing, paired with foolishness or folly. Since Thoth was often portrayed as an ape, I think of that humorous statue of a chimpanzee studying a human skull in his hand while sitting on a copy of Darwin's *Origin of the Species*. ("thothfolly making chilly spaces at hisphex affront of the icinglass of his windhame") McHugh translates this as "thoughtfully making silly faces at himself in front of the looking-glass of his window." Since this passage appears in the story of the "Ondt and the Gracehoper," the juxtaposition of "thought" and "folly" makes perfect Wakean sense. I wonder if Joyce was anticipating Michel Butor's novel, *Portrait of the Artist as a Young Ape* (© 1967), when coining "thothfolly," with its thought of Thoth and the foolishness or folly of thinking and knowledge.

throust *FW* 395.36 *v.* A forceful push or thrust into the passage from the mouth to the stomach or throat. As "when, as quick, is greased pigskin, Amoricas Champius, with one aragan throust, druve the massive of virilvigtoury flshpst the both lines of forwards (Eburnea's down, boys!) rightjingbangshot into the goal of her gullet." This is from Tristram and Iseult's steamy lovemaking scene onboard the boat in which Tristram is taking the Irish princess Iseult to Cornwall as bride to his uncle King Mark II. If the censors had taken the time and effort to decipher this passage, *Finnegans Wake* would have been banned as was *Ulysses*. Here's what they missed: "pigskin" is slang for a "football;" "Amoricas" is Tristram who came from French Brittany, also known as Amorica, and who is a champion in war and love; *aragan* is Armenian for "masculine" or "male," and *ouragan* is French for "thrust of the male reproductive organ;" McHugh gives "virilvigtoury" as "virile victory" and "flshpst" as "flash past," while "gullet" is another name for "throat." You can put these pieces together yourself. This steamy scene, and it gets steamier than these lines, is witnessed by the four old men, the Evangelists Matthew, Mark, Luke, and John, known in the *Wake* as "Mamalujo." Margot Norris compares their "salivating gusto . . . as they admire Tristan's erotic assault with the brutish enthusiasm of fans at an American football game."

thuartpeatrick *FW* 3.10 *n.* Thou art Patrick. From Jesus' pun on Peter's name, meaning rock, in *Matthew* 16:18: "Thou art Peter, and upon this rock I will build my church." When a friend complained of the constant punning in *Finnegans Wake*, Joyce replied, "The Holy Roman Catholic Apostolic Church was built on a pun. It ought to be good enough for me." A substantial part of Ireland is composed of peat and, when cut into bricks and dried in ricks, is used as fuel. In establishing the Catholic Church in Ireland, St. Patrick could punningly be referred to as St. Peatrick. ("nor avoice from afar bellowsed mishe mishe to tauftauf thuartpeatrick") St. Germanicus was Patrick's spiritual tutor, so Joyce used the German *taufen* for "baptize" to create "tauftauf." There are always reasons in what seems the *Wake*'s madness, though readers often fail to find them. In *Larva: Midsummer Night's Babel*, Julián Ríos references this Wakean wit with "Thou art Peter Pun." When Vladimir Nabokov described the *Wake* in his *Lectures on Literature* as "that petrified superpun," he might more accurately have described "thuarpeatrick" as that "patrified" superpun. (See **apun, patrified,** & **prepatrickularly**.)

thumbtonosery *FW* 253.28 *n*. To place one's thumb to one's nose at someone is a sign of disrespect and disregard. By way of rhyme, this suggests thumb to rosary, a string of beads used by Roman Catholics is reciting a series of prayers, and an indication of Joyce's rejection of his religious upbringing. ("reechoable mirthpeals and general thumbtonosery") Page 308 of *Finnegans Wake* has a crude drawing of a thumb to a nose in the right margin.

thuthunder *FW* 378.7 *n*. The stuttering sound of the loud noise following lightning or thunder, a sign of God's guilt, according to Joyce, in creating a flawed world. ("he horrhorrd his name in thuthunder. Rrrwwwkkkrrr!") (See **horrhorrd**.)

tighteousness *FW* 5.18 *n*. 1. Proper and just behavior or righteousness in which it is thought best to be stingy or tight. 2. Righteousness based on being drunk or, in slang, being tight. ("Stay us wherefore in our search for tighteousness, O Sustainer") Joyce was not "tighteousness" when it came to money, even going so far as to buy fur coats for his daughter in hopes it would positively affect her mental problems or giving lavish tips to waiters, but he was a fervent believer in "tighteousness" based on the consumption of alcohol and, to Nora's consternation, he seldom failed to order a second bottle of white wine at dinner.

timeblinged *FW* 612.21 *adj*. In *Joyce's Rare View*, Richard Beckman writes: "Human time is despised by the ideal and the members of its cohort, purity and eternity; for them, time is contemptible as are those that are 'timeblinged' (612.21), blinded or blinkered or blighted by time." ("for beingtime monkblinkers timeblinged completamentarily murkblankered")

todie *FW* 381.23 *v. & n*. To cease living or die now or today. The day of one's death. ("the blackberd's ballad *I've a terrible errible lot todue todie todue tootorribleday*") McHugh gives as a reference the song "I've a Terrible Lot to Do Today." (See **todue**.)

todue *FW* 381.23 *n*. What is expected or due now or today. As the sign on the boss's desk reads: "Of course I want it today. If I wanted it tomorrow I'd ask for it tomorrow." (*"I've a terrible errible lot todue todie todue tootorribleday"*) (See **todie**.)

tomarry *FW* 324.33 *v*. To wed or marry the day after today or tomorrow. The old song lyrics "I'll marry you tomorrow for a honeymoon tonight" may now be shortened to "I'll tomarry you for a honeymoon tonight." For "with local drizzles, the outlook for tomarry (Streamstress Mandig) beamed brider, his ability good," McHugh gives the Norwegian *mandig* for "manly" and "sexual potency" as slang for "ability," both in keeping with a marriage motif. The outlook for a marriage tomorrow looks good if "beamed brider" is read as a bride beaming brightly with happiness and a weather forecast for bright, beaming sunshine.

toonigh *FW* 11.13 *n*. This evening or tonight is too nearly upon us or nigh. ("But it's the armitides toonigh, militropucos, and toomourn we wish for a muddy kissmans") McHugh finds "armistice tonight" and in "militropucos" Esperanto's *milito* for "war" and *paco* for "peace." If "muddy kissmans" is read as "Merry Christmas," this passage becomes a reference to the Christmas Eve truce spontaneously declared by German and English soldiers during the First World War when these men, to the consternation of their officers, abandoned their muddy trenches to figuratively kiss and be friends. The thing to mourn is that on Christmas morn both sides would be back to militarily killing each other in the muddy, bloody war that didn't end all wars.

toborrow *FW* 455.12 *n.* To get with the idea of returning or to borrow from the day after today or tomorrow in order to get by today, something Joyce did as he frequently asked for advances on his wages from employers and for loans from his friends, all to be repaid in some distant tomorrow. As Wimpy in the Popeye comics was wont to say, "I would gladly pay you Tuesday for a hamburger today." In *Finnegans Wake* "toborrow" becomes a play on Macbeth's soliloquy, "Tomorrow and tomorrow and tomorrow," with "Toborrow and to toburrow and tobarrow! That's our crass, hairy and evergrim life, till one finel howdiedow Bouncer Naster raps on the bell with a bone and his stinkers stank behind him with the sceptre and the hourglass." HCE appears in this horribly grim glance at what awaits all of us on some tomorrow with "our crass, hairy and evergrim life."

tosorrow *FW* 563.36 *n.* The sadness or sorrow of the day after today or tomorrow, something that is sure to come. As Jack Kerouac writes in *The Dharma Bums*, "It all ends in tears, anyway." With Macbeth's sad soliloquy, "Tomorrow and tomorrow and tomorrow," we certainly know his tomorrow will most certainly be a "tosorrow." ("Adieu, Soft adieu, for these nice presents, kerryjevin. Still tosorrow!") We are thankful for the present, which may be nice, till the morrow whence comes sorrow.

tourible *FW* 344.13 *n.* Description of a journey or tour that is dreadful, awful, or terrible. The Titanic had a short but "tourible" voyage. That some tours of Europe are "tourible" can be found in the title of the film *If It's Tuesday This Must be Belgium*. ("I seeing him in his oneship fetch along within hail that tourible tall with his nitshnykopfgoknob") The last word here appears like something that would result from a monkey playing with a keyboard but, as a Wakean construction, it contains some interesting ideas. McHugh uncovers Nietzche, the Ruthenian (Ukrainian) *nichanyk* for 'night watchman," the German *Kopf* for "head," and "knob" as slang for "penis." Tying all of these together would make for an interesting contest.

towooerds *FW* 237.1 *prep.* In the direction of or towards seeking to marry or to woo. Candy and flowers are traditional gifts for romantic wooers traveling "towooerds" matrimony. ("accourdant to the coursets of things feminite, towooerds him in heliolatry") According to the course of things feminine, women once were laced into stiff corsets. Joyce complained of Nora's corset on their early dates and begged her to "leave off that breastplate," comparing it to "embracing a letter-box." She kept it on.

transaccidentated *FW* 186.3-4 *v.* 1. A mishap or accident while conducting or transacting a business deal or other transaction. 2. McHugh references "transaccidentation: transmutation of accidents of bread & wine in Eucharist." 3. In *Joyce's Rare View*, Richard Beckman writes: "Joyce's flip 'tranaccidentated' is a one-word retort to Kant's quasi-metaphysical positing of a world beyond the senses. The noumenal and the Ding-an-sich are prodigious guesses at the unknowables that underlie experience; but they imply faith in an indemonstrable coherence. The word 'transaccidentated' smiles away the transcendental, and nods toward a condition of being in which 'time and chance happeneth to . . . all.'" And in *Lots of Fun at "Finnegans Wake": Unravelling Universals*, Finn Fordham has more to say about this word coming "from the separation of 'accidents' from 'substance'" than can be recounted here, so I refer interested readers

280 | A *Finnegans Wake* Lextionary

to pages 47-48 of his book. ("reflecting from his own individual person life unlivable, transaccidentated through the slow fires of consciousness into a dividual chaos") McHugh defines "dividual" as "shared amongst a number," which works with his reference to the Eucharist in definition two above.

transfusiasm *FW* 425.15 *n*. A zeal or enthusiasm for the transfer or transfusion of a liquid from one container to another, generally thought of in terms of transfusions of blood. Count Dracula comes to mind as having the greatest "transfusiasm" in literature and films. ("with the allergrossest transfusiasm as, you see") McHugh gives the German *allergrösste* for "largest of all," which perfectly describes the Count's enthusiasm for transfusions of great quantities of the sticky red stuff. In the television comedy *The Munsters*, Grandpa had such a strong "transfusiasm" that he was always overdrawn at the blood bank.

traumscrapt *FW* 623.36 *n*. A written copy or transcript plus the German *Traum* for "dream," giving a transcript of a dream with the hint of some shock or trauma to it. *Finnegans Wake*, a transcript of a dream that caused trauma in the literary world, is a case in point. In the *Wake* the "tramscrapt" referred to is the "litter" or letter that the hen scratches up in the dump and that ALP uses to defend her husband, HCE, against charges that he did something improper in Phoenix Park. ("Rased on Traumscrapt From Maston, Boss.") The letter's envelope indicated it was sent from Boston, Massachusetts.

treeth *FW* 44.9 *n*. A tree combined with what is true or the truth. In the Garden of Eden it was the fruit from the Tree of the Knowledge of Good an Evil that was to open Eve and Adam's eyes to the truth, putting them on parr with God. Truth always has consequences, and the first couple paid dearly for violating this dietary restriction that kept doctors as well as God away. ("viersified and piersified may the treeth we tale of live in stoney") With "treeth" and "stoney," the tree/stone motif that so often recurs in *Finnegans Wake* is found. The tale that lives in story is that of Tristram or "Treestone" and Iseult as well as the time (tree)/space (stone) continuum woven into the *Wake*. Tree and stone also represent a phallic/testicular combination.

troublant *FW* 5.7 *adj*. Disturbance, disorder, or trouble that is violent, stormy, or turbulent. This is also the French spelling for "perturbing." Considering all the trouble Henry II of England had after wondering aloud who would rid him of that troublesome priest (Thomas à Becket achieved sainthood after being murdered by some of the king's supporters), he might have more accurately asked who would rid him of this "troublant" priest. ("His crest of huroldry, in vert with ancillars, troublant, argent, a hegoak, poursuivant, horrid, horned.") The coat of arms of Finnegan/HCE is described here. McHugh gives "Poursuivant' as "an officer of the College of Arms" and several heraldic terms such as "argent" for "silver." For those with a special interest in heraldry, I recommend Michael J. O'Shea's excellent volume, *James Joyce and Heraldry*.

trurally *FW* 357.34 *adv*. Genuinely or truly in the country rather than the city or rurally. Within "for relieving purposes in our trurally virvir vergitable (garden)" McHugh provides the Latin *vir* for "man," making this a most manly garden for vegetables the color of verdigris (See **vergitable**.), and "virvir" is another instance of stuttering in *Finnegans Wake* that so often indicates guilt. The first guilt associated with a garden is the Original Sin of Eve and Adam in the Garden of Eden, a "trurally" garden since there were no cities in sight at that time in history.

trystfully *FW* 317.36 *adv*. Having faith and confidence or believing trustfully in an appointed time and place for a meeting or tryst, usually involving lovers. In *Finnegans Wake* Tristram and Iseult have complete trust in seeing each other at the spot in King Mark's garden where they have arranged their tryst. ("still trystfully acape for her his gragh knew well in precious memory

282 | A *Finnegans Wake* Lextionary

and that proud grace to her, in gait a movely water") For "acape" and "gragh," McHugh gives the Greek *agape* and the Irish *gràdh* for "love." A manner of walking or running or a gait like lovely, moving water is one way to read "in gait a movely water," but it also recalls the spring that flowed from the base of a pine tree in the fenced orchard behind Kind Mark's castle. This spring-fed steam flowed out of the orchard, into the castle, and through Iseult's rooms. As a prearranged sign, Tristram would throw pieces of bark and twigs on these waters and Iseult, watching for them, would then know to meet her lover in the orchard. This signal system may seem primitive in our day of cell phones and text messages, but it's proven to be much safer.

twiminds *FW* 188.14 *n.* Of like mind such as is found in the minds of twins, especially identical twins, and even those separated at birth. ("you have become of twosome twiminds forenenst gods, hidden and discovered") McHugh gives *forenenst* as Anglo-Irish for "opposite." The twins in *Finnegans Wake*, Shem and Shaun, are definitely of two minds, being opposite in every way, but the only way they can overcome their father is to transcend their differences and join forces. This shared goal gives the twins "twiminds." (See **twwinns**.)

twowsers *FW* 276.F1 *n.* Two pairs of pants or trousers. Many suits were once sold with "twowsers" as trousers get more wear than coats, so a suit with "twowsers" allows the coat and trousers to wear evenly. ("never in these twowsers and ever in those twawsers")

twwinns *FW* 330.30 *n.* A visually-creative way to represent the word "twins." In *Finnegans Wake* an appearance by the Earwicker twins, Shem and Shaun, is often signaled by the use of doubled consonants. These quarreling, competitive siblings stand in for many other famous and infamous pairs throughout the *Wake*, beginning with Cain and Abel, whom Joyce said were the originators of war. (See **twiminds**.) This is seen in the Wakean joke: "Knock knock. War's where! Which war? The Twwinns." McHugh writes that Joyce said the second "w" in "Twwinns" stood for "without an apple" since Eve was born without an Adam's apple, leading to a related joke. "Knock knock. Woos without! Without what? An apple."

U

ultimendly *FW* 29.35 *adv.* Coming to the very end or ultimate limit of time as opposed to the end of space or any other measured item. Death, for example, comes when one's time is ultimately and "ultimendly" up. ("he is ee and no counter he who will be ultimendly respunchable for the hubbub caused in Edenborough") McHugh gives the Latin *timendum* for "to be feared," as the end of time so often is. He also gives the Hebrew *hibbub* for "love" and "Edenborough" as both "Edinburgh" in Scotland and the "Eden and Burgh Quays" that face each other on the Liffey in Dublin. The "hubbub caused in Edenborough" can be read as the uproar caused in the Garden of Eden when Eve and Adam ate the forbidden apple. (See **forebitten** & **applegate**.) HCE also created an uproar from his activities, whatever they may have been, in Phoenix Park that stands as a substitute for Eden in *Finnegans Wake*. Pigott's forged letter in which he attempted to incriminate Parnell in the Phoenix Park murders began, "Dear E . . . let there be an end of this hesitency." In appears as "he is ee" above.

ultravirulence *FW* 425.35 *adj.* Excessively or ultra deadly or virulent regarding the damaging power of sunlight's ultraviolet rays, such as severe burns and skin cancer. ("Because I am altogether a chap too fly and hairyman for to infradig the like of that ultravirulence.") Infrared rays that provide most of the sun's heat are part of the picture here. McHugh gives the Latin *ultra virulentiam* for "beyond a stink," which speaks to the stink given to suntans by dermatologists. He also references "hairyman" with *Genesis* 27:11: "Esau my brother is a hairy man."

umberella *FW* 530.29 *n*. A reddish brown or umber portable, circular cover from the rain/sun or umbrella. ("Bloody old preadamite with his twohandled umberella!") McHugh identifies "twohandled umberella" as the "two-handled sword" used by Sir Almeric Tristram that is on display in Howth Castle. Sir Almeric makes an early appearance in *Finnegans Wake* as the first word of the second sentence, though he shares that honor with an earlier Sir Tristram, the knightly lover of Iseult. He was part of Henry II's invasion fleet and landed on the hill of Howth on Saint Lawrence's Day. In commemoration of his victory over the Irish, he changed his family name to Lawrence and was made the first Earl of Howth. While umbrellas, mostly black, not umber, are now ubiquitous in London, the first person to be seen with one was stoned to death on the street, bringing up "Bloody" above. (For "preadamite," see **preadaminant**.)

umproar *FW* 273.26 *n*. A loud noise or roar when one who rules on plays in a game such as baseball or an ump, short for umpire, makes an incorrect or unpopular decision or call. "Kill the ump!" is a common "umproar." ("nith is the nod for the umproar napollyon and hitheris poorblond piebold hoerse") I won't argue that the obvious reference here is to the Emperor Napoleon on his roan horse but, since everything in *Finnegans Wake* relates to everything else and, since the Wakean phrase "the Yanks were huckling the Empire" naturally relates to "umproar" and, since both anticipate Kenneth Lash's "Finnegan Wakes at Yankee Stageum" (*The New Yorker*, April 9, 1984) that contains "—Oi! Keel the empire!", my definition is not outside the ballpark.

unasyllabled *FW* 183.15 *adj.* The 100 letter thunder words in *Finnegans Wake* are difficult to absorb or are unable to be assimilated because of the difficulty of breaking the words into syllables, making these very long words "unasyllabled" for most readers. In his filmed lecture on the *Wake*, Joseph Campbell gives a great rendition of the first thunder word that appears on the *Wake*'s first page, though others might sound it out differently. ("imeffible tries at speech unasyllabled") The clue here with "imeffible" suggests that many words in *Finnegans Wake*, while not technically too great to be described in words or "ineffable," are ones that can not be said with any assurance of competency. In *A Shorter "Finnegans Wake,"* Anthony Burgess arranges the syllables of the first thunder word in a verse pattern to assist readers in a syllabic pronunciation.

unaveiling *FW* 503.26 *adj.* Inexhaustible or unfailing though not successful or unavailing in revealing or unveiling. All the trials HCE is subjected to over his purported crime in Phoenix Park are "unaveiling," and readers know no more at the *Wake*'s end than at its beginning. Beckman writes: "An elegiac speaker starts to speak the phrase 'To the unaveiling [unfailing] memory of,' but then has to break off. So elusive is memory that invoking it makes the speaker forget what he is about to say. The truth slips out, and 'unfailing memory' comes out as 'unaveiling memory.' Unavailing is discouraging, but, worse, the veil in 'unaveiling' brings up the veil drawn by time and the phenomenon of screen memory." ("By tombs, deep and heavy. To the unaveiling memory of. Peacer the grave.") McHugh reads "tombs, deep and heavy" as "Tom, Dick, and Harry" and "Peacer the grave" as "Peter the Great." With the Latin *petrus* for "stone" (See **Prepatrickulary.**), "Peacer the grave" can be read as a "gravestone," perhaps inscribed with "RIP" for "Rest In Peace." With one last thought on "unaveiling," I submit a quatrain from *The Rubaiyat of Omar Khayyam*:

> There was the Door to which I found no Key;
> There was the Veil through which I might not see:
> Some little Talk awhile of Me and Thee
> There was—and then no more of Thee and Me.

unbespokables *FW* 496.31 *n.* Underwear or unmentionables that are made-to-order or bespoke. ("he came back with a jailbird's unbespokables in his beak") Only *Finnegans Wake* would have Noah's dove return to the ark with tailor-made underwear in its beak instead of an olive leaf. What that might portend is anybody's guess, as is the gender of the wearer of the underwear. Joyce did have a thing for women's undergarments and had a miniature pair of "unbespokables" that he could slip two fingers into as legs and walk them across a tabletop, a stunt he found funny.

uncouthrement *FW* 113.1-2 *n.* Furnished with clothing and/or equipment or accouterment that is crude, strange, or uncouth. ("But how many of her readers realize that she is not out to dizzledazzle with a graith uncouthrement of postmantuam glasseries from the lapins and the grigs.") McHugh references "postmantuam glasseries" with the Lewis Carroll's portmanteau words, forerunners of Wakeisms. In *Through the Looking Glass*, Humpty Dumpty recites, "Twas brillig, and the slithy toves . . ." and explains, "Slithy means lithe and slimy. You see it's like a portmanteau—there are two meanings packed into one word." When Alice asks if words can be made to do so many things, Humpty replies that it is simply a matter of who is to be master. The difference between Humpty and Joyce, who is the undisputed monarch of words, is that Joyce packs in so many meanings that it's difficult to fasten the portmanteau or, as the *Wake* puts it, "his portmanteau priamed full." I'll go far out on a limb with this last quote, so follow at your peril. Joyce produced a production of Oscar Wilde's *The Importance of Being Earnest* while living in Zurich during World War I. In the play it's discovered that Jack Worthing was mistakenly removed from his pram as an infant and placed in a hand-bag by his nurse, Miss Prism, who then left this portmanteau in the cloakroom of a London railway station. Even a small infant would have crammed the bag full. I give this to illustrate just how far one may go when deciphering *Finnegans Wake*.

unfallable *FW* 153.26 *adj*. Reliable, sure, or infallible of not dropping from a higher place or falling. Of the hundreds of characters in *Finnegans Wake*, none seem to possess an "unfallable" nature. Beginning with Tim Finnegan who falls from a ladder in the song that gives the *Wake* its title, to Adam and Eve's fall from grace in the first sentence, and continuing on with Satan falling from Heaven, HCE's fall in Phoenix Park, Napoleon's fall at Waterloo, to ALP's fall as rain over the Wicklow Mountains, everyone is set up for a fall. ("with his unfallable encyclicling upom his alloilable") McHugh provides the German *Unfall* for "accident" and "infallible encyclical" for "unfallable" Pope. This phrase once more (See **dhrone, improssable,** & **purscent**.) trots out Oscar Wilde's comment on foxhunting: "The unspeakable in full pursuit of the uneatable."

unglish *FW* 609.15 *n*. Offensive or ugly English. Politics, especially its campaigns and speeches, seems unable to function without liberal doses of "unglish." ("ricocoursing themselves, as staneglass on stonegloss, inplayn unglish") This may suggest not only "in plain English" but that the ugly in the English language is used in fun or play. The phrase may also suggest that those who live in stained-glass houses should not throw shiny or glossy stones. With "ricocoursing" McHugh brings in the Italian *ricorso* for "recurring," returning once again to Vico's reoccurring historical cycles.

unhappitents *FW* 258.22 *n*. Sad or unhappy dwellers or inhabitants. ("the unhappitents of the earth have terrerumbled from fimament into fundament and from tweedledeedumms down to twiddledeedees.") Within "fimament" McHugh gives the

Italian *fime* for "manure," giving a novel take on the heavens or firmament. You no doubt spotted Tweedledum and Tweedledee from Lewis Carroll's *Through the Looking Glass*.

unletched *FW* 459.26 *v*. To open or lift the latch, thus unlatch lust, lewdness, or lechery. *Finnegans Wake* unletches more than most innocent readers imagine and was mainly saved from the censors because, unlike the unlucky *Ulysses*, they couldn't understand or wouldn't bother to try to translate the lecherous passages before them. Here's the sentence "unletched" comes from: "Why I love taking him out when I unletched his cordon gate." If that doesn't set off your censor alarm, here's the sentence that precedes it: "I shouldn't say he's pretty but I'm cocksure he's shy." If you're still in the dark, see if several sentences that follow it will unletch your little gray cells: "He fell for my lips, for my lisp, for my lewd speaker. I felt for his strength, his manhood, his do you mind?" The real tip-off comes on lines 23-24 with "pity bonhom" that McHugh matches to the French slang *petit bonhomme* for "penis." If you are still uncorrupted after all this, I won't unletch any more, but you may find it helpful to read a few of the more racy romance novels.

unmerried *FW* 226.18 *adj*. Not only without a husband or wife or unmarried but not happy or merry about such a situation. When Joyce asked the young Nora Barnacle to leave Dublin with him, without the benefit of clergy, to live together on the continent of Europe, we know only that, unlike Eveline in Joyce's short story in *Dubliners* by that name, Nora did not hesitate a second. Whether she was "unmerried" about such a state is unknown. Joyce and Nora were officially married in London many years later, primarily for legal, inheritance purposes, though Joyce told his authorized biographer that they had been married in Trieste under assumed names in their early years together. ("For though she's unmerried she'll after truss up and help that hussyband how to hop.")(See **hussyband**.)

unnerstunned *FW* 378.22 *v.* To apprehend a meaning or understand while at the same time overwhelmed or stunned by that understanding. HCE was undoubtedly "unnerstunned" by the nasty rumors and allegations and the song circulating throughout Dublin about his activities the night before in Phoenix Park. ("We dinned unnerstunned why you sassad about thurteen to aloafen, sor, kindly repeat!") McHugh reads this as "we didn't understand why you said that about 32 11, sir" and also reads "thurteen to aloafen" as "13 & a loaf = Last Supper" and "13 = baker's dozen."

unpeppeppediment *FW* 463.11-12 *n.* Not having a stammer or speech impediment, while not being able to exert the overcoming of this condition without proving it false. It's as though saying, "I don't stustustutter." ("And his unpeppeppediment.") In *Finnegans Wake* Mr. Earwicker, as well as other characters, often stutters when caught in some wrongdoing. The sound of the first 100 letter thunder word on the *Wake*'s first page can be heard as a stutter, beginning with "bababa . . . " and, as thunder representing God's voice, it indicates His guilt in creating a flawed world and its creatures. (See **thuthunder**.)

upperturnity *FW* 366.21 *n.* A favorable time, chance, or opportunity for an improvement or upturn in conditions or circumstances. Mr. Micawber in Dicken's *David Copperfield*, with his firm belief that "something will turn up," finally found his "upperturnity" in Australia. ("e'en tho' Jambuwel's defecalties is Terry Shimmyrag's upperturnity, if that is grace for the grass what is balm for the bramblers") You probably recognized the old maxim,"What is sauce for the goose is is sauce for the gander," but may have missed the Irish maxim, "England's difficulty is Ireland's opportunity." McHugh also provides the Irish *Tír na Simearóig* for "Land of the Shamrock."

usylessly *FW* 179.26 *adv.* Ineffectually or uselessly in relation to the Greek hero of the Trojan War, Ulysses. Ulysses' careful thought and cunning in creating the Trojan Horse to quickly end a stalemated war and his clever strategies in overcoming the imposing conditions the gods created to delay his voyage home demonstrate just how "usylessly" ineffective his opponents' proved to be. ("making believe to read his usylessly unreadable Blue Book of Eccles") The obvious reference here is to Joyce's famous and infamous novel, *Ulysses*, that was bound in blue paper to represent the Greek flag. "Eccles" refers to the Dublin street address of Leopold Bloom who stands in for the original Odysseus/Ulysses during his, Bloom's, day-long, roundtrip travels from his home and back. And "usylessly unreadable" is Joyce's Wakean admission of the great difficulties involved in reading *Ulysses*, leading many readers to make believe they've read it when they haven't. Joyce's wife Nora is said to have given up some 30 pages in. Part of the joke here is that *Ulysses* seems easily accessible when compared with *Finnegans Wake*, a work that many critics labeled unreadable.

uterim *FW* 187.36 *n.* The time between conception and birth or the interim in which an animal embryo is held and nourished in the womb or uterus of a female. ("Where have you been in the uterim, enjoying yourself all the morning since your last wetbed confession?") McHugh gives "deathbed" as a reading for "wetbed," but I confess I immediately thought of the first page of *A Portrait of the Artist as a Young Man* where Stephen Dedalus remembers: "When you wet the bed first it is warm then it gets cold. His mother put on the oilsheet. That had the queer smell." I don't know if wetting the bed is Catholic confession worthy but, if this is read as a "wet dream," which has a closer connection to uterus, it very well might be.

V

vaast *FW* 338.14   *adj.* A degree greater or more immense than "vast." Our solar system may be considered vast, our galaxy "vaast," and the universe more vaaaaast by far. ("But da. But dada, mwilshsuni. Till even to aften. Sea vaast pool!") In context we have Sevastopol, the Russian port on the Black Sea, along with the suggestion that the sea is a gigantic, vast pool. Sevastopol was a major site of conflict during the Crimean War in which Buckley shot the Russian general. (See **gianerant**.) McHugh gives the Shelta, secret language of Irish tinkers (See **communicanting.**"), *mwil, mwilsa* for "I, me," and *suni* for "see," and *da* in "dada" as Russian for "yes" and German for "there." The modern art movement known as Dada began in Zurich during World War I, exactly the time Joyce and his family moved there after their removal from Trieste. Dadaism ridiculed and rejected all the accepted standards and conventions, and it would be surprising if Joyce didn't have this avant-garde group in mind as he wrote "But da. But dada, mwilshsuni," that I translate as, "But yes, yes I see, Dada's there for me." Naturally enough, *Finnegans Wake* would reject Dadaism itself. In a little rhyme Joyce wrote to promote the publication of part of the *Wake*, known then as *Work in Progress*, is the line: "Humptydump Dublin's granddada of all rogues." Robert Burns' line "Flow gently, sweet Afton" is worked in with "Till even to aften."

velivision *FW* 610.35 *v*. Seeing swiftly (Latin *viso* for "see," *visum* for "a spectacle," and *velox* for "swift") the spectacles on television. Television programs today are viewed, at least by men, with a liberal application of the remote control, flipping quickly through the 100 plus channels in a circular style resembling that of *Finnegans Wake*. Joyce may be the first novelist to mention television with the *Wake*'s "faroscope of television, (this nightlife instrument)," and "bairdboard bombardment screen." While televison was in its infancy when Joyce was writing, the remote control was not even remotely on the horizon, another example of the *Wake*'s predictive powers ("Peredos Last in the Grand Natural. Velivision victor.") McHugh brings in Caesar's *veni, vedi, vici* or "I came, I saw, I conquered." He also identifies *Peredos* as a horse in the English Grand National race and the Greek for "seat of the Gods."

venerections *FW* 356.33 *n*. 1.reverences or venerations for things straight up or erections. The great success of drugs and devices to correct erectile dysfunctions pays tribute to our society's "venerections" for things that are stiff and stand straight up. ("I have just been seeing, with my warmest venerectrions, of a timmersome townside upthecountrylifer") The Wellington Monument in Dublin's Phoenix Park is a venerection in granite to the Dublin-born duke. It certainly has phallic overtones throughout *Finnegans Wake* and is identified as Finn MacCool's erect penis in the giant's body spread under the Dublin landscape (See **marmorial** & **penisills**.).

ventruquulence *FW* 360.21 *n*. A scathing harshness or truculence that appears to come from a source other than the speaker who is "throwing" his/her voice or a ventriloquist. Many ventriloquists' dummies have become famous for their funny "ventruquulence." ("We knows his ventruquulence.")

verdigrassy *FW* 231.7 *n.* Grass the color of verdigris, a green or greenish-blue substance that forms on copper, bronze, or brass surfaces that are left exposed to the air over a long period of time. The implication of aged surfaces comes from the Old French *vert de grice* meaning "green of Greece." The description "verdigrassy" appears in *Finnegans Wake* as a stanza of poetry:

> —*My God, alas, that dear olt tumtum home*
> *Whereof in youthfood port I preyed*
> *Amook the verdigrassy convict vallsall dazes.*
> *And cloitered for amourmeant in thy boosome shede!*

This "sentimental poetry," as Joyce described it in a letter dated 22 November 1930 to Harriet Shaw Weaver, is a Wakean transformation of a poem that Joyce tells her he wrote at the age of nine: "My cot alas that dear old shady home where oft in youthful sport I played, upon thy verdant grassy fields all day or lingered for a moment in thy bosom shade etc etc etc etc." This demonstrates, if nothing else, that in the hands of a world-famous writer even youthful doggerel can be put to a high literary purpose.

vergitabale *FW* 357.34 *n.* A bluish-green or verdigris plant used for food or a vegetable. With the Latin *vir* for "man," there may be the suggestion of a man who lives with very little action, thought, or feeling, that is a vegetative existence. Broccoli may be the verdigris vegetable referred to with: "in our trurally virvir vergitabale (garden) I sometimes, maybe, what has justly said of old Flannagan" (See **trurally**.)

vibroverberates *FW* 249.15 *v.* A sound that combines vibration and reverberation. A quivering or vacillating of a sound while echoing back or reechoing. A vibraphone may produce such a sound in a musical composition or a voice in yodeling. ("It vibroverberates upon the tegmen and prosplodes from pomoeria.") McHugh references "tegmen: hardened wing cover of some insects. Those of some Orthoptera resonate to the song."

vicereversing *FW* 227.19 *v.* Inverting or reversing evil or vice. Responding to evil with good or doing the opposite (vice versa) so as to cancel out vice with virtue. ("But vicereversing thereout from those palms of perfection to anger arbour") Jesus' example of voluntarily carrying a man's cloak for two miles when one is only required to carry it for a mile is an instance of "vicereversing."

vicewise *FW* 286.29 *adv.* Also wise or likewise knowledgeable concerning evil or likewise vice. If Eve was sinful in eating the apple, then Adam was "vicewise." This just shows that the problem was not with the apple on the tree but with the pair on the ground. ("Nor was the noer long disappointed for easiest of kisshams, he was made vicewise.") McHugh provides the phrase "easy as kissing hands" for "easiest of kisshams" and notes that it contains Ham, one of Noah's sons.

volupkabulary *FW* 419.12 *n.* 1. A stock of words used by a person or profession, in this instance the vocabulary that comprises the artificial language Volapük. ("How farflung is your fokloire and how velktingeling our volupkabulary!") McHugh references "fokloire" with "folklore," the river "Loire," and the Irish *foclóir* for "vocabulary." Wakese itself may be thought of as an artificial or constructed language, though one only completely mastered by its creator, James Joyce. While Johann Martin Schleyer said that God told him to create Volapük (1879-1880) as an international language, some readers no doubt think that the devil told Joyce to combine the world's languages to create *Finnegans Wake*. 2. A vocabulary full of sensual delights or voluptuousness. The word "velktingeling" that describes "our volupkabulary" is referenced by McHugh with the Danish *velklingende* for "euphonious" or "leasing to the ear," Joyce's overriding concern in his construction of the *Wake*.

voyce *FW* 536.22 *n.* The speech or voice of Joyce. James Joyce was, as described in *Finnegans Wake*, "quite a musical genius in a small way and owner of an exceedingly niced ear with tenorist voice to match." Nora would have preferred that her husband earn their living with his voice rather than his pen. A recording of Joyce reading from the Anna Livia Plurabelle chapter is available on the internet for those who want a direct experience of "voyce." ("The boyce voyce is still flautish and his mouth still wears that soldier's scarlet") McHugh reads "boyce voyce" as a "boy's voice" which is feeblish and/or flattish (German *flau*). He identifies "boyce" as "Boyce," one an English composer and chorister and another a Lord-Mayor of Dublin.

W

warewolff *FW* 225.8 *v.* Be conscious of or aware (archaic "ware") and wary or to beware of someone who can change into a wolf or a werewolf. ("Warewolff! Olff! Toboo!") McHugh reads "Toboo!" as "taboo" and as the Irish *abu* meaning "to victory!" Simply to shout "boo" is not enough to ward off a werewolf. It takes a silver bullet to be victorious.

warhorror *FW* 91.30 *n.* Dread or horror of fighting by armed forces or war. If there were more horror of war, the world would be a more peaceful place. ("with his heroes in Warhorror if ever in all his exchequered career") Valhalla, the Scandinavian banqueting hall where heroes killed in battle feast forever with Odin, is suggested in context here. Such a reward for brave warriors mitigates "warhorror." HCE's initials are also scrambled in this passage.

warpon *FW* 615.19 *n.* An instrument used in fighting by armed forces or a weapon of war. ("he was with a twohangled warpon") The "warpon" referred to is the two-handled sword wielded by Sir Amory Tristram, later the first Earl of Howth, during Henry II's invasion by invitation of Ireland. This "warpon" is

300 | A *Finnegans Wake* Lextionary

on display in Howth Castle that is situated on Howth Head, Dublin's promontory that is referred to in the *Wake*'s first sentence with "Howth Castle and Environs." This is also the first appearance of the *Wake*'s primary male protagonist, Humphrey Chimpden Earwicker, most often found in some order of his initials, HCE.

warld *FW* 345.31 & 608.34 *n.* The earth or world fighting or at war. World Wars I and II are as close as the world has come to a "warld," though not all the countries and peoples were fighting, but the Bible's long prophesized Battle of Armageddon should do the word "warld" proud. ("Theres scares knud in this gnarld warld a fully so svend" & "Into the wikeawades warld from sleep we are passing.") For the first quote McHugh references Thomas Moore's song, "The Meeting of the Waters," with the line, "There is not in this wide world a valley so sweet." In the *Wake*'s version the world appears as a little knotted, twisted, or gnarled. In the second quote ALP is heard who, as the Liffey, is flowing from sleep and the dream world of *Finnegans Wake* into the wide awake world and reunion with her father, the Irish Sea.

washup *FW* 628.11 *v.* Reverence or worship by cleansing with water or washing up. Some Christian churches practice the custom of foot washing as demonstrated by Jesus washing his disciples' feet or his own feet washed by a woman's tears. Baptism could also be considered a form of "washup" by cleaning up one's act when one is born again. As Poor Richard reminds us, "Cleanliness is next to Godliness." ("I sink I'd die down over his feet, humbly dumbly, only to washup.") McHugh also reads "washup" as "wake up," bringing in the *Wake*'s resurrection theme, which is fitting for the last page where a dying ALP as the Liffey flows to her father, the Irish Sea, with full faith that she will be resurrected at the book's beginning. (See **returnally**.) Humpty Dumpty makes the last of numerous appearances here before washing up on the first page with "humptyhillhead . . . tumptytumtoes."

waywords *FW* 369.1 *n.* Willful, disobedient, or wayward words that have lost their way. Words that have turned from their original sense or meaning such as "gay," which is still in a sort of linguistic limbo. So many of the *Wake*'s words seem like "waywords" that most readers become waylaid and never get past the first page. In my introductory essay, Humpty Dumpty tells Alice that with portmanteau words it is all a matter of who is to be master, but Joyce lets his created words wander around in any way they like and mean as much as they like. In *Finnegans Wake* words have freedom to be all that they can be, which for readers is both frightening and liberating. ("one percepted nought while tuffbettle outraged the waywords and meansigns of their hinterhand suppliesdemands")

weekreations *FW* 585.1 *n.* 1. Amusements or recreations enjoyed during the week rather than on weekends when most recreations occur. 2. Amusements or recreations enjoyed for one week, as on vacations. ("exclusive pigtorial rights of herehear fond tiplady his weekreations, appearing in next eon's issue")

wetting *FW* 260.17 & 314.33 *n.* McHugh gives "wetting" as slang for "fucking," so the combination here of wedding and sexual intercourse, two activities that are joined less closely today than in less liberal times, is apt. ("The marriage of Montan wetting his moll" & "twilled alongside in wiping the rice assatiated with their wetting") As a bonus, here is a better understanding of *FW* 585.31 when, after the failed coitus of HCE and ALP in the early morning hours, she remarks, "You never wet the tea!"

whant *FW* 603.32 *interj. pron.* Contraction of what and want or what do you want. ("Where is that blinketey blanketer, the quound of a pealer, the sunt of a hunt whant foxes good men!") Many cuss words can be contained in blankety blank, and McHugh writes that "pealer" is slang for "policeman." For "sunt of a hunt" he reads son of a gun.

whatarcurss *FW* 225.12 & 225.13 *n.* 1. What happens or occurs as the result of wishing harm or evil on someone or a curse 2. What happens or occurs are surly, snarling people or curs. ("Breath and bother and whatarcurss." & "Then breath more bother and more whatarcurss.") McHugh's translation as "bread & butter & watercress" is no doubt more correct in the context here since bread and butter and watercress sandwiches are staples at an English tea, but *Wake* words are never content with only one meaning. In *Scandinavian Elements of Finnegans Wake*, Dounia Bunis Christiani gives the Danish *karse* and the Middle English *Kerse* for "cress."

whirrld *FW* 147.22 *n.* The earth or our world with emphasis on its spins or whirls on its axis as it whirls around the sun. ("Bright pigeons all over the whirrld will fly with my mistletoe message round their loveribboned necks") The *Wake* later speaks of "whorled without aimed," suggesting that all our "whirlworlds" are going nowhere in particular and without meaning.

whisping *FW* 148.1 & 384.32 *n.* A mere shred or wisp of whispering softly and covertly under the breath. ("Why do you like my whisping?" & "Isolamisola, and whisping and lisping her about Trisolanisans") For the second quote, McHugh writes "Isola: sister of Oscar Wilde; died at age of 9"and adds that *isola* is Italian for "island." Paired with "Trisolanisans" is Isolde who is thinking of her young lover, Tristan.

wholume *FW* 48.19 *adj.* The whole or entire book or volume. The "wholume" of *Finnegans Wake* comprises 628 pages of text. ("which, thorough readable to int from and, is from tubb to buttom all falsetissues, antilibellous and nonactionable and this applies to the whole wholume") Joyce here defends *Finnegans Wake* as a book that is readable end to end and from top to bottom and any suggestion that it is otherwise is a false issue, a tissue of falsehoods, and factitious. He recognizes that, despite the libelous remarks critics have made against his work, he won't be able to take any action against them. But this is also HCE's attitude toward the terrible rumors circling Dublin about his supposedly spurious actions one night in Phoenix Park. If the meaning I give has merit, then Joyce was redundant when writing "whole wholume." But then redundancy is one of the primary features throughout the "wholume" of the *Wake*.

whome   *FW* 138.30, 296.31, 332.27, & 379.3   *n*. The uterus or womb as a dwelling place or home. Given a choice, a fetus would probably prefer to remain where it was rather than be born, feeling that be it ever so humble, there's no place like "whome." If an incubator is a womb with a view, it is also an artificial "whome." ("when he's come whome sweetwhome," "I'll make you to see figuratleavely the whome of your eternal geomater," "those oathmassed Fenians for whome he's forcecaused a bridge of the piers," & "We don't know the sendor to whome.") In the first quote is found the song title "Home Sweet Home" and in the second Shem figuratively removes the fig leaf (See **figuratleavely**.) from his mother's pubis to explain female sexual geometry to his brother Shaun. In the third quote McHugh explains that the "Gaelic Athletic Association (games in Phoenix Park) forecast a breach of the peace" and he reads the fourth quote as "sender to whom."

whorable   *FW* 438.17   *adj*. Terrible or horrible in the sense of a shocking situation related to prostitutes or whores. Had they known of it, Joyce's parents and priests would have considered his first sexual experience with a prostitute at the age of fourteen as something "whorable." ("It would be a whorable state of affairs altogether")

whorse   *FW* 84.27 & 610.2   *adj*. Less good or worse than a horse. Walking is "whorse" than riding a horse, for example. As a *Wake* word, it can't be overlooked that the "whore" hiding here is a reference common *in Finnegans Wake* and open to creative interpretation. ("not one of the two hundred and six bones and five hundred and one muscles in his corso was a whit the whorse for her whacking" & "*Juva:* Bulkily: and he is fundementially theosophagusted over the whorse proceedings.") McHugh reads "corso" in the first quote as "torso" and gives the Italian *corso* for "in progress" and *corpo* for "body." He sees "whorse proceedings" in the second quote as a "horse race." (See **theosophagusted**.)

whorship *FW* 547.28 *v.* Reverence or worship of prostitutes or whores. Playing on a line from the marriage ceremony, "With all my body I thee worship," the *Wake* changes it to "with all my bawdy did I her whorship." Joyce's first sexual experiences began with Dublin prostitutes at the age of fourteen and he did, in a real sense, forsake his worship of God, at least the Catholic God he had grown up with, in exchange for devotion to ladies of the evening. (See **bawdy** & **whorable**.)

whouse *FW* 221.15 *pron.* The possessive form of who, a word used in asking a question about a person or persons, or whose dwelling place for a family or a house. ("whouse be the churchyard or whorts up the aasgaars") Here is found yet another reference to Le Fanu's novel, *The House by the Churchyard*. (See **cohortyard** & **hearseyard**.) McHugh identifies "aasgaars" with Asgaard, home of the Nordic gods. Given the scabrous nature of some Wakean allusions, the question of what's being taken up the ass can not be discounted.

whyre *FW* 115.19 *adv.* At what place and for what reason or where and why rolled into one word. ("whyre have you been so grace a mauling and where were you chaste me child") This where and why question is being asked of Grace O'Malley, who appears in many guises in *Finnegans Wake*. She is an Irish princess and/or piratess who was denied hospitality at Howth Castle and, therefore, kidnapped the Earl of Howth's son until the Earl promised to keep the castle doors open during dinner. This somewhat historical account makes a Wakean transformation into The Tale of Jarl van Hoother and the Prankquean in which the "queen of pranks" riddle, "Mark the Wans, why do I am alook alike a poss of porterpease?", echoes throughout the *Wake*.

wildcaps *FW* 383.19-20 *n*. The white foam of wave crests in wild and windy weather, better known as whitecaps. ("And there they were too, when it was dark, whilest the wildcaps was circling, as slow their ship, the winds aslight") In this context, "wildcaps" makes sense paired with "whilest," which combines "white" and "whilst" to give the common word "whitecaps." This line comes from the page with the famous opening line, "—*Three quarks for Muster Mark!*", that tells the love story of Tristram, Iseult, and King Mark II and provided physicist Murray Gell-Mann with the name for the fundamental constituents of the nucleon, quarks. (See **quarks**, **amotion**, & **charmaunt**.) A wine cup is also suggested as McHugh references the song "The Winecup is Circling" from Thomas Moore's *Irish Melodies* ("tummy moor's maladies"). Though it's far fetched, "wildcaps" conjures up the wild, mapcap catchphrase of a Dublin comic that appears throughout *Finnegans Wake* in many guises, "Take off that white hat" ("Tick off that whilehot").

wilelife *FW* 113.3 *n*. Wild animals, plants, or wildlife that trick or deceive through cunning or wiles. ("Nuttings on her wilelife!") McHugh reads this as "Not on your life." In *Finnegans Wake*, the serpent in the Garden of Eden is the first example of "wilelife" to be found. Through his wiles to Eve and hers to Adam, the apple is the instrument of their original sin and thus expulsion from paradise. In nature, all sorts of plants and animals have evolved wiles that protect them from predators or ensure their success as predators. A chameleon that can change its coloring to match that of its setting is but one of many examples. The cartoon character Wile E. Coyote, the Roadrunner's nemesis, is "wilelife" in popular culture.

woesoever *FW* 576.19 *pron*. Whosoever and grief or woe combined to indicate that whatsoever person or persons are in a sorrowful state. ("Prospector projector and Boomooster giant builder of all causeways woesoever") McHugh gives the German *Baumeister* for "master builder" and references Ibsen's play *The Master Builder* that plays an important part in *Finnegans Wake*. In keeping with the *Wake*'s falling motif, the famous builder falls to his death from a tall tower he designed. There is also a Giant's Causeway in County Antrim, Northern Ireland.

wohly   *FW* 349.19   *adj.* Completely, totally, or wholly sacred, devoted to God, or holy. Of all the accusations made against *Finnegans Wake*, it has never been described as a "wohly" book. ("*the figure of a fellowchap in the wohly ghast*") This is best read as "fellowship of the Holy Ghost," and McHugh references Philippians 2:1: "fellowship of the Spirit."

woice   *FW* 240.6   *n.* A vocal expression of great grief or distress or a voice of woe. We hear such a "woice" on the first page of *Finnegans Wake* with the word "Oconee" that suggests the Irish word *Ochon* for "alas" or "woe is me," a cry often heard at the American Wakes given for Irish emigrants leaving home forever. It also appears in the *Wake* as "Ochone!," "Ocone!," and "O Home!" and *Ulysses* introduces "Ochone!" as a "banshee woe." (See **farwailed**.) ("But low, boys low, he rises, shrivering, with his spittful eyes and his whoozebecome woice.") McHugh reads "whoozebecome" as "woebegone" which matches well with "woice." He references the lines "Low, boys, and up she rises" from the sea shanty "What Shall We Do with the Drunken Sailor?"

woid   *FW* 378.29 & 596.21   *n.* A sound or group of sounds with meaning or word and vacuum or void combined. The Bible's "In the beginning was the Word" (John 1:1) is parodied in the *Wake* with "In the buginning is the woid, in the muddle is the sounddance and thereinofer you're in the unbewised again, vund vulsyvolsy." McHugh gives the German *unbewiesen* for "unproved" and reads "vulsyvolsy" as "vice versa." Joyce may be suggesting that the "Word" was actually empty space or a vacuum, that the "Word" was devoid of substance or meaning. Joyce wrote that he had made *Ulysses* out of next to nothing but that he was making *Finnegans Wake* out of nothing, so the world, too, may have been created from the void. As science columnist K. C. Cole writes, "When nothing changed, the universe was born." The *Wake* does have some Nietzschean streaks of nihilism, and the philosophical definition of nihilism is the denial of all existence. But then "woid" may only be "word" spoken with a Brooklyn accent. ("the gren, woid and glue been broking by the maybole gards") With this second quote McHugh gets green, white & blue, but I wonder if it might not also be, in keeping with the *Wake*'s American motif, red, white, and blue.

wooman *FW* 170.14 *v.* To seek to win, marry, or woo an adult human female or woman. ("when lovely wooman stoops to conk him, one of the littliest said me, me") McHugh provides two literary references—Goldsmith's *She Stoops to Conquer* and "When lovely woman stoops to folly" from *The Vicar of Wakefield*. The conquering seems to be done by conking or hitting him on the head. When Joyce was a little boy, his younger brother, Stanislaus, reports watching him come downstairs with his nursery maid while shouting, "Here's me. Here's me."

worrild *FW* 258.21 *n.* To be uneasy or worried about our earth or world. For those who want to worry about the world, our present age seems to offer an almost endless assortment to select from, beginning with global warming and on to species extinction, which includes us among the other animals. ("For the Clearer of the Air from on high has spoken in tumbuldum tambaldam to his tembledim tombaldoom worrild") McHugh finds "tumbledown" in "tumbuldum" and in "tembledim" finds "Tem: creator in *The Egyptian Book of the Dead*." So the suggestion seems to be that it is correct to worry about our created world tumbling down and, despite all the warnings, Congress seems unlikely to do anything about clearing the air of this climate controversy.

wrestless *FW* 143.21   *adj.* Uneasy or restless about struggling or wrestling. In *Finnegans Wake* "the wrestless in womb, all the rivals to allsea" are the biblical twin boys Jacob and Esau who in *Genesis* 25:22 struggle together in Rebekah's womb. Jacob is holding on to his brother's heel during the delivery, thus the name Jacob meaning one who takes by the heel or supplants. Obviously Jacob was not restless or "wrestless" about supplanting Esau in the matter of his birthright later in the story. (See **ashaped, eatsoup,** & **peacisely**.)

wright *FW* 597.11   *adj.* Beckman comments that "the *w* added to 'right' signifies that the 'wright' has some 'wrong' in it. Right and wrong are not binary opposites and neither side of a tapestry is the right one." ("there are two signs to turn to, the yest and the ist, the wright side and the wronged side") McHugh finds not only the east and the west here but "yest" as "yesterday" or "the past" and the German *ist* representing "the present."

wroght *FW* 595.19   *adj.* At once incorrect or wrong and correct or right. Answers to questions are often "wroght" when they combine both true and false (or omitted) information. For example, to say that slavery was the sole cause of the War of Southern Secession is primarily right but also partially wrong in that it oversimplifies by neglecting several other contributing causes. Wrought may also be implied as something fashioned or formed from both the right and wrong materials. ("You are alpsulummply wroght!") I wonder if this sentence implies the ideas of either doing something right for the wrong reason or something wrong for the right reason. Anna Livia Plurabelle (ALP) makes an appearance here, absolutely.

wunder *FW* 84.10   *prep.* Beneath or under something strange, surprising, or a wonder. There is a wild theory that a fabulous secret is hidden "wunder" the wonderful Egyptian Sphinx, but it's more likely that "wunder" the wonder of the Sphinx lies nothing more than sand. ("bore up wonderfully wunder all of it with a whole number of plumsized contusiums") The German *wunder* meaning "wonder" is also at work here.

X

Xero *FW* 574.12 *n.* 1. "X" as a symbol for an unknown quantity replacing the "Z" of zero suggests that the quantity unknown is not just nothing to sneeze at but nothing itself. Joyce said that he had created *Ulysses* out of next to nothing but that he was creating *Finnegans Wake* out of nothing (See **woid**.). This is the same situation physicists face as they attempt to determine the makeup of our universe. If, as Bruno of Nola believed, everything must evolve its opposite, what scientists term matter and antimatter and, if, as is currently thought, these two forces can be shown to be equal, then the sum total of the universe equals zero. Yes, the "Big O," or in Wakese, "ah! O!" and "a great big oh." But for the indefinite "now" we must be content with an answer of "Xero." 2. An unknown hero. If you remember the ending to every adventure of the Lone Ranger, someone always asked, "Who was that masked man? I wanted to thank him." Lana Turner, starring in that tearjerker of a film *Madame X*, is a female version of a "Xero" or, the closest thing in the *Wake* to it, a "zeroine." ("The fund trustee, one Jucundus Fecundus Xero Pecundus Coppercheap, counterclaimed that payment was invalid") McHugh translates from the Latin *jucundus* for "pleasant," *fecundus* for "fruitful," and *pecuniosus* for "rich," all wonderful attributes for a "fund trustee," but the "Xero" in the name makes me hesitate to let him manage my funds. The Romans had the habit of occasionally giving their children a number for a name, such as Sextus for the sixth child, so the "Xero" included in the name here might be in remembrance of an earlier stillborn child. Far out, yes, but one can never be too fanciful in reading *Finnegans Wake*.

xxoxoxxoxxx *FW* 456.23 *n.* Joyce's representation of the sound of chewing. ("All the vitalmines is beginning to sozzle in chewn and the hormonies to clingleclangle, fudgem, kates and eaps and naboc and erics and oinnos on kingclud and xoxxoxo and xxoxoxxoxxx till I'm fustfed like fungstif") Louis Gillet describes this passage as "the description of a meal where some spoonerisms, some reversed syllables, *naboc* (bacon), kingclud (duckling), eaps (peas), represent the act of chewing, while the onomatopoeia xxoxoxxoxxx is a funny portrayal of a mouth occupied by a gruel of potatoes. This kind of verbal humbug gave him (Joyce) exceeding pleasure." The last four words here may be read as "I'm stuffed like Falstaff," Shakespeare's fat, comic character from *Henry IV*.

In his *Dictionary* Dr. Johnson asserts that "X is a letter, which, though found in Saxon words, begins no word in the English language." Time has modified his assessment. *Finnegans Wake* has only seventeen entries under "X" and only two I am able to define.

Y

yestures *FW* 267.9 *n.* Positive or affirmative motions of the limbs or body, gestures that, nonverbally, say "yes." ("Whence followeup with endspeaking nots for yestures") McHugh's reading of "endspeaking" as "unspoken" and "nots" as "nods" works well with "yestures" as affirmative gestures.

youlldied *FW* 308.17 *v.* To have perished or died during the Christmas season or Yuletide. ("With our best youlldied greedings to Pep and Memmy and the old folkers below and beyant") This is from the "NIGHTLETTER" that Shem, Shaun, and Issy send to their parents, HCE and ALP, after finishing their homework lessons. "Yuletide greetings" would be a conventional reading. Perhaps because I live not so far away down from the Suwannee River, I find Stephen Foster's famous song in "old folkers below."

yoxen *FW* 18.32 *n.* Oxen that are fastened together by a wooden frame or a yoke and are therefore ready for work. ("earthcrust at all of hours, furrowards, bagawards, like yoxen at the turnpaht") McHugh gives the Greek *boustrophedon* for "turning like oxen in ploughing: writing with lines read left-right, then right-left &c."

Z

zeemliangly *FW* 415.24 *adv.* Apparently or seemingly as in a deceptive appearance. James S. Atherton, in his essay in *A Conceptual Guide to Finnegans Wake*, gives a quite wonderful analysis of the opposite meanings of "zeemliangly": "It means, of course, 'seemingly,' or seems to, but it combines the Russian *zemlya*, 'land, earth,' here to be taken as 'Space,' with the Chinese *liang*, one of the meanings of which is 'Time.' Joyce has summed up his Space-Time fable in one word which employs the language of the vast spaces of Russia for one aspect and Chinese with its immense antiquity for the other. Nothing could be neater, or more astonishing." ("Erething above ground, as his Book of Breathings bed him, so as everywhy, sham or shunner, zeemliangly to kick time." McHugh references "Book of Breathings: a funeral ritual in *The Egyptian Book of the Dead*" and has "Shem or Shaun" "seemingly to kill time."

zeroine *FW* 261.24 *n.* The most important female character or heroine in a fictional work whose role is still pretty much of no importance or a zero. Since a majority of literary works in past centuries were written by men, it should be no surprise that the "zeroine" outnumbers the "heroine." This would seem to be the case when Lord Illingworth refers to Mrs. Arbuthnot as "a woman of no importance" in Oscar Wilde's play of the same name. But by the play's end it's found she is no "zeroine" but a true heroine, and his lordship is shown to be, as Mrs. Arbuthnot puts it, "No one in particular. A man of no importance." ("Ainsoph, this upright one, with that noughty besighed him zeroine.") Referencing "zeroine" within its Wakean context, McHugh gives "Ainsoph" as "Ain-Soph: Kabbalistic name of the unmanifest Diety" and writes that "Kabbalistic doctrine regards woman as intrinsically passive." This passage suggests that the "zeroine" sighing beside him is not only naught/nought or nothing/zero, but also improper or naughty.

znore *FW* 266.7 *n.* A harsh, rough sound made during a snooze or a snore that is often visualized in cartoon drawings by a string of "Z's." ("In our snoo. Znore.") McHugh suggests "zoo" for "snoo" but also gives the Czech *snu* for "dream" which works well in this context. I hear the first part of "snooze" as well, and all these associations fit since this passage is coming just 20 pages after the lovely Phoenix Park nocturne (*FW* 244-246). While walking with Joyce one evening to the Zurich zoo, Eugene Jolas relates that Joyce suddenly began quoting from the *Wake* "the magnificent Nocturne of Phoenix Park, with the verbal magic of animal sounds dying in the gathering night." One of these sounds might well have been heard as a "Znore."

Works Consulted

Works by James Joyce

A Portrait of the Artist as a Young Man. Edited by R. B. Kershner. Boston/New York: Bedford Books of St. Martin's Press, 1993.

Dubliners. New York: Penguin Books, 1976.

Exiles. Mineola, NY: Dover Publications, Inc., 2002.

Finnegans Wake. New York: Viking, 1939.

Letters of James Joyce: Vol. 1, ed. Stuart Gilbert 1957, new ed. 1966; vols. II and III, ed. Richard Ellmann. New York and London: The Viking Press and Faber & Faber, 1966.

Stephen Hero. New York: New Directions Publishing Corporation, 1963.

Ulysses. Edited by Hans Walter Gabler. New York: Random House, Inc., 1993.

Works on *Finnegans Wake*

Atherton, James S. *The Books at the Wake: A Study of Literary Allusions in James Joyce's "Finnegans Wake."* New York: Viking, 1960.

Beckett, Samuel, et al. *Our Exagmination Round His Factification for Incamination of Work in Progress.* Paris: Shakespeare and Company, 1929.

Beckman, Richard. *Joyce's Rare View: The Nature of Things in "Finnegans Wake."* Gainesville: University Press of Florida, 2007.

Begnal, Michael H., and Senn, Fritz, eds. *A Conceptual Guide to "Finnegans Wake."* University Park: The Pennsylvania State University Press, 1974.

Bonheim, Helmut. *A Lexicon of the German in "Finnegans Wake."* Berkeley: University of California Press, 1967.

Boorstin, Daniel J. *The Creators: A History of Heroes of the Imagination.* New York: Vintage Books, 1992.

Brivic, Sheldon. *The Abiko Annual* #22, 2002: 56-57.

Burgess, Anthony, ed. *A Shorter "Finnegans Wake."* New York: The Viking Press, 1968.

Campbell, Joseph, & Henry Morton Robinson. *A Skeleton Key to "Finnegans Wake."* New York: Viking, 1961.

Christiani, Dounia Bunis. *Scandinavian Elements of "Finnegans Wake."* Evanston: Northwestern University Press, 1965.

Crispi, Luca, and Slote, Sam, eds. *How Joyce Wrote "Finnegans Wake:" A Chapter-by- Chapter Guide.* Madison: The University of Wisconsin Press, 2007.

Devlin, Kimberly J. *Wandering and Return in "Finnegans Wake."* Princeton: Princeton University Press, 1991.

DiBernard, Barbara. *Alchemy and "Finnegans Wake."* Albany: State University of New York Press, 1980.

Ellmann, Richard. *James Joyce.* Oxford: Oxford University Press, 1983.

Epstein, Edmund Lloyd. *A Guide Through "Finnegans Wake."* Gainesville: University Press of Florida, 2009.

Fargnoli, A. Nicholas, & Gillespie, Michael P. *James Joyce A to Z: The Essential Reference to His Life and Writings.* New York: Oxford University Press, 1995.

Fordham, Finn. *Lots of Fun at "Finnegans Wake": Unravelling Universals*. Oxford: Oxford University Press, 2007.

Gordon, John. *"Finnegans Wake": A Plot Summary*. Syracuse: Syracuse University Press, 1986.

Hart, Clive. *A Concordance to "Finnegans Wake."* Minneapolis: University of Minnesota Press, 1963.

Hayman, David, and Anderson, Elliott, eds. *In the Wake of the Wake*. Madison: The University of Wisconsin Press, 1978.

Herr, Cheryl. *Joyce's Anatomy of Culture*. Urbana: University of Illinois Press, 1986.

Knowles, Sebastian D. G., ed. *Bronze by Gold: The Music of Joyce*. New York: Garland Publishing, Inc., 1999.

McHugh, Roland. *Annotations to "Finnegans Wake."* revised edition. Baltimore: John Hopkins University Press, 1991.

McLuhan, Eric. *The Role of Thunder in "Finnegans Wake."* Toronto: University of Toronto Press, 1997.

Nabokov, Vladimir. *Lectures on Literature*. San Diego: A Harvest Book, 1982.

Norris, David, and Carl Flint. *Introducing Joyce*. Cambridge: Icon Books, Ltd., 2000.

O'Shea, Michael J. *James Joyce and Heraldry*. Albany: State University of New York Press, 1986.

Potts, Willard, ed. *Portraits of the Artist in Exile*. Seattle: University of Washington Press, 1979.

Sartiliot, Claudette. *Citation and Modernity*. Norman and London: University of Oklahoma Press, 1993.

Sawyer-Lauçanno, Christopher. *The World's Words: A Semiotic Reading of James Joyce's "Finnegans Wake."* London: Alyscamps Press, 1993.

Škrabánek, Petr. *Night Joyce of a Thousand Tiers: Studies in "Finnegans Wake."* Prague: Litteraria Pragensia, 2002.

Strong, L. A. G. *The Sacred River: An Approach to James Joyce.* New York: Pellegrini & Cudahy, 1951.

Tindall, William York. *A Reader's Guide to "Finnegans Wake."* Syracuse: Syracuse University Press, 1996.

Acknowledgements

Special thanks are due to Brandy Kershner, Joycean extraordinaire at the University of Florida, for untiringly answering the many questions I put to him and for directing me to valuable resources, both books and people. John Gordon, author of *"Finnegans Wake": A Plot Summary,* was such a person, not only for his excellent book but, especially, for permission to use his limerick in my definition of "bedst." Once again, as they did with my previous book, *Riverrun to Livvy: Lots of Fun Reading the First Page of James Joyce's "Finnegans Wake,"* Lindsay and Jason Cliett did a fantastic job with the design of both book and cover and its transfer to Kindle accessibility. Good friends Jack and Selma Wassermann of Vancouver generously gave the two things writers want most (other than seven figure advances and studio fights over film rights), praise and encouragement. Also in the praise and encouragement department are two book-loving friends, Margaret Perkins and Kate Doster. While any errors are mine, Judith Kendall's copyediting skills corrected many mistakes I made along the way. Daniel Gardiner provided much needed technical support, making the entire process so much simpler. And, once again, I express my sincere appreciation and indebtedness to Roland McHugh for his truly great gift to Wakeans everywhere, the invaluable *Annotations to "Finnegans Wake."*